Metaphors and Climax

Reminiscences On The Drama And Theatre Of Ogonna Agu

Published by
Adonis & Abbey Publishers Ltd
St James House
13 Kensington Square
London
W8 5HD
Website: http://www.adonis-abbey.com
E-mail Address: editor@adonis-abbey.com

Year of Publication 2014.

British Library Cataloguing-in-Publication Data
A catalogue record for this book is available from the British Library

ISBN: 978-1-909112-46-9

Metaphors and Climax

Reminiscences On The Drama And Theatre Of Ogonna Agu

Edited by

Charles Nwadigwe, Molinta Enendu & Canice Nwosu

TABLE OF CONTENTS

Acknowledgements

In the course of putting this book together, we have incurred a debt of gratitude to many people. We wish to acknowledge our departed colleague, friend and brother, the Late Dr. Ogonna Anaagudo-Agu (Associate Professor) whose invincible spirit sparked the fire for this project. In that vein, we wish to thank his immediate family, particularly his wife, Mrs. Evelyn Agu (Barrister at Law), for her moral support to the project.

Our effusive gratitude equally goes to the contributors who authored the various chapters of the book. These scholars, in answering the call for papers, had to put up with continual harassments from the editors to answer queries from paper reviewers; revise papers accordingly and meet tight deadlines.

The editors are quite grateful to Prof. Kalu Uka for accepting to share his wealth of experience by writing the introduction to the book. Prof. Uka taught Dr. Agu in his undergraduate years and later mentored him when he began his academic career. We are equally grateful to Prof. Osita Okagbue who agreed to write the preface to the book even at short notice. He also offered vital logistic support to the project and linked us to the book publishers.

The editors must also acknowledge the efforts of the publishers, Adonis and Abbey Ltd., who in accepting to publish the book worked within deadlines with needle-point precision. We cannot leave the acknowledgement podium without recognizing the immense but unsung efforts of our families who provided us with moral, emotional and material support and endured inconveniences while we worked on the project.

There are many other people that gave us ancillary support towards the project. While we remain eternally grateful, we can only hope and pray that all those who assisted us in one way or the other will equally find support and assistance in their time of need.

Preface

Progenies of Idemili: Ogonna Agu and I

I have a very peculiar but fascinating personal relationship with Dr Ogonna Agu, the scholar-artist-activist whose life and work this book, *Metaphors and Climax...*, celebrates; it is almost an intimate relationship in that fact that I feel that I know Ogonna Agu reasonably well, especially through his work. Yet, I never met him in person before his death in 2012. Ogonna Agu and I, it seemed always and as it eventually turned out, were never destined to meet, but he was always a shadow and presence that ever successfully managed to leave a place as I entered it, or seen the other way, I always stepped into a place as he was leaving it. And, Ogonna Agu was always able to leave intellectual and creative echoes, imprints and mementoes of himself, wherever he has been; he always marked a territory with his indomitable and evanescent personality and signatures.

I will now explain this uncanny yet easily plausible relationship of knowing but not meeting, intimate yet distant; we are both sons of Idemili (Ogonna Agu hailed from Nnobi and I from Nkpor). Idemili is that Igbo deity whose name 'means Pillar of Water ... [which holds] up the Raincloud in the sky so that it does not fall down'', as his chief priest, Ezidemili, informs his friend, Chief Nwaka, in Chinua Achebe's *Arrow of God* (Achebe 1964, 1974: p.41) and whose symbol, messenger and physical manifestation is the royal python, ever graceful, mysterious, sinuous, utterly inscrutable and regally unperturbed in its movement. Idemili, Ezidemili continued, 'was there at the beginning of things', when the world was in its infancy; his messenger, *Eke Idemili* (the royal python) in turn proclaims in Ezeulu's nightmarish tragic dream:

> I was born when lizards were in ones and twos.
> Child of Idemili. The difficult tear-drops

Of Sky's first weeping drew my spots.
Being Sky-born I walked the Earth with royal gait...' (Achebe 222)

It seems to me from descriptions by those who knew him, worked with him, have seen him perform on stage or through his own artistic creations that Ogonna Agu possessed some of these same attributes of the child of Idemili. In addition, he seemed to have embodied some of the deep religiousity, the oftentimes creative unpredictability and sometimes terrifying destructiveness of *Agwu*, that other Igbo deity/spiritual agency who marks those it touches with the ability to have rare visions and knowledge which place them quite often beyond the mundane realms of human imagination and understanding. *Agwu's* touch is a call to priesthood, to supreme service and total devotion to society/community. Those who reject this call or attempt to ignore this touch usually pay heavily for it. Such individuals are different because they have the eyes of the gods; but they also are destined to be restless because they are trapped in an earthbound human form. It appears also through testimonies by those who met and/or knew him personally that Ogonna may have had *Agwu* as his guiding muse, the invisible flutist who played the inaudible music-to others-which he danced to through his work and which seemed to have guided the life that he lived. But let me return to my baton-less intellectual relay with Ogonna Agu.

Ogonna Agu became an undergraduate student in the Department of English, University of Nigeria, in 1972 and he graduated with an English/Drama degree in 1975; I came to the Department in 1976, but via the Vice-Chancellor's Office as a Clerical Officer in 1974. I lived with a close relative of mine, the late Professor Emmanuel Obiechina and it was through him, as I have pointed out earlier, that I heard of the artistic exploits of Ogonna Agu, the late Professor Ossie Enekwe, Professor Sam Ukala, and host of other talented members of that immediate post-Biafra War generation of undergraduates of the English Department at Nsukka, as well as the Oak Theatre which I became a member of and later very proudly headed in the third year of my undergraduate study. In 1986 I left Nsukka on a Commonwealth Scholarship to study for a doctorate at Leeds University under Professor Martin Banham, and behold, Ogonna Agu had been there studying for and obtaining his Masters in 1978; and again, tales of Ogonna's stay were still being told by all those who were there at the time.

Between 1982 when he began his Ph.D. at SOAS (University of London; we also have the University of London in common as I now teach at Goldsmiths, a UoL college) and 1992 when he returned to Nigeria we shared six years being together in the United Kingdom. Yet, we never met; but as ever, I heard of him through friends and colleagues such as the late Dr Esiaba Irobi, Dr Olu Oguibe, Sam Ukala, Professor Chimalum Nwankwo, Professor Olu Obafemi, Martin Banham and Terry Enright who had been Ogonna's course mate on Professor Banham's African Theatre programme at Leeds University. In 1990, I joined the Theatre and Performance teaching team at the Polytechnic South West (this became the University of Plymouth in 1992) and Terry and I became colleagues and friends. It was my animated discussions with Terry throughout the eleven years I was at Plymouth that made the image of Ogonna Agu yet again intrude and settle in my academic horizon for such a long time.

Terry Enright had done the Leeds African Masters and claimed at the time that he struggled to grasp what basically qualifies a theatre or play (such as J. P. Clark's, Wole Soyinka's, Lewis Nkosi's, Ola Rotimi's, Ama Ata Aidoo's, Efua Sutherland's, Ngugi wa Thiong'o's, Athol Fugard's or Barney Simon's) to be called African. He informed me that it was what he had argued/debated with Ogonna Agu for the twelve months they were together on the Leeds African programme. Since Ogonna Agu had not been able to convince him, he was hoping I could. So, Ogonna Agu left an unfinished task for me to complete with 'educating' our mutual English/Welsh friend and contemporary. I directed Wole Soyinka's

Death and the King's Horseman (with Esiaba as assistant director/research cover), work-shopped *The Lion and the Jewel,* directed Bode Sowande's *A Sanctus for Women*; Efua Sutherland's *The Marriage of Anansewa*; I devised *The Sea Woman*, I did an African dance drama, and led numerous African dance workshops with Ayodele Scott; and I also taught numerous African plays with the help of colleagues such as Dr Victor Ukaegbu, Esiaba Irobi, Peter Badejo, Mary Yirenkyi, Dr Mary-Blossom Okafor, and even Professor Dapo Adelugba came to the University of Plymouth as External Examiner and a guest lecturer. But Terry was not convinced that he had been helped by all these to understand and this then became one of the central elements and aspiration of my research and teaching-to make non-African students and colleagues of mine come to grips with what African theatre is.

So, thanks to Ogonna Agu and his 'unfinished' business with Terry Enright, I came to acquire an abiding teaching and research philosophy which recently culminated in the African Theatre Association (AfTA) Annual Conference which I co-hosted with a Ugandan colleague, Dr Sam Kasule, of the University of Derby, UK at Goldsmiths and Derby in July 2013; the theme was: *What is African Theatre?* This is an indication that I am still searching for this definition of what African theatre really is, but that I am now doing so with the help of other contemporary African scholars and theatre makers. And perhaps, *Metaphors and Climax...* will contribute to this search for meaning and definition.

The essays presented here, in their different ways and collective iterations, capture the flavour and spirit of the man and artist that Ogonna Agu was. Both Professors Kalu Uka and Molinta Enendu paint for the reader intimate portraits of Ogonna Agu as a student, budding dramatist, poet, novelist and actor, dancer, painter, film maker/TV presenter, Igbo cultural activist, social crusader, ethnographer, and evocatively by Uka, as a 'stranger on the shore'; while Professor Charles Nwadigwe in his essay uses the concept of the virtuoso to explain Agu's diverse range of creative artistry as he 'traverses the various media of literary, visual and performing arts' (p.39) Nwadigwe also highlights Ogonna Agu's qualities as a practical man of the theatre who sought to engage with the economics of theatre as a professional practice, a business and an industry capable of providing employment for a multitude of people in Nigeria. For Ogonna Agu, the theatre in Nigeria needed to move out of university buildings and settings if it was ever going to realise its potential of becoming a commercially and socially viable enterprise that can transform lives and communities in the country.

All the other essays in their respective engagements with and interrogations of various aspects and different plays of Ogonna Agu, provide for the reader a dense but exciting picture and memory of the creative talent, the man of vision, a poet of the street, that this Igbo, Biafran (the idea and dream of Biafra never quite left Ogonna's imagination and that of many others who like him experienced Biafra physically and emotionally, as John Iwuh demonstrates in his essay which looks at Agu's two Biafra war plays, *Symbol of a Goddess* and *Cry of a Maiden* and as other contributors such as Charles Okwuowulu, Emeka Ofora, Uche-Chinemere Nwaozuzu, Canice Nwosu *et al*, Ofonime Inyang and Edet Essien who also looked at these two plays), Nigerian and African artist he was and will continue to live and be celebrated in the works that he has left behind.

In concluding this preface which I felt honoured to be asked to write, it seems to me, therefore, through reading the varied responses which Ogonna's plays, the numerous other creative works and cultural activism which are presented in this book, that in seeking to synthesise what is essentially a composite theatre/per formance/artistic aesthetic, Ogonna Ana-agudo Agu was in his unique and complex way, philosophically and practically answering that nagging question that Terry Enright and I mulled and argued over at every opportunity for the eleven years that we were colleagues at the University of Plymouth Department of Theatre and Performance.

Professor Osita Okagbue
Department of Theatre and Performance
Goldsmiths, University of London
United Kingdom
January 2014

Work Cited

Achebe, Chinua. *Arrow of God*, London, Ibadan, Nairobi, Sydney: Heinemann: (1964, 1974),

Introduction

Stranger on the Shore: A Personalized Reminiscence Introducing, The life of Ogonna Chibuzo Anaagudo Agu, Teacher, Artist and Explorer

Kalu Uka

Prologue

Let me introduce the subject of this whole book, *OGONNA* to you. The man who perambulated round the shores of Igbo civilization-to paint, write, sing his dirges, envision his dramas, and parade his masquerades.

Let me introduce him to you-because you only think so when you claim you know him. You don't. I do.

You've only, perhaps, read some of his works for the stage and articles in journals to boost a curriculum vitae for promotion. Maybe you met him at a Society of Nigerian Theatre Artists (SONTA) conference. Maybe you glimpsed him teaching dance arts and choreography, wearing his priestly anklets, in the old-fashioned Department of Theatre Arts University of Calabar Dance Studio where resident dance-artistes of the University of Calabar Performing Company (UCPC) practised and learnt their occupational trade since the days of Darlene Blackburn and Orville Johnson, and latterly of Arnold Udoka. Maybe you saw Ogonna as Director of a play conceived and written by himself in one of the Department's categories of venue: - the Courtyard Studio Theatre, or the Garden Theatre or the (New) Chinua Achebe Arts Theatre built as model proscenium in 1980 by Apio and Associates during Dexter Lyndersay's watch as H.O.D and Art Director.

Introduction | *Kalu Uka, in*
Charles Nwadigwe, Molinta Enendu & Canice Nwosu (Eds.)
Metaphors and Climax, Reminiscences on the Drama and
Theatre of Ogonna Agu
London , Adonis & Abbey Publishers

Maybe you breathed excitement as you saw Ogonna venture in bold experimentation out into Calabar's "11-11" (the Cenotaph, Roundabout, resplendent with the giant Gold Gong that J.D. Ekwere had won in 1974 for the old South-Eastern State at that year's NAFEST in Lagos, with Wole Soyinka's *The Lion and the Jewel* which he turned into an Efikland fairytale moving operatta in the title, "Esen Owo" ("Stranger"/"Visitor") at once reminding the modern theatre scholar-historian of Friedrich Durrenmatt's captivating fictive play, *The Visit*). Maybe you saw Ogonna as apprentice actor in Kalu Uka's production of Efua Sutherland's *Edufa*, the iconic Greek-derivative classic, linking the scholar to Euripidean *Alcestis*.

Oh, yes, my friend, you need a special imagination and sympathy of a kindred spirit to know that MAVERICK and CREATOR that *was* Ogonna-Agu-because even with his physical desiccation now in death, compelling inevitable absence, you must FEEL him, if you knew him. He remains a PULSE of the artistic. Only imagination, of those around whom his aura reflected small small streaks of theatrical light, can stimulate again Ogonna's artistry in you, to reach the CREATIVITY in him, grounding the forms of it in your environment, Nigeria; the flow of it in your Exhibition Gallery; the thrill of it when a performer personalizes his fictional characters; when a learner-student is challenged by it, and post-production post-mortems roll out interminable questions on significances and significations.

Ogonna exhumed and enlivened the deadness of humdrum existences; his artistic soul exhaled a breath of freshness that held imaginations captive. A one-time Dean of the Faculty of Arts, Godfrey Uzoigwe the Historian, exhaling a swirl of tobacco smoke from the curve of his pipe-bowl acknowledged this much at the end of the performance of *The Return of a Night Masquerade* in 1986. Why? How? Well, by the cohesive entirety of his creations.

Introduction | *Kalu Uka, in*
Charles Nwadigwe, Molinta Enendu & Canice Nwosu (Eds.)
Metaphors and Climax, Reminiscences on the Drama and Theatre of Ogonna Agu
London , Adonis & Abbey Publishers

Ogonna created such a totality as only a discerning maverick at work could embody in eliciting the essence of a civilization.

You never saw him at his work. I did. As he prepared his thoughts; as he reflected on the "Igboness"-or, as Pol Ndu had once phrased it, the "Ivoriness"-of the Igboman in Nigeria; as Ogonna, at 12 Azikiwe Street, in Calabar, bemoaned fate and brooded over the demise of his baby.

What is death to the artist? Thomas Mann volunteered a philosophic answer with *Death in Venice*. For Ogonna, it is the artist contemplating his *Chi*. Or, isn't it? Is a madman an irrational being? When your pet bird confined, escapes out of the cage, never to return, (like Noah's lost dove after the flood; like Emenike's eagle after the soldiers' attack in Agu's *Symbol of a Goddess*), should depression not be ousted by hope? Should a low spirit send you wandering the streets, or propel you into becoming a motivational television star speaker, an entertainer exuding joy from depths of frustration, as the angry English young men's playwrights' group of the late 1950s and the early 1960s led by John Osborne would picture it in Jimmy Porter?

Ogonna drew dream pictures when the University of Calabar Administration ostracized him in a pet psychological warfare, he stuck to his conviction that innocence would always be vindicated as right despite the passage and wastage of time. Now, follow me.

Movement I: A Flashback

Follow me to 1971. The embers of the devastating Nigeria-Biafra War were still smouldering. In heaps, the ashes and the debris, the cesspool of hatreds, the ruins and dilapidations of structures still lay heavily around, stinkingly palpable all over the once paradisiacal Nsukka, town and University alike, and Vincent Ike's PPMC was exerting itself at resuscitation. Artists were on the fringes-hard at work. Obiora Udechukwu, Bons Nwobiani and the

Introduction | *Kalu Uka, in*
Charles Nwadigwe, Molinta Enendu & Canice Nwosu (Eds.)
Metaphors and Climax, Reminiscences on the Drama and
Theatre of Ogonna Agu
London , Adonis & Abbey Publishers

celebrated charcoal art group, precursors of the Nsukka Art School were around, capturing on board, wood and canvas the "SILHOUETTES" of a damaged civilization in need of repair. The nation's politicians called it "REHABILITATION", one leg of General Gowon's famous tripodal slogan.

Ogonna was in tune with the artists. Their minds were all like stilettos. They were trying to re-embroider, re-knit, the legacy of Nnamdi Azikiwe. Indeed, Zik had, with singular peculiar vision endowed a legacy of a many-splendoured light, the light of education, education to "restore the dignity of man" in the Nsukka environment and beyond. Some of us, with Nwamife Publishers in Enugu, replacing the failed dream of an Okigbo-Achebe projected publishing house, undertook poetic reminiscences, "seeing the silver in an evening drop of rain"; while others would be rubbing their scars as Wole Soyinka characterized the postwar agonies in the lyric, "Apres la guerre". Out of the shattered shards of the crushed, but unbowed nation of Igboland, Ogonna, by now an upcoming brooder, was brooding, moodily poring over matters, searching the soul for the divine soothing balm and blessing ointment of art such as postwar and slavery Israel sought for souls in Gilead.

A song, and a dirge, later refined and enshrined in Igbo Musicology by Nelly Uchendu, welled forth from Ogonna's Nnobi folkways:

> Nne nne m o
> Udu m alaputa m o
> Udum oma
> Udum ji chuo mmiri
> Ma mu amaro n'udu awaa . . .[1]

Thus, his first play, in 1973, "Broken Pots" took shape. For a debut drama by a youthful undergraduate, the imagery of *Broken Pots* was telling and apt, by anchoring the central action in the

---

Introduction | *Kalu Uka, in*
Charles Nwadigwe, Molinta Enendu & Canice Nwosu (Eds.)
Metaphors and Climax, Reminiscences on the Drama and Theatre of Ogonna Agu
London , Adonis & Abbey Publishers

image of the virgin damsel whose waterpot is shattered by a conglomerate of distractions on her way back from the stream. Ogonna recalls all the diversionary gimmicks that Western missionary education and commercial attractions in the newness of the radio set used to captivate the mind of innocent Africa. A virgin is ravished by the dogs of war, a war waged when those superficialities of innovations beyond and including the portable radio, like sugar and sweets and canned sardines, were used to lure away the soul.

It was not only a pleasure for me to direct that play on the stage at Nsukka in 1973, but "Broken Pots" signalled the coming together to re-create Igboland by a band of dedicated, not broken souls, on the auspices of the once famed Oak Theatre Group. The Oak Theatre was founded by Ossie Enekwe, but the staff of the Department of English adopted it as a platform for show-casing the new spirit of endeavour. Successive Heads of the Department- D.I. Nwoga, M.J.C Echeruo, Emma Obiechina-ensured that Kalu Uka, as Patron and Drama leader, of Oak Theatre, was given the facilities with which to realize the deep-sighted creations of such aspiring playwrights as Ogonna.

He has proved his mettle. In his classmates, men and women, Ogonna's first play reached beyond Nsukka and the likes of Amobi Adirika, Rose Ani and Sam Ukala became famous as centrestage and touring actors. The burden of using Igbo art to lift the soul became a delightful challenge that Ogonna would respond to time and time again via his plays. For that effort, Ogonna possessed an unassailable arsenal of a totality of weapons: he was a *painter*; he was a *visual artist* in *sculpting* characters; he was a *poet*; he was a scribbler of notes; he was a *worshipper* in a personalized shrine; he had a quill-feather pen; above all he has a special vision, the trajectory along which he believed Igbo life and art must be realized: a philosophical picturization of the power within the

Introduction | *Kalu Uka, in*
Charles Nwadigwe, Molinta Enendu & Canice Nwosu (Eds.)
Metaphors and Climax, Reminiscences on the Drama and Theatre of Ogonna Agu
London , Adonis & Abbey Publishers

individual soul. Maybe, that is why all his plays and stories whatever their setting are all concretely *visual*.

Movement II

The first people to accord Ogonna a rightful acknowledgement of place in Igbo arts were people who awarded him the prize in California, USA. In the early 1980s a book came out on Igbo arts. It was put together by H.M. Cole and C.C. Aniakor, and was titled, *Igbo Arts: Community and Cosmos* published by the Museum of Cultural History, UCLA, Los Angeles. In a "foreword" to that book, Chinua Achebe wrote:

> ... Another reason why it is important to the Igbo to renew their art frequently is their view of the world as never standing still. "No condition is permanent" is the contemporary assertion of this view. In Igbo cosmology even gods could fall out of use and new forces were liable to appear without warning in the temporal and metaphysical firmament. The practical purpose of art is to channel a spiritual force into an aesthetically satisfying physical form that captures the presumed attributes of that force. It stands to reason, therefore, that new forms must stand ready to be called into being as often as new-threatening-forces appear on the scene. It is like "earthing"-grounding-an electrical charge to ensure safety.[2]

If Achebe focuses on the *macro* matrices of an Igbo civilization affected by European invasive intrusion and intervention, from the slave trade to warrant chieftaincies, Ogonna Agu reminds us of the importance of "little drops", the *micro* matrices. A tree may be felled, but when the brushes and undergrowths are also swept away, a "desert not only encroaches", but may take over and a windswept sand empire replace a rainforest vegetation. So, in all his subsequent excursions, Ogonna focused on this complementing dimensional aspect of Igbo cultural concerns. To reach the *soul* of it, let us go on an imaginary journey.

Introduction | *Kalu Uka, in*
Charles Nwadigwe, Molinta Enendu & Canice Nwosu (Eds.)
Metaphors and Climax, Reminiscences on the Drama and Theatre of Ogonna Agu
London , Adonis & Abbey Publishers

Movement III

Just imagine. Imagine, I insist, that you are a scout on an excursion. You see before you a long stretch of a beach. It is a "coastline". Let's now give it a name: it is the lonely celebrated beach-line of Agulu Lake. As if you stood on the Awka-end of the highway, northwards of the lake, Nnobi and Nnewi are to the south. You've heard of the mystery monster crocodiles of the lake. Take in the fresh breeze of the landscape. Forget the crocodiles. If they do appear, ignore them. You are a good man, not a saboteur. They will ignore you too. They are part of the mystique.

"There are more things in the world than are dreamt of in your philosophy", Hamlet told Horatio. Imagine it. As in Shakespeare's Elizabethan England, so in Ogonna Agu's Peter Obi's Anambra State, there are mysteries beyond expanses of murky waters and sluggish lakes, sluggish waters-where do they flow into? Or, from? Blue skies, and sky-blue green waters who colours them? Whose eyes are they? Knowable and unknowable, which sailor has fathomed them? Still they are there, fascinatingly alluring.

So, now, see behind you, on the edge of the hills in the background, there stands a *man. This* man, - or is it his *shade*, rather his *substance*? He descends gracefully down to the shore. He begins to move along the beach line. In the south pacific they would have called him a beachcomber, a loafer, such as Achebe said Unoka was.

But I'll tell you who this one is. If you grew up with my generation, you'd recall a golden music guy of the 1960s, a famous Alto Saxophonist. He was called Acker Bilk. His most memorable music was titled, "Stranger on the Shore". Ogonna Agu was Acker Bilk's "alter ego" in terms of making music on the strange shores of his world. He understood and wrote in defence of the mysteries of OKIJA SHRINE. He danced to his own music, and when he threw that side or backward or forward step we call "itu nkwu" it

Introduction	*Kalu Uka, in* Charles Nwadigwe, Molinta Enendu & Canice Nwosu (Eds.) *Metaphors and Climax, Reminiscences on the Drama and* *Theatre of Ogonna Agu* London , Adonis & Abbey Publishers

was with the grace and agility of a gazelle. "Ana-Agu-Udo" was the soil on which the smart soul of hallowed ground grew peace and harmony for a people to establish their niche in the world. When he played "Madman" in Calabar on NTA, or read "Mad Poems", it was that imagination seeking to find that "thing" Achebe has called "force" of aesthetics seeking concrete form for attributes society can identify.

Ogonna Ana-agudo Agu, now slate in hand, left hand, held as a mermaid holds up a monitoring mirror, as the Greek Medusa-slaying champion held it, becomes the creative leopard casting an image, his own image, upon slate and state of mind. You may not recognize the man any more, as if it was an "atali" in the dance arena. But the man *sees*, in a double vision. He throws an aura of a strange feeling over the onlooker, he is simultaneously peering over your back and over your head to beyond the beach creatures. His soul is surfing the waves. Acolytes emerge: an assortment, in assorted attires – bikinis, hotpants, bare-breasts, long black hair dripping water rivulets. The waves carry them up, hide them briefly, throw them to the sun. Now you see a play of dolphins; a swim of sharks. The power and strength of "forest boy" is matched with the power and strength of water dwellers.

Ogonna Agu was romantic in imagination and painted romantic, images. His skies remind you of a Vincent van Gogh's sea-and-land-scapes. Add to these the altosaxophonic timbres and you have your mystic Ogonna.

Movement IV

Here then is he: Ogonna Chibuzo Anagudo Agu. I have introduced him to you. I have, I believe in a style that he would have endorsed, let you *know* and now you could *touch*, not the *ghost*, but the *substance*, of the Ogonna you knew only in part. If he

Introduction | *Kalu Uka, in*
Charles Nwadigwe, Molinta Enendu & Canice Nwosu (Eds.)
Metaphors and Climax, Reminiscences on the Drama and
Theatre of Ogonna Agu
London , Adonis & Abbey Publishers

were to do it himself, all you would have seen would be a broad, thicklipped, jagged toothy smirk on his wry face.

That is what he gave me the day in January 1989 when he came for me to endorse by recommendation his application to the Foreign and Commonwealth Office for a scholarship[3] to study for a Ph.D. in an aspect of Igbo civilization that excited him. In that Application Form, you could see the authentic Agu you never knew. You could see his burning desire; his application proposal painted vividly the colour of his mind. Indeed, it was like what Esiaba Irobi would have called "the colour of rusting gold".

Epilogue

From here, then, you will read the rest of what you need for this exemplary, heartfelt book commemoration exercise initiated by Professor Charles Nwadigwe. To foster a memorabilia of this magnitude is more than "labour of love", it is a dedicated encomium to the memory of a great soul. In all subsequent perusing you will do of Ogonna's dramatizations, fictions, poetry, critical essays or of his paintings, and other artworks with which he survived in England by selling them to raise money when sponsorships ended, you will be savouring *phases* and reflections of Ogonna the dreamer's search for significations and significances; you will probably be able to define his role better; determine his place and how he has grounded "Chi" and "Ana" in the stabilizing forces of Igbo culture, as exemplified in, *The Return of a Night Masquerade* (Achebe's "Ogbazulobodo" in *Arrow of God*) and why the masquerade is a central player in the Igbo cosmos. Again Achebe ramifies by asserting that;

> . . . what makes the dance and the masquerade so satisfying to the Igbo disposition is, . . . that artistic deployment of motion, of agility, which informs the Igbo concept of existence. The masquerade . . . moves spectacularly . . . Those who enjoy its motion . . . must follow its progress up and down the arena: ". . . ada akwu ofu ebe enene mmuo". . .The

Introduction	*Kalu Uka, in* Charles Nwadigwe, Molinta Enendu & Canice Nwosu (Eds.) *Metaphors and Climax, Reminiscences on the Drama and* *Theatre of Ogonna Agu* London , Adonis & Abbey Publishers

kinetic energy of the masquerade's art is . . . transmitted to a whole arena . . .[4]

Ogonna saw that arena when in 2000, I commissioned him to write the (25th year) Silver Jubilee performance script for Unical which produced the play, *Dawn in the Academy*, which has since been semiotically directed to give scholars both M.A. and Ph.D. degrees. Ogonna came fully into his own after that and, in a novel, imaged himself, beyond a "Stranger on the Shore", as *The Strong Boy of the Forest*-but death, the final diction and dictator reckons with no "strong boys", but must come when it must. Remember Ogonna Chibuzo Anaagudo AGU. Ph.D. 1948-2011.

Notes

1. A popular Igbo folk song.
2. Culled from Okey Ikenegbu's write-up on Achebe in the Enugu-based LIMCAF Artists' tribute booklet to Achebe; *Chinua Achebe: Visual Expressions* (Enugu, 18-20 May, 2013).
3. Original copy recovered from my personal archives as I was researching for this paper following Prof. Nwadigwe's "order" that I contribute, however belatedly. I thank him for his and the co-editors' patience with me.
4. See Note 2 above, p.2 of *Visual Expressions*.

Introduction | *Kalu Uka, in*
Charles Nwadigwe, Molinta Enendu & Canice Nwosu (Eds.)
Metaphors and Climax, Reminiscences on the Drama and Theatre of Ogonna Agu
London , Adonis & Abbey Publishers

Chapter One

Ogonna Anaagudo-Agu: The Dynamism of a Versatile Artist

L.O. Molinta Enendu

Preamble

Perhaps, no practising theatre artist or theatre scholar quite closely fits the hypothetical logo for a theatre ensemble workshop, showing a theatre artist at work, than Ogonna Anaagudo-Agu. This illustrative and imaginative image is described below:

> An abstract elongated human figure in a backwards tumble, is supported on his two open feet and the elbows. Between the exaggerated toes are, dexterously held; a painting brush, a drawing pencil, a spanner, a drumstick, a screw driver, mathematical calculator, a hammer and a sewing needle with thread. In between his two legs, from the laps down towards the ankle are held; a local skin-drum, a local calabash guitar, a wooden gong, and closest to the ankles, is a carved totem of a dancing female figure. Balanced on the bent body trunk, between the groin and the neck, are a computer screen, a video camera, a lantern, a horn speaker, all tied to the trunk by a network of cables and connectors. On his neck, worn like a pendant, is a cordless microphone. The waist and ankles are decorated with dancing rattles; between his lips is a wooden flute. An open book, positioned in between his hands, or so it seems, faces his two pronounced eyeballs set on a very cheerful, calm physiognomy.

A study of this figure shows a stylized, physical human representation, depicting the versatility and flexibility of a theatre artist; the sheer diversity of his professional tools and the unlimited, dexterous deployment of the body, and the senses in professional theatre endeavour. Perhaps, Ogonna Anaagudo-Agu lived his life, a prototype of a profound theatre artist portrayed above.

Chapter one | *L.O. Molinta Enendu, in*
Charles Nwadigwe, Molinta Enendu & Canice Nwosu (Eds.)
Metaphors and Climax, Reminiscences on the Drama and Theatre of Ogonna Agu
London , Adonis & Abbey Publishers

Background

Ogonna Anaagudo-Agu was born in 1948, in his hometown Nnobi, in Anambra State, Nigeria, to the family of Mr. and Mrs. Gilbert Anaagudo-Agu. He enjoyed a sound educational foundation, attending one of the best Mission Schools in the then Eastern Nigeria, the Dennis Memorial Grammar School (DMGS), Onitsha. His Bachelor of Arts Degree in English and Drama was earned at the University of Nigeria, Nsukka, from 1972-1975. With the British scholarship scheme, he started a Masters Degree programme in the University of Leeds and obtained it in 1978. He proceeded to the University of London, School of Oriental and African Studies (SOAS), in 1982 with a Study Fellowship grant from the University of Calabar, Nigeria, and studied for a Doctorate Degree (Ph.D.) in Igbo culture. He returned to Nigeria in 1992 and joined the University of Calabar, where he had been employed, in 1979, as a pioneer staff. Serving at various capacities, Agu was the Director of the University of Calabar Performing Company (UCPC), (2002-2004) - the demonstration and teaching support unit of the Department. Here, he experimented on dance and music theatre composition. As a member of the Theatre Graduate Studies Committee, he taught and supervised graduate theses and dissertations mainly on, but not limited to, cultural studies, playwriting, adaptation and directing. He was the Head of Department from 2004-2006.

Focus

This piece is a study based on the academic and professional theatre practice of Ogonna Anaagudo-Agu, over a period of about thirty-five years. From an introduction to his background, the study benefits from the experiences of working with him in the same Department for several years; this writer also worked as a designer in the stage production of Agu's plays. The writer also interacted personally with Agu on some social, traditional and

Chapter one | *L.O. Molinta Enendu, in*
Charles Nwadigwe, Molinta Enendu & Canice Nwosu (Eds.)
Metaphors and Climax, Reminiscences on the Drama and Theatre of Ogonna Agu
London , Adonis & Abbey Publishers

cultural issues as *"Nwa Nnaa"*, coming from the same State and geographical location, and shared same cultural and traditional practices, even when they lived far away from home. Most importantly, the study is anchored on the writer's view of Agu as a versatile, visionary, all-purpose, multi-talented (virtuoso) theatre artist. The study benefits from the very close mutual relationship that existed between the writer – a designer, and Agu- a director, from his newest beginning, to his distinction as an experienced veteran.

Agu as a Playwright

Ogonna Anaagudo-Agu has seven full-length published plays; several uncompleted play manuscripts (and even unpublished drama sketches) and one award winning playlet, *House of Death.* His plays, *The Last of the Biafrans*, (1996); *Dance of the Deer*, (1998); *The Return of a Night Masquerade*, (1998); and *I Fear for Kattie* (2000), were all published by Baaj Publishers. *Symbol of a Goddess*, published by the University of Calabar Press, in 2005, was actually one of Agu's earliest plays. *Cry of a Maiden* was also written much earlier, immediately after the Nigeria-Biafra War, in 1970, revised in 1973 and produced by the University of Nigeria, Nsukka as directed by the veteran Kalu Uka. Agu noted in the 2000 definitive published version of the play that it was Professor M. J. C. Echeruo, "who was the first to see the merits of the play, and decided to place it on the production list of the English Department. This singular encouragement has contributed to inspire me in my creative efforts".

Dawn in the Academy, was also published in 2001 from the stable of Baaj publications. In this play, Agu takes a bold look at the persistent problems, conflicts and chaos facing the University systems in Nigeria. He looks at the problems from several angles and dimensions with each posing as a major factor of the decadence. Hence, in the introductory section to the play, Agu

Chapter one | *L.O. Molinta Enendu, in*
Charles Nwadigwe, Molinta Enendu & Canice Nwosu (Eds.)
Metaphors and Climax, Reminiscences on the Drama and
Theatre of Ogonna Agu
London , Adonis & Abbey Publishers

explains that "... from unionism and government, to informal characters who impart learning and learn-the problem is one of selection, structuring and adaptation of the mass of material to make compulsive, cogent theatre, at once fascinating and engaging".

In May 2000, *Dawn in the Academy* was commissioned and sponsored by the University of Calabar as part of the ceremony marking its Silver Jubilee Celebration. The production Director was Affiong Okon, while production design was executed by this writer. In fact, Okon used the production's directorial experience as the basis for her Masters Degree practical project and thesis: "A Semiotic Approach to the Direction of Ogonna Agu's *Dawn in the Academy*".

In an experimental design project in 1981, supervised by Dexter K. W. Lyndersay, the chosen playlet was, *House of Death*, by Ogonna Anaagudo-Agu. It was this writer's first contact with Agu's work, and the project required giving a stage explication of the play's scenographic demands. The setting was a fireplace in an Igbo cultural milieu and traditional architecture; where a mother is using traditional medication to treat an *Ogbanje* child in a purely realistic setting. The resulting design was expository, innovative and enthusiastic, according to Mr. Lyndersay's evaluation.

Generally speaking, the wide acceptability of the plays of Agu may be traced to his mastery of the language which is considered beautiful and forceful. His works are uniquely exceptional with some experimental flavour and stylistic innovations in the theatrical composition. His human, spiritual, supernatural characters-gods, goddesses, deities, are highly developed as convincing stage characters. Agu in his writings and compositions, at times, breaks conventional boundaries but he does this with conscious, enterprising, expeditory, artistic spirit, and returns with successful aesthetics and innovative results. There are

Chapter one | *L.O. Molinta Enendu, in*
Charles Nwadigwe, Molinta Enendu & Canice Nwosu (Eds.)
Metaphors and Climax, Reminiscences on the Drama and
Theatre of Ogonna Agu
London , Adonis & Abbey Publishers

outstounding instances of this in *Dance of the Deer, Return of the Night Masquerade* and, *I Fear for Kattie.*

Agu as a Poet

Perhaps, Agu's first international recognition was with his poetry. In 1972, his "Lonesongs at Dawn", a collection of poems, entered for the All African Arts Competition organized by the University of California at Los Angeles, emerged a winner. Part of this collection was later published in *African Arts*. Other works of poetry include, *Odu Okike, (Horn of Creation: An Igbo Epic of Creation,* and a poem written in Igbo language, *"Aguma by Nwapolici",* which was published in *Uwa Ndi Igbo* by Nsukka Odunke Publishers in 1986.

Ogonna Agu was an accomplished poet and he used this genre, mostly for the propagation of Igbo worldview and philosophy particularly to comment on Igbo cosmology as well as other topical social issues. These are exemplified in *Odu Okike* and, *Hymn to the Lady of Red Eyes,* published in 1991, by Wsafiri, Canterbury, Kent, England.

Agu as a Novelist and Short Story Writer

In all the major literary genres, drama, poetry and novel, Agu has shown reasonable resourcefulness with significant returns. *The Strong Boy of the Forest,* published by *Odinaala-ka* in 1999 was his first published novel. A volume of 132 pages, the novel is in twelve chapters, with eleven full-page illustrations by the author. It is a story of a young dumb boy, Ohaezueme, who struggles to achieve heroic personality by his exploits in the forest, but with equally great cost to his life. Agu dedicates the work to his mother, Madam Uzonwa Patience Agu, whom he said, contributed to the framing of the story.

Chapter one | *L.O. Molinta Enendu, in*
Charles Nwadigwe, Molinta Enendu & Canice Nwosu (Eds.)
Metaphors and Climax, Reminiscences on the Drama and Theatre of Ogonna Agu
London , Adonis & Abbey Publishers

Agu's other novel, *Adiaha the Beauty Queen*, published in 2002 by Baaj Publishers, was inspired by the quashed World Beauty Pageant that was hosted in Calabar in Cross River State, Nigeria, in 2001. The Cross River State Ministry of Education soon after recommended *Adiaha the Beauty Queen* as a literature text for Junior Secondary School curriculum, and it is still in use till date.

Agu and the Promotion of Igbo Culture and Tradition

Ogonna Anaagudo-Agu's most outstanding literary contribution perhaps may be found in his love for, and the promotion, propagation and preservation of Igbo cultural heritage and tradition. This view is highlighted in his research interests, his use of language, and in his deployment of astounding traditional (Igbo) metaphors, music, icons, symbols and relics. There is also immeasurable strengthening in his theatrical interpretation of the Igbo mythology and cosmology, and in stage representation of the deities, gods, goddesses, and the supernatural especially in the dramatization of Igbo story of the origin of creation.

Agu's preoccupation and interest for African culture stem from his childhood adventures in his village, Nnobi, where he was said to have taken active part in several cultural and social activities. In the University, he enrolled as a member, and championed the cultural programmes, of learned traditional associations like, the Society for the Promotion of Igbo Language and Culture (SPILC). He later trained in the School of Oriental and African Studies (SOAS) where he took his Doctorate Degree (Ph.D.) in Igbo tradition. He became a dynamic member of different societies for the promotion of Igbo language, heritage, values and tradition.

In 1983, Agu's research on "*Chi* and Role Differentiation in Igbo Culture and Tradition", and his findings were presented in the International Colloquium on Igbo Language and Culture held at the University of Nigeria, Nsukka under the auspices of the Society for the Promotion of Igbo Language and Culture (SPILC).

Chapter one | *L.O. Molinta Enendu, in*
Charles Nwadigwe, Molinta Enendu & Canice Nwosu (Eds.)
Metaphors and Climax, Reminiscences on the Drama and Theatre of Ogonna Agu
London , Adonis & Abbey Publishers

This was followed by further work and research on, "The Teaching of Igbo Drama", delivered to teachers of Igbo language at the 3rd International Colloquium hosted at the University of Nigeria, Nsukka, by the same organization in 1984. Confirming the feeling that his research is culture based, Agu goes further to work on, "The *Ikenga* as the Archetype of Hero in Igbo Cultural Tradition". This was presented at the Faculty of Arts Seminar series, University of Nigeria, Nsukka in 1986. *Ikenga* as a notable Igbo cultural and religious symbol, occurred in over eight of Agu's works, in several different usages. For instance, in his novel, *The Strong Boy of the Forest*, Agu sees *Ikenga* as, "a carved two horned figure . . . sometimes in a sitting position, holding a matchet in the right hand, and a skull in the left, used as a symbol for expressing the indomitable will of a man to achieve success in life. A symbol used in representing the *Chi* of a man" (128).

The Igbo Water Goddess was the focus of Agu's research in 1988. In a paper, "The River Goddess as the Mother-figure of the *Idemmili* Igbo", Agu drew a striking, and inspiring analogy between a typical Igbo mother's responsibilities to her children, with that of the spiritual motherhood of *Idemmili* Goddess to her children. His classic work, "*Uli* Essence and Symbols in the Development of an Indigenous Igbo Script," presented at a conference of Nigerian Artists, form the backbone for Agu's development of "Indigenous Igbo Alphabets". The figures used in his *Aka Umuagbara*, are original Igbo alphabets of his own creation, as a rejection of the English alphabets. The *Aka Umuagbara* in *Uli* Essence could best be explained as a form of ideogram, created by Agu, comprising written and printed characters. They are used in making up words that symbolize the idea or action. The *Uli Essence* also dominates his literary, theatrical and visual artworks.

Agu's love for the masquerade tradition permeates his literary works and his dance theatre. This is manifest in his plays, *The Return of the Night Masquerade, Dance of the Deer, Symbol of a Goddess*

Chapter one | L.O. Molinta Enendu, in
Charles Nwadigwe, Molinta Enendu & Canice Nwosu (Eds.)
Metaphors and Climax, Reminiscences on the Drama and Theatre of Ogonna Agu
London , Adonis & Abbey Publishers

and some of his poetry. He uses it as a medium to project the Igbo ritual, mythology and for the enhancement of his dramatic composition. Agu is versed in Igbo traditional masquerade songs which he sees as "mythos" of drama, and "myth" as framework of action. Agu's encounter with Western culture for the years he sojourned in United Kingdom did not diminish his interest nor divert his attention from Igbo cultural values. He envisioned an annual Festival of Igbo Drama and Theatre to be instituted at Nri, the ancestral home of the Igbo. This was meant to coincide with the yearly New Yam Festival of the Igbo and thus blossom into an international tourist attraction. He enlisted the support and collaboration of Prof. Charles Nwadigwe and some other theatre artists and cultural devotees of Igbo extraction and they began consultations with stakeholders on the Festival Project but this could not be accomplished before his transition to the ancestral world.

Agu as Painter, Artist, Dancer, Actor and Drummer

Ogonna Anaagudo-Agu was a talented painter and fine artist. His paintings and artistic symbols are culture inspired, simulating what he has severally called the "Uli Essence and Symbols". He employs these metaphors and symbols as vehicle for his artistic expression and for Igbo cultural evangelism. His paintings on canvas, framed with polished hard, wooden, battens abound in public and private places in the country, but more in Cross River State capital, Calabar: in banking halls, in reception halls of government establishments, and private sitting rooms of the nobles. Agu also, using this language of forms, personally illustrated most of his books-*Adiaha the Beauty Queen*, *Cry of a Maiden* and *The Strong Boy of the Forest*.

As a staff of the University, he has directed almost all of his plays as Departmental experimental works for the stage. In such stage experiments, Agu reserves a role for himself, either as an

Chapter one | *L.O. Molinta Enendu, in*
Charles Nwadigwe, Molinta Enendu & Canice Nwosu (Eds.)
Metaphors and Climax, Reminiscences on the Drama and
Theatre of Ogonna Agu
London , Adonis & Abbey Publishers

actor or a dancer or a drummer: which ever, he has always justified his participation by sheer excellence of his attempts, which are seen, as unique with significant artistic imagination. He was indeed a man of several parts-Ogonna of all trades and master of all. He employed mime, nonverbal codes, free vocalization, dirge, songs and lyrical arts with innovative melodic force joggled in his performances.

Agu as Film Maker/TV Programme Star/Social Crusader

Ogonna Anaagudo-Agu was a filmmaker and director. In 1986, Agu initiated a one-man television serial production in which he was the only actor, the scriptwriter, the production designer and the director. He called it *I Be Mad Man*. It was a programme that drew inspiration from his versatility in different arts of theatre – acting, dancing, miming, creative use and command of language, vocalization supported by drumming, entertainment technology and realistic costume and make-up. His solo TV Show greatly captivated the audiences every week. While holding the audience spellbound, he launches satirical attacking messages that are directed towards the expositions and the correction of the ills of the society-coming from the lips of a mad man, who spoke mainly 'Broken English'. He struck at his audience with words, but pacified them with rhythmic dance, throbbing music and mime.

Agu also tried his hands on a number of films working on his own scripts, as an adventure into the new film culture. In 2006, his experiment was greatly rewarded when the story he put into film script, directed by him using entirely a cast selected from the students of Theatre Arts Department, University of Calabar, won the Star Prize in the All Nigeria Universities Challenge, organized by BOBTV. This success and the attendant recognition became a great source of inspiration and frustration to him as well. Inspired by the Award, he set more goals for himself and worked on more film scripts but got frustrated by some complex domestic politics

Chapter one | *L.O. Molinta Enendu, in*
Charles Nwadigwe, Molinta Enendu & Canice Nwosu (Eds.)
Metaphors and Climax, Reminiscences on the Drama and Theatre of Ogonna Agu
London , Adonis & Abbey Publishers

and conflicts that enmeshed the Award. Hence, he could not realize those cinematic goals till his demise.

Agu as an Ultraconservative Traditionalist

Agu's intensive research and studies on traditional Igbo cultural values and lore have deep influence on his day-to-day conduct. Given any opportunity, he reiterates how deeply he loves the Igbo culture despite his encounter with foreign cultures. Quite often, he protests, in his own way, the influence of foreign cultural practices on Igbo cultural norms and traditional values. It is only by very close association and study that this was made manifest. On language, religion and ideology, Agu posits quite emphatically that:

> The language crisis is seen to be a consequence of the displacement of African ideological basis of language usage generally by English thought, mercantilist ideology and technology. There is need for the retention of African cultural ideology as the superstructure on which to base language usage in creative writing particularly for their poetic quality. ("Religion and Igbo Ideology . . ." 16)

He developed, with time, a cultural revolutionary spirit and argues strongly that:

> With the development of Western canons of art, the pattern of development of African arts, has been disturbed . . . the argument is that African pattern of expression could have found its own pattern of development but for the intrusion of Western patterns which produced a profound retraction in trend. ("Background and Development. . ." 228)

Agu contended that the African (Igbo) encounter with the colonial forces stalled the march of African civilization, and contributed to the retardation of the development of many African scripts such as the *Bamum* in Cameroon and *Uli* in Nigeria. He saw the present English alphabets (A-Z) as being inadequate for

Chapter one | L.O. *Molinta Enendu, in*
Charles Nwadigwe, Molinta Enendu & Canice Nwosu (Eds.)
Metaphors and Climax, Reminiscences on the Drama and Theatre of Ogonna Agu
London , Adonis & Abbey Publishers

grappling with the complex tonal structure of African languages, Igbo in particular.

Agu then followed this with the invention of *"Aka Umuagbara"* as the alphabets (signs) for writing Igbo language ("Uli Essence. . ." 161). He was constantly in search of the African (Igbo) traditional values through religions, ideology, systematic observation and analysis of traditional African religious liturgy.

Agu's vision of Igbo culture and his related cultural research often interrogated the underlying modes of worship using colonial religious liturgy. He saw this as Eurocentric; another dimension of culture-religious domination that cannot, and need not, be universally binding on Africans (Igbos). This view stirred much smoke and dust around, blurring the people's views and perception of his new religious posture. Some concluded, with exaggeration, that it was a question directed on the existence of God. Blinded with such opinions, that were mere corrugation of facts, some saw it as mere heresy, and switched off. But again, Agu's occasional use of Igbo traditional accoutrement and accessories, especially, the wearing of *elili ukwu,* (ankle rope or anklet), made it difficult for some to fully clarify his true position on religion unless with very intimate closeness. Agu, however, was only pursuing a cultural evangelism of Igbo tradition that was to secure emancipation from the Eurocentric cultural subjugation and hegemony.

Conclusion

This study has focused on the creative arts of Ogonna-Anaagudo Agu, (1948-2011); from a brief mention of his background and educational career, attention centres on his thirty-five years of multi-faceted, professional practice as a poet, playwright and novelist. His numerous successful creative adventures as a man of several parts-a filmmaker, television star, a painter, an actor, a drummer, a dancer, a dirge vocalist, a traditionalist, and a cultural

Chapter one | L.O. Molinta Enendu, in
Charles Nwadigwe, Molinta Enendu & Canice Nwosu (Eds.)
Metaphors and Climax, Reminiscences on the Drama and Theatre of Ogonna Agu
London , Adonis & Abbey Publishers

evangelist-are fully delineated upon. Agu's seven published plays, two novels, several poems and numerous research papers, in both national and international journals, form the major reference points. His cultural revolutionary questions on some "Eurocentric patterns" in religion, language, worship, and plastic arts are examined and his alternative-"Uli Essence", "Aka-Umuagbara" are thoroughly studied and clarified. This "personal statement" on Agu's philosophy and professional practice concludes that Agu's formidable literary, cultural, performative and scholarly attainments, with more inquests in future, need to be truly instituted and immortalized.

Looking back on Agu's career of about thirty-five years in the theatre, one sees a man of extraordinary courage and innovative capabilities. He was a man imbued with bold, formidable, and creative sensibilities for experimental works in literary, plastic, performing arts as well as in media, cultural and anthropological studies. Perhaps, his strongest tools included his unique, forceful and expressive language and imaginative versatility. A playwright, a poet, a novelist, a painter, a dancer, an actor, a drummer, a filmmaker, a social crusader, a director and above all, a radical mind: lover and crusader for traditional African culture and values. Perhaps, with time, as more literary inquests are directed on the formidable attainments of this brilliant and bold spirit in creative and cultural arts, his immortality as a rare, talented, thorough-bred artist with continuous expanding frontier will be more truly established.

Works Cited

Agu, Ogonna C. "House of Death."*African Arts*. Ed. J. Poveys. California: University of California at Los Angeles, 1973. 26-27.

Chapter one | *L.O. Molinta Enendu, in*
Charles Nwadigwe, Molinta Enendu & Canice Nwosu (Eds.)
Metaphors and Climax, Reminiscences on the Drama and
Theatre of Ogonna Agu
London , Adonis & Abbey Publishers

Agu, Ogonna C. "Dance Theatre Ritual and the Igbo Drama." *Nigeria Magazine* 55:2 (1978): 78-84.

Agu, Ogonna C. "*Chi* and Role Differentiation in Igbo Culture and Tradition", Paper Presented at the 2nd International Colloquium of the Society for the Promotion of Igbo Language and Culture, (SPILC), University of Nigeria, Nsukka, 1983.

Agu, Ogonna C. "The Teaching of Igbo Drama", Paper Presented to Igbo Language Teachers, at the 3rd International Colloquium of the Society for the Promotion of Igbo Language and Culture, (SPILC), University of Nigeria, Nsukka, 1984.

Agu, Ogonna C. "The *Ikenga* as the Archetype of Hero in Igbo Cultural Tradition". Paper Presented at the Faculty of Arts Seminar Series, University of Nigeria, Nsukka, 1986.

Agu, Ogonna C. "Background and Development of Contemporary Arts in Nigeria."*Nigeria Heritage*. Ed. J. U. Obot. Calabar: Wusen Publishers, 1987. 225-235.

Agu, Ogonna C. "Songs of War: The Mixed Messages of Biafran War Songs."*Journal of African Languages and Cultures* 4:1 (1991): 5-19.

Agu, Ogonna C. *The Last of the Biafrans*. Calabar: Baaj Publishers, 1996.

Agu, Ogonna C. *Dance of the Deer*. Calabar: Baaj Publishers, 1998.

Agu, Ogonna C. *The Return of a Night Masquerade*. Calabar: Baaj Publishers, 1998.

Agu, Ogonna C. *The Strong Boy of the Forest*. Nimo: Odinala-ka Publishers, 1999.

Agu, Ogonna C. *I Fear for Kattie*. Calabar: Baaj Publishers, 2000.

Agu, Ogonna C. *Cry of a Maiden*. Calabar: Wusen Publishers, 2000.

Agu, Ogonna C. *Dawn in the Academy*. Calabar: Baaj Publishers, 2001.

Agu, Ogonna C. "Religion, and Igbo Ideology: The Language Crisis in the New Order." *NDUNODE: Calabar Journal of Humanities* 3:2 (2002): 19-30.

Chapter one | *L.O. Molinta Enendu, in*
Charles Nwadigwe, Molinta Enendu & Canice Nwosu (Eds.)
Metaphors and Climax, Reminiscences on the Drama and Theatre of Ogonna Agu
London , Adonis & Abbey Publishers

Agu, Ogonna C. "Political Ideals and Public Space in the Pre-literate Igbo Society: Masquerade Enactment as Socialization Process Among the Nri Igbo." *Lwati: Journal of Interdisciplinary Studies* 4:2 (2010): 50-58.

Anaagudo-Agu, Ogonna. *Symbol of a Goddess*. Calabar: University of Calabar Press, 2005.

Anaagudo-Agu, Ogonna. *"Aka Umuagbara: Uli* Essence and Symbols in the Development of an Indigenous Igbo Script". *The Parnassus: University of Uyo Journal of Cultural Research.* 2 (2005): 152-162.

Chapter one | *L.O. Molinta Enendu, in*
Charles Nwadigwe, Molinta Enendu & Canice Nwosu (Eds.)
Metaphors and Climax, Reminiscences on the Drama and Theatre of Ogonna Agu
London , Adonis & Abbey Publishers

Chapter Two

Cultural Promotion and the Economics of Theatre: The Ogonna Agu Perspective

Charles E. Nwadigwe

Introduction

The organic nature of theatre as a composite art is not debatable. In pursuit of this functional reality, Ogonna Agu further postulates that art, as an entity should not be balkanized and isolated. This is the philosophy behind the concept of the virtuoso-a kind of super artist who could harmonize and deploy various artistic genres to communicate and render an aesthetic experience. Perhaps, this explains Ogonna Agu's interest and practical incursion into diverse but interrelated genres of art, thus wearing the multifaceted toga of actor, playwright, director, musician, painter, dancer, critic, poet, cinematographer and art administrator.

The artistic canon of the virtuoso is anchored on the personality of the artist as the hub and driving force of every artistic creation. This watershed reinforces the ideal of creative freedom in which the artist is neither fettered not controlled by external forces in terms of what to create, how to create as well as the artistic and technical details of a creative work. In line with this artistic unity in diversity, Ogonna Agu as a virtuoso artist oscillates and traverses the various media of literary, visual and performing arts. In fact, Bellman affirms that it is "the artist and his psyche" that actually "looks through his eyes, feels with his nervous system and ponders with his brain". In essence, since "only an individual can inject that human quality into an art work" it ultimately affects "the *general* nature of the artist's activity, the

Chapter two | *Charles E. Nwadigwe, in*
Charles Nwadigwe, Molinta Enendu & Canice Nwosu (Eds.)
Metaphors and Climax, Reminiscences on the Drama and
Theatre of Ogonna Agu
London , Adonis & Abbey Publishers

mode of artistic communication within which he works, the elements which characterize the symbolic devices of the art, and the general steps which must be followed if any art work is to result" (297).

Following these general principles, the artist creates, using any medium of his choice, not merely to savour the aesthetic satisfaction that comes with artistic creativity but to propagate a culture, share experience and communicate meanings. In these objectives, Ogonna Agu contends that economic viability and sustenance of livelihood must be embedded directly or indirectly within the theatrical activity so that the promotion of culture and allied values of the arts will be sustainable especially in the contemporary world in which theatre is competing with other existential needs of human society. Scholars and practitioners of theatre, arts and culture have repeatedly stressed the need to "promote arts and culture as veritable economic business with revenue earning objectives" (Asagba 25). Similarly, Buratai affirms that in view of the national and global economic challenges as well as "the uncertainties associated with oil economy", Nigeria should "tap and harness the gains of her numerous culture industries as a revenue-earner and strategy for sustainable development" (99). These concerns relating to culture and economy have equally engaged Ogonna Agu's critical mind as reflected in his writings and professional practice.

Historical Reflections

As a theatre critic, Ogonna Agu emphasizes the centrality of history in understanding and managing contemporary challenges. In some of his recent studies, Agu traces the historical development of theatre business in Nigeria, its challenges and prospects and argues that the path to sustainable progress in the theatre industry lies in evaluating and learning from the mistakes

Chapter two | *Charles E. Nwadigwe, in*
Charles Nwadigwe, Molinta Enendu & Canice Nwosu (Eds.)
Metaphors and Climax, Reminiscences on the Drama and
Theatre of Ogonna Agu
London , Adonis & Abbey Publishers

of the past, recognizing current global trends and developing practicable approaches that best suit the peculiarity of the local situation.

In his discourse on theatre audiences, church congregations and revenue generation to sustain the performing arts industry, Agu observes that the Church made some historical contributions in the development of theatre in Nigeria and the Western world. Nevertheless, he observes that in recent times, a conflict of interest exists between church worship and public theatres in Nigeria especially in the areas of fund generation, use of performance venues and the crucial issue of audience engineering and retention ("Theatre Audiences Versus Church . . ." 26).

In a recent historical reflection presented as a bulwark for his analysis of contemporary trends in the theatre industry, Agu focused on the tradition of gate-taking and Box Office management. While citing Iyorwuese Hagher for corroboration, Agu traces the historical foundations of the Box Office as a Western tradition since, as Hagher states, in traditional African performance "theatre is not performed in a special building neither does performance become a commercial enterprise for a fee paying audience" (4). To reinforce the argument, Agu goes back in history to cite earlier studies such as the one by Bakary Traore, published about four decades ago, in which Traore asserts that the idea of building physical structures specifically to house a performance and institutionalize the culture of gate fees was alien to indigenous Africa (56). Based on these positions, Agu submits that:

> Hence, the Box Office tradition is a system derived from Western theatrical practice whereby fees are charged before spectators are allowed into the theatre building to watch a play. Gate-taking, by which this practice is known, being an imported phenomenon, it is pertinent to examine how it is fast changing the way theatre is practiced in Africa in the present times. ("The Rise of the Box Office. . ." 1)

Chapter two	*Charles E. Nwadigwe, in*
	Charles Nwadigwe, Molinta Enendu & Canice Nwosu (Eds.)
	Metaphors and Climax, Reminiscences on the Drama and
	Theatre of Ogonna Agu
	London , Adonis & Abbey Publishers

Since the modern African theatre was considerably borrowed from European traditions, Agu attempted a historical and economic analysis of how theatre survived in "pre-modern" and "pre-colonial" era. He observed that theatre in both cultures (Africa and Europe) thrived mainly on charity. His "comparism of the pre-modern Western theatre with African performance experience" in the areas of performance venue, space configurations and funding shows a significant similarity in both traditions since most of their theatres were open "like the arena stage". In addition, in both traditions, the "performers had to depend on the generosity of the public"("The Rise of the Box Office . . ." 2).

However, relying on historical evidence, particularly from the English theatre, Agu explains that with the rise of modernity, the proceeds from generous spectators, patrons and the State began to dwindle considerably. In fact, these were some of the economic impacts of a fast-industrializing capitalist society characterized by the promotion of free enterprise. Thus, the construction of buildings exclusively for theatre performance, especially in "the heydays of the Elizabethan era" was linked to the rise of professionalism and commercialization in theatre which logically "ushered in the era of gate-taking"' necessitated by the need "to offset the cost of the production" ("The Rise of the Box Office . . ." 1). It is therefore understandable that the first English Theatre was built in 1572 as a business venture by James Burbage, an Actor-Manager, who was desperately seeking for a sustainable revenue base to maintain his production cast and crew and free his company from the vagaries and uncertainties of depending on the whims of donors and charitable patrons. Indeed, *The Theatre* as Burbage's new performance venue was named, was constructed specifically to block bystanders from seeing the performance unless they are admitted into the house after paying the gate fee.

Chapter two | *Charles E. Nwadigwe, in*
Charles Nwadigwe, Molinta Enendu & Canice Nwosu (Eds.)
*Metaphors and Climax, Reminiscences on the Drama and
Theatre of Ogonna Agu*
London , Adonis & Abbey Publishers

This was a marked departure from the inn-yards which were open and people could freely watch the performance from the balconies of the inns (Lane 35).

While concluding his historical reflections on Box Office development, theatre practice and professionalism, Agu submits that:

> A historical review of the rise of professionalism in the theatre would indicate that a number of considerations are responsible for it. We have linked the rise of professionalism in England with the establishment of *The Theatre* in Shoreditch in 1572. However, about a hundred years earlier, in 1478, the first professional acting company ever in history came into being in Spain. ("The Rise of the Box Office . . ." 4)

Beyond the European theatre experience, Agu maintains that a logical link exists between the development of English theatre and that of the modern Nigerian theatre which was hinged on the colonial experience. In fact, this linkage is amply reflected in the practice of Concert and Theatre in the late 19th century Lagos society (Echeruo 357).

Nonetheless, Agu contends that though the root of professional theatre practice in Nigeria can equally be traced to some indigenous groups such as the *Alarinjo*, *Wawan Sarki* and numerous masque-dramaturges, these groups had limited economic pursuit, "yet, there was professionalism in spite of this" since "some form of proceeds [in cash or kind or both] accrued from the performance as an enterprise on which the group lived" ("The Rise of the Box Office . . ." 6). The advent of the Western concert, vaudeville or revue as well as the subsequent emergence of Ogunde's theatre further consolidated the development of modern professional theatre in Nigeria even though their pioneering example "has not been sustained due to a number of factors" particularly, "the nature of modern economies" and their impact in "the development of the theatre as a professional

Chapter two | *Charles E. Nwadigwe, in*
Charles Nwadigwe, Molinta Enendu & Canice Nwosu (Eds.)
Metaphors and Climax, Reminiscences on the Drama and
Theatre of Ogonna Agu
London , Adonis & Abbey Publishers

venture" ("The Rise of the Box Office . . ." 6). The advent of literary dramatists in the mid-twentieth century was expected to uplift and sustain professional theatre practice in Nigeria but their works were often limited to the Universities.

Performance Venues

The designation of spaces and construction of physical structures as performance venues are fundamental prerequisites for the perpetuation of theatre as agency in cultural promotion and livelihood sustenance. Therefore, theatre deserves a home, its own place, a venue specifically delineated for theatrical expression. In Europe, theatre found its permanent home since the Renaissance era when it left open courtyards, inns, and other found spaces. In indigenous African settings, theatre has always been at home in the village and community squares which have always served as permanent performance venues. Hence, Nwadigwe has stressed that:

> The site of the performance is largely a cultural expression defining the physical surrounding and conditions in which the audience and performers interact. Similarly, the character of the theatrical occasion is often shaped by the place designated for the event. In contemporary practice and discourse, the concept of theatre has widened, giving rise to flexible spaces and fluctuating perceptions of performance venue. ("Meet us at the Other Side . . ." 64)

It is therefore common for scholars and practitioners to adopt the loose and avant-gardist concept of theatre as any space that accommodates a performance. But in view of the technological advancements of contemporary society and its considerable impact on modern and postmodern theatre practice, it has become increasingly difficult, if not impossible, to run a viable theatre industry without a standard theatre plant, a theatre building with the basic facilities, spaces and installations to accommodate and

Chapter two | *Charles E. Nwadigwe, in*
Charles Nwadigwe, Molinta Enendu & Canice Nwosu (Eds.)
Metaphors and Climax, Reminiscences on the Drama and
Theatre of Ogonna Agu
London , Adonis & Abbey Publishers

enhance the planning, presentation and organization of theatre business. Consequently, it has been observed that:

> It is also only in Nigeria and Nigeria alone that the National Troupe of the country is without a home. It has been swindled out of its natural habitat and now begs for a rehearsal hall from a landlord ruled by unpredictable mood swings. (Ojewuyi 27)

In line with this reality, Ogonna Agu maintains that professionalism in theatre and cultural promotion cannot be achieved and sustained without the provision of good performance venues to serve as centres of theatre business and symbols of a people's cultural identity. Furthermore, Agu presents a comparative analysis between the English and Nigerian experiences in terms of professionalism and development of permanent theatre structures. Based on this comparism, he submits that "for professionalism to arise in England, permanent structures were set up for performances where gate-takings could be ensured". But Nigeria's experience "defies this pattern of economic development" since "the first professional theatre in Nigeria-that of Hubert Ogunde-was a travelling theatre that was not domiciled in any theatre building". But Agu equally observes that, nevertheless, Ogunde "performed in closed buildings at which the company had to pay some rent" such as the Glover Hall in Lagos ("The Rise of the Box Office. . ." 2-3).This affirms the interdependence between permanent theatre houses and the sustenance of professionalism in the industry. In fact, one can cite some examples where theatre structures were erected to facilitate private commercial theatre enterprise in Nigeria. These include the New Culture Studio Theatre of Demas Nwoko in Ibadan, the PEC Repertory Theatre of Pepper and Ebun Clark-Bekederemo in Lagos, the Rosy Arts Theatre, Owerri built by Hilary Njoku and the Yelwa Club Theatre erected by J.C. Folley in Bukuru, Jos.

Chapter two | Charles E. Nwadigwe, in
Charles Nwadigwe, Molinta Enendu & Canice Nwosu (Eds.)
Metaphors and Climax, Reminiscences on the Drama and
Theatre of Ogonna Agu
London , Adonis & Abbey Publishers

In essence, professionalism is not merely tied to the formation of a theatre company, how they are organized as artists, and their modes and styles of production. Professionalism is chiefly determined by the self-sustaining capacity of the troupe, their economic base, their managerial structure and procedures that enhance revenue generation, self-reliance, economic viability and sustainability, and artistic identity. All these are tied to the performance venue which becomes a home for artists; a production plant and marketing outlet for artistic goods and services; a rendezvous for investors and stakeholders in the industry; and a metaphor for a people's regard (or disregard) for their cultural identity. Thus, Agu affirms that "certain basic needs constituted the condition for the establishment of professional theatres". These "needs" and "condition" are "applicable anywhere in the world" and fundamentally, "they included, first and foremost, a theatre building where plays are mounted for audiences to watch on payment of the required fees" ("The Rise of the Box Office . . ." 3). Therefore, Ojewuyi denounces the poor attitude of most Nigerian governments to theatre structures and cultural promotion and asserts that the government through its Ministry of Tourism, Culture and National Orientation needs to "embark on the building of new Theatres across the states to engineer the renaissance of theatrical life and culture in Nigeria" (33). This is quite logical because even when a troupe or Theatre Company is itinerant, they will need a performance venue, at every destination, to display and market their product.

Theatre as Business

Without equivocation, Ogonna Agu declares that if theatre is recognized as an industry, then the consideration of "theatre as a business venture" should be "the heart of the matter" in professional practice. In this regard, theatre industrialists and

Chapter two | *Charles E. Nwadigwe, in*
Charles Nwadigwe, Molinta Enendu & Canice Nwosu (Eds.)
Metaphors and Climax, Reminiscences on the Drama and
Theatre of Ogonna Agu
London , Adonis & Abbey Publishers

investors must not make any apologies for being pragmatic and shrewd since business involves "capital and profitability" ("The Rise of the Box Office. . ." 3). Within the capitalist mode of production, business is all about taking risks (investing one's capital) and expecting the investment to yield optimal dividends. The theatre is no exception.

In fact, in general business administration, it is often quoted and accepted that "there is no free lunch". This implies that every expenditure is a kind of investment that should yield interest either immediately or in the near future. In the same vein, there should be "no free show" in theatre. A clear demonstration of this axiom in theatre practice is the convention where artists and members of cast and crew are encouraged to buy tickets for their invited guests rather than trying to bring them in for free. This tradition helps the non-theatre persons to imbibe the culture and consciousness of buying tickets to watch performances in future. The axiom of "no free lunch" or "no free show" has nothing to do with stinginess or miserly disposition as it is sometimes perceived. It is merely a reminder that for every "free lunch" or "free show" we enjoy, someone has picked the bill. In line with this philosophy, professional theatre practitioners sometimes offer or subsidize certain value-added services as a bait to attract wider patronage.

However, on the issue of Box Office and gate-takings, Agu observes that "African theatre will have a hard time growing into a professional status". He anchors his argument on the fact that "African performance tradition derives from a communal culture whereby private ownership of the theatre is not normative". Hence, some people still find it difficult paying to see a performance which traditionally has always been offered to the public free of charge in various communities. A second factor adduced by Ogonna Agu as the reason for the difficulty in entrenching professional (commercial) theatre in Nigeria is that:

Chapter two | *Charles E. Nwadigwe, in*
Charles Nwadigwe, Molinta Enendu & Canice Nwosu (Eds.)
Metaphors and Climax, Reminiscences on the Drama and
Theatre of Ogonna Agu
London , Adonis & Abbey Publishers

Most modern performance theatres exhibit works of literary dramatists domiciled in the universities and this, by implication, has not made theatre popular in Nigeria. Faced by this dual stasis-the traditional one based on communal ethos and the modern based on the fact that theatre is not in touch with the (mass) living society, modern African theatre is more or less unpopular. ("The Rise of the Box Office . . ." 4)

Furthermore, Agu opines that transforming African theatre practice into "modern professional companies" will require a keen "sense of professionalism" as well as "the security to make it part of the vibrant economic system". Although it can be argued that the needed "sense of professionalism" is not lacking in the Nigerian theatre, there is still insecurity for investments in the industry due to the socio-economic and political climate of the country. Therefore, potential investors are often reluctant to plough their capital into such risky ventures like theatre because profitable returns cannot be guaranteed in the prevailing circumstances.

While presenting an analysis of the political economy of theatre business in Nigeria, Agu observed that it lacked distinct and enforceable "legal instruments of rights and authority". This absence of "legal security for the performing groups" is an allusion to the obsolete legal codes in the industry. In some instances, there are no legal provisions to regulate theatre practice and protect the investors, artists and their profession. Consequently, pirates and charlatans continue to pillage the industry to the detriment of trained professionals. Indeed, theatre is virtually the only skilled profession in Nigeria that does not require a licence to practice. As government supervision remains poor and sometimes non-existent, it is difficult to foresee the needed update and full implementation of the Nigerian Cultural Policy. Hence, Agu maintains that "based on all these, it would be safe to conclude that there was no economic index to define these performances or

Chapter two | *Charles E. Nwadigwe, in*
Charles Nwadigwe, Molinta Enendu & Canice Nwosu (Eds.)
Metaphors and Climax, Reminiscences on the Drama and
Theatre of Ogonna Agu
London , Adonis & Abbey Publishers

suggest the direction of capital growth and development" ("The Rise of the Box Office . . ." 5-6). On the contrary, what obtains in the Nigerian situation is the trend of "culture-nomics", an anomalous condition "where profit is at the expense of culture and the arts" (Ojewuyi 28).

Beyond the external challenges which relate to government policies, poor economic base, investor apathy and socio-political instability, Agu appears to indict the Nigerian theatre artist for the content of their works and attitude to their professional calling. He explains that most of the productions of modern theatre practitioners are unpopular with the wider audience because the contents are often elitist and alienating to the masses. In addition, many of the artists themselves have not shown sufficient commitment, fortitude and acumen needed to nurture the theatre business in a traumatized economy such as Nigeria's. Using the theatre of Hubert Ogunde as a reference point, Agu demonstrates how the populist content of theatrical performances and the dogged spirit of industry can translate to a successful professional career in theatre.

From a professional business perspective, Ogunde took various measures to establish and run his theatre company in line with "the demands of a professional enterprise". He ensured that "the company was formally registered with all the rights to operate as a legal body". Ogunde equally spent money and time on "vigorous advertisements" and publicity as vital resources for optimal marketing of his company and its productions. In addition, "the labour relations was organized the way cottage industries were done" making his key staff to be "collective shareholders in the Company" thereby ensuring commitment and "industrial harmony' ("The Rise of the Box Office . . ." 7). In fact, Clark also informs that Ogunde ploughed his capital into human resource development and acquisition of equipment to improve the quality

Chapter two | *Charles E. Nwadigwe, in*
Charles Nwadigwe, Molinta Enendu & Canice Nwosu (Eds.)
Metaphors and Climax, Reminiscences on the Drama and
Theatre of Ogonna Agu
London , Adonis & Abbey Publishers

and market value of his productions and thereby maintain an edge over his competitors. Indeed, Ogunde arrived from his training tour of the United Kingdom in the 1940s with theatrical equipment worth Two Thousand Pounds Sterling (Clark 302).

Having considered the antecedents of Hubert Ogunde as "an astute businessman" that is always eager to "move with the tastes of the time", Agu insists that such professional dedication, perseverance, industrial pragmatism, strategic business planning and innovative spirit are rare among contemporary Nigerian theatre practitioners. Thus, the emergence and sustenance of a viable professional (commercial) theatre industry that can guarantee Box Office success in the country remains uncertain in the present time.

Conclusion

In his diverse writings as a theatre scholar and critic, Ogonna Agu has beamed his critical searchlight on various aspects of the theatre and creative arts. This chapter has made an analytical review of the opinions of Ogonna Agu in the areas of theatre business, professional practice and the promotion of culture through the agency of the performing arts. Incidentally, this was his last publication before his transition to the Great Beyond. The cardinal view of Ogonna Agu is that any nation desirous of promoting her arts and cultural heritage must promote the theatre which is the centerpiece of the arts. Agu also advocates that self-reliance can be achieved in cultural preservation and promotion if Africans look inwards and explore their heritage as the Asians have been doing rather than following the Western trends and tenets blindly. For instance, Agu had used the "Igbo *uli* symbolic designs" to illustrate the possibility of developing a script, a form of writing and communication code that will be expressive of Igbo values and "solve some of the perennial problem of tonation [in] writing

Chapter two | *Charles E. Nwadigwe, in*
Charles Nwadigwe, Molinta Enendu & Canice Nwosu (Eds.)
Metaphors and Climax, Reminiscences on the Drama and
Theatre of Ogonna Agu
London , Adonis & Abbey Publishers

and reading of African languages". In this regard, "African traditional heritage is seen as the basic superstructure" on which African civilization and transformation can "derive its strength and energy" ("Aka Umu Agbara . . ." 161).

Furthermore, Agu admonishes theatre practitioners to embrace the spirit of professionalism and commitment and work towards the sustainable development of the industry. He draws a historical analogy between the theatrical experiences of England and Nigeria using the achievements of pioneer professional theatre practitioners, James Burbage and Hubert Ogunde, as paradigms. Thus, Agu argues that though these practitioners existed at different historical epochs as well as diverse socio-economic, cultural, political and environmental conditions, both Burbage and Ogunde succeeded in establishing and running viable professional theatre companies. They achieved these commendable results by following diligently the cardinal principles of entrepreneurship and doggedly holding onto the spirit of enterprise and business ethics despite the odds. Therefore, Agu recommends the experiences and successes of Burbage and Ogunde as veritable models and catalyst to fire the imagination and entrepreneurial spirit of contemporary Nigerian theatre practitioners.

Basically, the governments are expected to support the arts and cultural promotion through the enactment of supportive laws, formation and implementation of arts-friendly policies, maintenance of public utilities and creation of an enabling environment for the arts to thrive. In this vein, Asagba affirms that "statutorily, the Federal Government has the responsibility to chart and set the atmosphere and pace for cultural re-orientation and revivalism in the country through effective policy formulation and implementation" (18). This is the norm all over the world. A recent study in the United Kingdom found that:

Chapter two | Charles E. Nwadigwe, in
Charles Nwadigwe, Molinta Enendu & Canice Nwosu (Eds.)
Metaphors and Climax, Reminiscences on the Drama and
Theatre of Ogonna Agu
London , Adonis & Abbey Publishers

6.2% of the UK's local economy (GVA) comes from the creative industries, the arts provide over two million jobs and are mentioned by 8 out of 10 tourists as a reason for their visit. Not only do the arts contribute massively to the UK economy, they do so whilst doubling the money invested in them (qtd. in Ojewuyi 20).

The UK experience is a good example of how governments can support and equally benefit from the arts and cultural subsector of the economy. The famous cultural economist, David Throsby in his landmark book, *The Economics of Cultural Policy*, outlines the basic criteria for assessing the economic contribution of the culture industries. According to Throsby:

> The most basic approach is to measure the contribution that the industry makes to the usual macroeconomic aggregates: gross value of production, value added, fixed capital formation, employment, exports, and so on. Such statistics can be used to indicate the size of the industry, expressed, for example, as a certain percentage of whole-economy aggregates such as GDP. Studies of the economic contribution of the cultural industries carried out along these lines may be effective in demonstrating that the cultural sector is not some minor economic backwater, but a significant component of the economy. (93)

Throsby emphasized that such indices and "data-gathering exercises" are useful but "can also be misused" if they are merely used to play up the economic impact of cultural industries without being used "to provide any special case for policy intervention" (94). In essence, the cardinal objective of measuring the economic contributions of the creative industries in a country should be to facilitate growth in the cultural sector by identifying areas and criteria for policy intervention. Nonetheless, Agu opines that theatre practitioners should be in the vanguard of promoting their profession and industry. By so doing, they earn the respect of others which will help to attract external support through funding and investments in their industry.

Chapter two | *Charles E. Nwadigwe, in*
Charles Nwadigwe, Molinta Enendu & Canice Nwosu (Eds.)
Metaphors and Climax, Reminiscences on the Drama and Theatre of Ogonna Agu
London , Adonis & Abbey Publishers

Indeed, it is not by mere accident that the process of preparing and presenting performances to an audience is called "production". The term "production" is an industrial process involving the manufacture of goods in a factory. In fact, the three industrial stages, production, distribution and consumption, are all applicable to the theatre whether it is presented through the medium of stage, radio, or the screen. The theatre is unarguably an industry but its industrial character is often overlooked by Nigeria's policy makers and uninformed analysts. In an earlier study, Nwadigwe emphasized that "theatres are public and industrial places and in Nigeria they are covered by the Factories Act of 1990 (Cap 125) *Laws of the Federation of Nigeria"* as amended ("Hazards and Safety Considerations. . ." 189). Hence, in modern theatre, as Nwadigwe explains, "the backstage area is analogous to the production line of a manufacturing firm, which must be well-equipped, staffed, maintained, and functional" ("Hazards and Safety Considerations . . ." 191). For this industry to thrive, Agu maintains that its primary stakeholders and investors (theatre practitioners) must nurture, practice and invest in it.

In a nutshell, the arts and cultural sector, in particular theatre, is big business. The economics of theatre presupposes that the industry responds to the laws of demand and supply and its practice as an enterprise in a free market economy implies that it oscillates with the vagaries of market forces. Consequently, Ogonna Agu recommends that the theatre industry needs a physical plant, a basic factory to operate from; "its chief motivating factor being the need for more permanent theatre houses to be put up; structures in which to house a production. In such an outfit, gate-taking could be made possible and secure, and not random and arbitrary" ("The Rise of the Box Office. . ." 9). To this end, Agu challenges theatre practitioners in Nigeria to brace up for the challenges of the contemporary society because "the era of free-for-

Chapter two | *Charles E. Nwadigwe, in*
Charles Nwadigwe, Molinta Enendu & Canice Nwosu (Eds.)
Metaphors and Climax, Reminiscences on the Drama and
Theatre of Ogonna Agu
London , Adonis & Abbey Publishers

all-performance" that usually "depend[s] on the generosity of the amorphous public" has become "a thing of the past". To be ready for the 21st century challenges of the theatre and culture industry, then "theatre groups with business initiatives" will need "to secure their existence through legal means". This will ultimately "enable them partner with potential sponsors" to revive and sustain the industry ("The Rise of the Box Office . . ." 9).

Therefore, Ogonna Agu sees the survival of theatre from the perspective of private sector initiative and investment which is the norm all over the world since governments are not quite good at doing business. In a related discourse, Duruaku avers that in the quest to promote Nigeria's cultural heritage through the arts, "governments alone cannot carry the burden". He opines that "the private sector should develop better commercial orientation" (23-4). Nevertheless, the government must make the business atmosphere favourable through policies, legislations, capacity building, human resource development and allied institutional support. Incidentally, the Nigerian governments are yet to meet these expectations. Instead, government officials habitually quote the World Bank, UNDP and UNESCO Annual Reports estimating the financial value of the Nigerian arts and entertainment industries to be worth millions of US Dollars. Therefore, they sit back, expecting these millions of dollars to magically flow into government coffers as revenue without commensurate investment.

Consequently, the lukewarm attitude and misplaced priority of the Nigerian government towards cultural promotion has been frequently criticized. Such attitudes can even be inferred from the provisions of the Nigerian Constitution and the Mission Statement of the Ministry of Tourism, Culture and National Orientation. The provisions and articulations in these documents seem to suggest that "if culture does not fit into the plan for the provision and manipulation of labour and capital for fiscal profit, it has no

Chapter two | *Charles E. Nwadigwe, in*
Charles Nwadigwe, Molinta Enendu & Canice Nwosu (Eds.)
Metaphors and Climax, Reminiscences on the Drama and
Theatre of Ogonna Agu
London , Adonis & Abbey Publishers

relevance" (Ojewuyi 12). In essence, the quest for consistent professionalism and improved entrepreneurship in the theatre industry, as advocated by Ogonna Agu, should not be misunderstood or used as a smokescreen by the government to abdicate its responsibilities to the arts and cultural sector. For now, as regards the fulfillment of those responsibilities, the Nigerian government is still performing below par.

Works Cited

Agu, Ogonna. "The Rise of the Box Office and Professionalism in Nigerian Theatre: The Economic Dimension."*Applause: Journal of Theatre and Media Studies* 2:1 (2011): 1-10.

Agu, Ogonna. "Theatre Audiences Versus Church Congregations: Paradigm for Social Transformation in Nigeria."*CAJOLIS: Calabar Journal of Liberal Studies* 2:1 (2008): 26 -50.

Anaagudo-Agu, Ogonna. *"Aka Umuagbara: Uli* Essence and Symbols in the Development of an Indigenous Igbo Script." *The Parnassus: University of Uyo Journal of Cultural Research* 2 (2005): 152-162.

Asagba, Austin. O. *Cultural Reorientation Peace Building and National Development.* Abuja: National Institute for Cultural Orientation, 2011.

Bellman, Willard. *Lighting the Stage: Art and Practice.* 2nd Edition. New York and London: Chandler Publishing Company, 1974.

Buratai, Mohammed. "Cultural Industry and Sustainable Development in Nigeria." *Perspectives on Cultural Administration in Nigeria.* Eds. Olu Obafemi and Barclays Ayakoroma. Ibadan: Kraft Books, 2011. 84-102.

Clark, Ebun. "Ogunde Theatre: The Rise of Contemporary Professional Theatre in Nigeria 1946-72."*Drama and Theatre in*

Chapter two | Charles E. Nwadigwe, in
Charles Nwadigwe, Molinta Enendu & Canice Nwosu (Eds.)
Metaphors and Climax, Reminiscences on the Drama and Theatre of Ogonna Agu
London , Adonis & Abbey Publishers

Nigeria: A Critical Source Book. Ed. Yemi Ogunbiyi. Lagos: Nigeria Magazine, 1981. 295-320.

Duruaku, Toni ABC. *Cultural Festival as a Tool for National Development in Nigeria*. Abuja: National Institute for Cultural Orientation, 2011.

Echeruo, Michael. "Concert and Theatre in Late Nineteenth Century Lagos."*Drama and Theatre in Nigeria: A Critical Source Book*. Ed. Yemi Ogunbiyi. Lagos: Nigeria Magazine, 1981. 357-369.

Hagher, Iyorwuese. "Introduction: Theatre and the Community Through the Ages."*The Practice of Community Theatre in Nigeria*. Ed. Iyorwuese Hagher. Jos: Society of Nigerian Theatre Artists, 1990. 3-13.

Lane, Peter. *The Theatre*. London: B.T. Batsford, 1975.

Nwadigwe, Charles. "Meet us at the Other Side of the River': Performance Venue and Community Education Among Migrant Fisherman in Southeastern Nigeria."*Research in Drama Education* 12:1(2007): 65-77.

Nwadigwe, Charles. "Hazards and Safety Considerations in the Design of Performance Venues."*Applause: Journal of Theatre and Media Studies* 1:2 (2006): 177-195.

Ojewuyi, Olusegun. *Katanfuru: The Illogic of Culture-Nomics in Nigerian Cultural Administration*. Abuja: National Institute for Cultural Orientation, 2011.

Throsby, David. *The Economics of Cultural Policy*. Cambridge: Cambridge University Press, 2010.

Traore, Bakary. *The Black African Theatre and its Social Functions*. Ibadan: University Press, 1972.

Chapter two | *Charles E. Nwadigwe, in*
Charles Nwadigwe, Molinta Enendu & Canice Nwosu (Eds.)
Metaphors and Climax, Reminiscences on the Drama and Theatre of Ogonna Agu
London , Adonis & Abbey Publishers

Chapter Three

The Patriot as a Villain: Biafra's Dashed Dream in Ogonna Agu's Two Plays

John Iwuh

Introduction

War and its ugly experiences are hardly ever forgotten by those involved in it one way or the other. In progressive societies, volumes of books, stage plays and films continue to emerge such that expose various dimensions and evils of such wars with a view to enlightening not only the people but also correcting some of the misconceived issues about the war, the heroes and the villains thereof. America is one good example where theatre and film have continued to reveal the roles of individuals in their various wars either of unification of over two hundred years ago or their ever unending battle for national security. Max Hastings had compiled some war classics in his "Ten Best Books about War"[1]. These books are: William Wheeler's *The Letters of Private Wheeler, 1809-28 (1948)*, Churchill's *My Early Life* (1930), *Sagittarius Rising* (1936), Philip Caputo's *A Rumor of War* (1977), and *Nella Last's War* (1981). Others which made Hastings list are Frederic Manning's *The Middle Parts of Fortune* (1929), Nicholas Monsarrat's *The Cruel Sea* (1951), Irene Nemirovsky's *Suite Française* (2004), Guy Sajer's *The Forgotten Soldier* (1967), and George MacDonald Fraser's *Quartered Safe Out Here* (1992), which like Ogonna Agu's *Cry of a Maiden* was influenced by the Burma War. The list shows that anyone who experienced a war in any form, ranging from World Wars to wars

Chapter three | *John Iwuh, in*
Charles Nwadigwe, Molinta Enendu & Canice Nwosu (Eds.)
Metaphors and Climax, Reminiscences on the Drama and Theatre of Ogonna Agu
London , Adonis & Abbey Publishers

on terrorism could tell a story that can change society or influence government decisions.

Considering the scanty works, and given the gravity of suffering experienced by the Igbo, it had been observed in 2011 on the occasion of the conference of Igbo Studies Association[2] that:

> Forty years after the material execution of the war, the mental agonies and the new destinies of survivors have received discourses at various levels. In all these, it appears that the role of drama in telling the story of the war and its unending impacts on Ndi-Igbo has not fully been explored if it has been explored at all. If not, it means that the role of "drama as history, history as drama"[3] is not clear to many, hence the need to use it as a tool to penetrate the minds of people especially the youth. (Iwuh 2)

It is disappointing to note that only a handful of books have attempted to chronicle the ugly occurrence of a war that claimed over two million Nigerians of mainly Igbo origin. But each did approach the issue from their personal perspectives. One of the first was Frederick Forsythe's *The Making of an African Legend (1969)*. Indeed:

> It is a book about Chukwuemeka Odumegwu Ojukwu, the then army colonel who led the Southeast to a civil war against the rest of the Nigerian nation (1967-1970)...The book in many ways describes the Igbo man with passion, his drive, personality and industry. As true as Forsythe's view may seem, and as objectionable as it may seem to non Igbo in the Nigerian nation, it could only be true of Ndi-Igbo; their courage and belief in the quest for self determination at the time. No doubt, it is historically and ethnologically different if compared to other personal accounts like Wale Ademoyega's *Why We Struck*, Ojukwu's *Because I'm Involved*, and Obasanjo's *My Command*; from whatever standpoint the war stands to be justified. The key players have spoken, what about those who were not privileged to write because they fell at battle fronts while the rest had to surrender? (Iwuh 2)

Chapter three | John Iwuh, in
Charles Nwadigwe, Molinta Enendu & Canice Nwosu (Eds.)
*Metaphors and Climax, Reminiscences on the Drama and
Theatre of Ogonna Agu*
London, Adonis & Abbey Publishers

There were also some literatures on the subject which include Flora Nwapa's *Never Again*. One of the many angles of Nwapa's work was to look at the trial which a war places on citizens who dare to engage inter-ethnic marriage; the trauma and agony of realizing tribal and cultural differences, and the dilemma of deciding to be an outcast should love go sour. The war had given the impression of an everlasting impenetrable gulf between the east and the rest of the country. Of course, there are more politically focused ones like Achebe's *Anthills of the Savannah* which centres on the many forces against the so-called giant, indivisible country rescued from Civil War in order to sustain that myth. There is also the more recent *There was a Country* which elicited hyper reactions of objectionable and sentimental kinds from both enlightened and ignorant minds alike. The works that have elicited controversies have come largely from writers of Igbo origin owing to personal pains. The accounts usually give the impression of oppression and genocide meted out with inhuman drive for total annihilation.

The reason for scanty books on the Civil War was because the war was fought on Biafran soil. No ethnic group outside the then eastern soil experienced the genocide, the starvation and the destruction of lives and property which the Igbo suffered. On the other hand, among the major reasons for the paucity of literature on the Civil War based on actual experience was due to little education by Igbo soldiers who fought the war, as did ordinary citizens who experienced the injustice of the war. At the end of the Civil War, such men and women were more eager to pick up the pieces toward self-restoration than literary documentation. Among the very literate minds of the arts expected to have written were men like Christopher Okigbo who did not survive the war.

Playwriting was even worse affected. However, a few plays still emerged on the Nigeria-Biafra War. Again, James Ene-

Chapter three | *John Iwuh, in*
Charles Nwadigwe, Molinta Enendu & Canice Nwosu (Eds.)
Metaphors and Climax, Reminiscences on the Drama and
Theatre of Ogonna Agu
London, Adonis & Abbey Publishers

Henshaw's *Enough is Enough* (1976) was among the earliest to come up in print. From the cover review, its publisher wrote that *Enough is Enough* is "about the tragedy, triumph, aspiration and despair of some of the dramatic personae like detainees and their guards. . . Particularly, it is about the reactions of men to the circumstances they founded themselves in the last months of the civil war". While Henshaw's play was based on interactive discussions with war prisoners, a few other plays had come out of experience by direct victims of the war; indigenes of the core east. One of such is Chukwuma Okoye's *We the Beast* (2002).

The war was like Chinua Achebe's reference to the moon, which every Igbo man saw and felt in his own clan with no less pain and anguish; somewhere in Igbo land, someone had lost a father or mother, sister or brother, uncle or niece. In the play, *We the Beast,* Okoye paints the image of a child brutally gunned down by a fighter jet while playing in his father's house. As was usual with such air raids, bodies were chopped and flung into different directions by bomb blasts. There were hundreds of such raids around people's homes. That air strike was typical of many throughout eastern Nigeria, and it defined the unfolding transformation of Ike and his wife, the degradation and eventual wreck of a family, mentally and morally, over a thirty-month period. Okoye in *We the Beast* had looked back at his experience as a child and agreed that:

> Authentic stories can only be told by those who experienced it, not by those who will imagine it. There is need, therefore, to recreate the image of every one of the two million soldiers lost in that war; his dreams and aspirations, his wishes even while in the throes of death, the pains gone through by his family and loved ones, and finally the destinies of those he left behind. (Iwuh 4)

Considering the various subjective angles from which non Igbo authors had sidetracked the issue of genocide due to political

Chapter three | John Iwuh, in
Charles Nwadigwe, Molinta Enendu & Canice Nwosu (Eds.)
Metaphors and Climax, Reminiscences on the Drama and Theatre of Ogonna Agu
London, Adonis & Abbey Publishers

reasons, and even made light of the matter especially by ethnic-minded researchers, Iwuh in a programme note to the production of the play, *Birthright* (2011), wrote that "the war that researchers read and write about from various subjective angles, took place around people's homes and villages. No amount of academic research and postulations can match eyewitness account".

Like Okoye did, childhood experience of the war among illiterate and helpless villagers, the enthusiasm of youth and the pride to defend the eastern territory became a theme for "Birthright". From the production Programme Notes by the playwright, "'Birthright' looks at the Nigeria-Biafra war from the common man's point of view. The illiterates and villagers in the rural areas who could not at any time tell why the war broke out. The immediate consequence was the drafting of young men from the villages to join the war".

It was on this note that the tragedy of Ijeogu, the play's hero, began. He lost his three sons to the war, his two daughters in order to survive became sex tools to soldiers while Ijeogu degenerated from schizophrenia to suicide. Such were the lot of a typical Igbo family during the war. But in all these literary works and their characters, none can be compared to Ogonna Agu's *Symbol of a Goddess*. This view is not based on the technicality of playwriting but from its experiential perspective of a Biafran soldier who tasted the battle front and relieved his anguish, frustration and crushed hopes in Emenike, the protagonist.

Beckoning Rays of the Biafran Sun

The Narrator in *Symbol of a Goddess* begins on a spiritual note when he voices that "it is by a streak of chance that man is born to carry his cross in this great wide world, more so, if he is a man of destiny" (6). Destiny has its strong foundation in a spiritual belief while consciousness is the awareness of it. It might be said that

Chapter three	*John Iwuh, in*
	Charles Nwadigwe, Molinta Enendu & Canice Nwosu (Eds.)
	Metaphors and Climax, Reminiscences on the Drama and
	Theatre of Ogonna Agu
	London, Adonis & Abbey Publishers

belief is the tool for the entrenchment of destiny while society creates the platform for the interpretation of its conditions. In all, birth is merely the first culprit in the journey toward death, and family in turn wears the portrait that the society would mourn or celebrate. War is akin to the beckon of the loo; the urge will take pre-eminence over all other emergencies.

Propaganda may have aided the interest of young men to enlist in the war, but it was more of the love to defend their fatherland that gave them additional impetus. News had penetrated the whole of southeast especially through the BBC, that the Igbo were being massacred in the northern part of the country; pictures were carried by the few newspapers at the time, particularly *The Daily Times*. In the midst of the worry came the declaration of the State of Biafra by Emeka Odumegwu Ojukwu and call for war in defence of the east.

The dream was to fight, defeat the enemy, free the east and come out as heroes as did Hercules through Hades.

The Biafran flag mounts in the background, soaked in the deep colours of both hope and uncertainty. In the sun, it rejoiced with that belief on which it is crafted, constantly announcing with boldness the sovereignty of a nation desirous of self-determination. The flag did not retain its brilliance too long. According to the Narrator, it is a reminder of "desolation, grief and anguish among the children of men" (6). An unsavory scene of exchange of gunfire is acted out on stage showing Emenike's gallantry as a soldier. But the war has been won and lost. Hence, "those that could not run became prisoners in their own land. Some turned deaf and dumb, many died in the fields of battle..." But it did happen that opposite forces soon embrace one another indicating the end of the war. Notwithstanding, Ogonna Agu reveals that Biafra became a land of "the sick, the hungry...the maimed and deformed", and the angry like Emenike.

Chapter three	*John Iwuh, in*
	Charles Nwadigwe, Molinta Enendu & Canice Nwosu (Eds.)
	Metaphors and Climax, Reminiscences on the Drama and
	Theatre of Ogonna Agu
	London, Adonis & Abbey Publishers

When Hercules rescued Alcestis from Hades, Athenian citizens thought that such an arduous task was impossible by mortal ability. It was not too difficult for them to conclude that only a god could defy the dangers of hell to come out victorious. That amazing act of bravery indeed gave rise to the popular phrase of "herculean task". It thus justified why Hercules got the status of a titan. Thence, his arrivals received the general greeting of "Hercules, son of Zeus!" However, before Agliaia, he still chose the part of modesty for fear of treachery when he said, "I am a man, just an ordinary man, I tell you". Yet, in order to register the impact of his achievement in case the reality was yet to dawn on Hercules, Agliaia had maintained her question, "God or man, Hercules, what do I see?" (Wilder 86)

Hercules did not just become a hero; he conquered opposition and became a god before the people. If he had failed, the trauma would have haunted him for life as well as his generations. This personal exploit is founded on the belief of one's ability and hope that the mission ahead was surmountable. Hercules' belief and hope reflect such bravery which every soldier possesses. It is the belief to conquer and come out victorious. Emenike and indeed every Biafran soldier had imagined himself in the personality of Hercules and expected the kind of honour bestowed on him. This was not to be. It becomes traumatic if an army embarks on a war and its soldiers do not come back as heroes. Victory then is the first dream in battle while defeat takes away a soldier's pride and threatens his people's liberty. This unenviable slide becomes Emenike's unintended personae at the dawn of Biafra's surrender. Perfectly fit, the author informs in the back page blurb of the book that "Emenike is a young war veteran just back from the battle field. Smarting from the loss of Biafra and itching for vengeance, he starts with unleashing a reign of terror in the village".

Chapter three | *John Iwuh, in*
Charles Nwadigwe, Molinta Enendu & Canice Nwosu (Eds.)
Metaphors and Climax, Reminiscences on the Drama and Theatre of Ogonna Agu
London, Adonis & Abbey Publishers

Emenike's quest for *vengeance* is mere *transfer of aggression* on those he sought to liberate for thirty months that he fought.

Sensing the ominous and expressing the mind of every easterner at the end of the war, Ogonna Agu whom education had prevented from being "an Emenike" had expressed joy at the end of the war but did put a rhetoric question to the authorities through the Narrator:

> Home. Home at long last. War has ended. But there is danger. The soldier going home with a gun, what is he going to do with it? What are we to expect? Armed robbers or what? What will happen when they get to their villages . . . these angry men who still refuse that the war has ended what are we to do with them ladies and gentlemen? (9)

Beautiful Dream and Cold Reality

Every war veteran usually would have great expectations. The first is gratitude to mother luck for surviving the war. The second is learning to be a civilian once again and perhaps, settle down to normal life. But having surrendered to the Federal forces, these two expectations become a nullity for Emenike. Thus, Ogonna Agu's *Symbol of a Goddess* (2004) comes out clear as one of the few dramatic notes of the civil war. Emenike is a young man obsessed with the idea of realizing Biafra. For him, the beagle of war would never stop sounding until the dream of Biafra materializes. This expectation kept his warring spirit alive even outside the physical realm of thought. Emenike appears misunderstood because in his assessment, "they say I've done evil, simply because I want Biafra to survive in our minds" (24). Before long, Emenike's dream is breached and his authority challenged.

One man who feels Emenike's excesses must be curbed states his reasons: "Emenike is too dangerous to be in this village. He will ruin this village. If you leave him he will set the whole place on fire. What do you say to a man who carry gun and terrorize the

Chapter three | John Iwuh, in
Charles Nwadigwe, Molinta Enendu & Canice Nwosu (Eds.)
Metaphors and Climax, Reminiscences on the Drama and Theatre of Ogonna Agu
London, Adonis & Abbey Publishers

whole village? ... Another point. All the *efulefu* in this village, Emenike is organizing them. All the jobless people..." This reference is to Emenike's forceful gathering of tramps and touts to drum and masquerade, often to realize his world, and sometimes to ridicule anyone who opposes his lifestyle. He displays to onlookers what he calls "dance of the guinea fowl, dance of my victory over the enemy. . ." while looking for his "queen lost in the clouds. . ." through the long wooden drums (24). Ironically, Iluka feels herself being mourned alive by her son, and each time, she becomes distraught and sorrowful.

One way of breaking Emenike's backbone is to destroy the powerhouse which holds the armoury of his dreams. This is a bedroom where his symbolic enemy (the birds) is bemoaned by his symbolic love (the masquerade). In this room, Emenike's hallucination attains its peak. In order to achieve this, the commandant of the Federal force is invited to carry out the destruction:

> They push and the hut breaks apart revealing a mask head, with all the paraphernalia of a masking tradition. Holding on to the skin of *agboghomuo* masquerade the man covers his nakedness. (28)

In addition, they release the birds and severe immediate contact with his symbol of psychological peace and transmutation. From this moment and sadly too, Ide becomes Emenike's mortal enemy for daring to invite the Commandant of the Federal forces to emasculate his unending Biafran dream. Thus, apart from the Federal forces, Ide represents another dimension of one of the symbolic forces against the realization of the sovereign state of Biafra which Emenike desires to control (47). Evidence of this sabotage is two-fold. First is the invitation of the Commandant to scuttle his influence. The second is the birds which were released from the cage. Emenike considers these acts treasonable against his

Chapter three | *John Iwuh, in*
Charles Nwadigwe, Molinta Enendu & Canice Nwosu (Eds.)
Metaphors and Climax, Reminiscences on the Drama and
Theatre of Ogonna Agu
London, Adonis & Abbey Publishers

authority. Symbolically, the release of the birds marks the final reality which Emenike dreads. The birds were like prisoners of war, and the physical hold of his enemy. It was a dream dashed, releasing the birds without a treaty or corresponding pact for his loss (85). In all, Emenike believes that his bedroom is the "bridal chamber" which will bear the fruits of future Biafrans with traditional wisdom.

Emenike has built his life around Biafra and foreclosed his future within it. It was traumatic and psychologically devastating not only to imagine but also to see that hope fading away. So, from the hope of delivering a new independent nation to his people, the community experiences the reverse of frustration of their son who lived thirty months in isolation from reality, battling for glory. It is compounded by the fact that the Biafran soldier has become hunted even within his community by the Nigerian soldiers. Consequently, the soldier who was a freedom fighter minutes before ceasefire becomes a rebel in the former enclave where they were patriots. The reason is obvious, they have lost the hope of becoming the core personnel of the military of the nation that never was. The immediate option was to build, hold and secure an image of comfort and safety in a world that only they can live in. For Emenike, "His whole being is in fact, with that woman of deep waters, symbol of Biafra he championed and fought for" (back page).

Emenike has become a mere shadow psychologically distributed between vain worlds; the skies, earth and the deep waters, responding each time to a different god. Iluka thinks that one way of making her son sane again is through marriage. But Emenike's extreme obsession defies touch with such reality. In his moment of apparition, he conjures up images of the wild to discredit the held reality. For instance, he calls the goddess of the

Chapter three | *John Iwuh, in*
Charles Nwadigwe, Molinta Enendu & Canice Nwosu (Eds.)
Metaphors and Climax, Reminiscences on the Drama and Theatre of Ogonna Agu
London, Adonis & Abbey Publishers

sea whose beauty he imagines to surpass that of any woman, to reduce Akudiri's acknowledged beauty to that of beasts (37-38).

Emenike is a poet whose loss renders estranged lines of alien voices. He lives in a world shared by no one but dead veterans who inhabit that realm ruled by the sea goddess (45). Emenike's symbolic world is beyond the perception of people of his community especially with references to an unrealistic inhabitant of the sea and other insignificant creatures like birds. These beings form the inhabitants of the new world which gives him consolation for the lost nation of Biafra.

Strangely enough, Act 2:2 is devoted to homely love play which shows Emenike embracing reality for the first time. This ambience of love and welcome appear sudden and premature if we consider Emenike's aggressive and rigid stance as an angry man, and one who does not wish marriage with any earthly woman having declared himself an avowed husband of the sea goddess.

Sins Against the Kingdoms

Soyinka had said that whom the gods will kill, they first make mad. Emenike, in this delirious state, no longer takes instruction from any one including the priest of the oracle. Before the gods, he declares himself as "eze k'ibe" (a king above all) and makes demands reserved for titled men. His preference is that which bars him from marrying any earthly woman (19). But as if blinded by the gods, his desecration and aided by his return since escaping the Commandant, Emenike met a sudden attraction from Akudiri (40). However, the resultant pregnancy and the idea of church wedding was another sacrilege to his dream world. Not even his mother's taunt or Akudiri's pleas would make him yield (49).

However, it is Iluka who first successfully played a mind game on Emenike by attacking her son's pride and male ego. This

Chapter three | *John Iwuh, in*
Charles Nwadigwe, Molinta Enendu & Canice Nwosu (Eds.)
Metaphors and Climax, Reminiscences on the Drama and
Theatre of Ogonna Agu
London, Adonis & Abbey Publishers

challenge dented his physical strength and put a major crack in the walls of his phantom kingdom when she nailed his fears: "You're afraid . . ."This is the reality that Biafra was lost when he unknowingly saw that woman of the red eyes in Akudiri and slept with her (52). But the pregnancy is the reality and responsibility he would not accept. She also brought up the worst albatross Emenike dreads to confront; the church. Marriage is a burden to imagine, but wedding in the church is a far concept to comprehend.

Emenike's character is akin to the living spirit behind the Movement for Actualization of Sovereign State of Biafra (MASSOB), the only body manifest which erupted and sustained the call for the resuscitation and actualization of the failed state of Biafra. Emenike's psychological trauma has become so evident that his life has come to be slightly less important to him, and the reason for his determination.

This realization becomes clearer to Igbonekwu, who is the first to note that Emenike deserves pity and support for his chosen masquerade acts which engage his mind. But he has incurred the wrath of the community deep enough for that sentiment to hold. For instance, Okobe was merely waiting for Emenike's debacle because he foresaw that Emenike would not succeed in his quest for two major reasons. One is that he disrespected Okobe's domain of authority when he demanded the *Ozoship* mantle and took the sacred ankle string under duress. Two is that he is not an initiate of the masquerade cult which he forcefully took control of. These two breaches pitched him against the spiritual forces of the community's ancestral belief system. From this moment he weakened and severed the pivot which holds the bipolar spiritual link between him and the gods of Biafran land that he fights to defend.

Chapter three | John Iwuh, in
Charles Nwadigwe, Molinta Enendu & Canice Nwosu (Eds.)
Metaphors and Climax, Reminiscences on the Drama and Theatre of Ogonna Agu
London, Adonis & Abbey Publishers

Same Image: Two Canvas Paintings

The two plays in this review are coincidentally war-inspired. The issues raised in them show that man remains the focus of dramatic engagements by those who bother about the fate of others owing to the action of stronger institutions. *Symbol of a Goddess* and *Cry of a Maiden* show Ogonna Agu's deep concern for individuals whose rewards fall either contrary to expectations or correspondingly low compared to the patriotic services they have rendered to defend the sovereignty of a state.

In *Cry of a Maiden,* Chidum suffers disconnect due to a few years absence as a soldier who fought for the British Empire. It was a period which also gave him a lot of exposure that contrasts with the traditional life he left behind. The playwright's notes already did the expose for his readers:

> Chidum returns from Burma a new man. He has made contact with foreign land, mixed with people of other lands and socialized with them. Thus, socially, his horizon has widened, his outlook expanded with the accompanying cultural and technological imperatives. New ideas and values, new way of looking at the world and new attitudes of lifeall these help to forge a character at crossroads. (ii)

Five years of being away from home brought the reality that he was due to have entered a new phase in his life. Chidum's intention to get married and settle down to active family life pitched him against his elder brother, Okolo, who does not see marriage as a "priority" in the face of more urgent productive venture facing the family. Okolo insists that the family *Obi* must be rebuilt. Although valid, the reason is a selfish dimension because Okolo should have rebuilt the *Obi* long before this time had he been a "responsible" man. The words "priority" and "responsible" separate the two brothers which each capitalized on to advance

Chapter three | *John Iwuh, in*
Charles Nwadigwe, Molinta Enendu & Canice Nwosu (Eds.)
Metaphors and Climax, Reminiscences on the Drama and
Theatre of Ogonna Agu
London, Adonis & Abbey Publishers

their sides of the story to win sympathy before the community elders in a hidden mind game.

The issue was the *Obi*; a little structure with strong cultural significance. The concept of the *Obi* in Igbo traditional life got proper reference in Chinua Achebe's *Things Fall Apart*. The *Obi* is a general shelter or common porch to receive all visitors to the family compound. Often, visits of non-personal nature are entertained and dispensed with in the *Obi*, particularly in large compounds. It also allows for personal pleasantries without entering individual family units. While the community welcomes the idea of marriage for every mature male, a home starts from the *Obi*.

At Okolo's age, he should have been married like his mates but rather he took to drinking and easy life. With such a lifestyle, he could not engage in an occupation that is productive enough to position financially to take up family responsibilities. Thus, marriage does not cross his mind, consequently, the community does not count him as a responsible man. Being placed in such a category, the community does not imagine him to prioritize and fulfill family obligations as they normally would expect a responsible man. In the traditional parlance, a responsible man is a focused person who lives up his responsibilities as do men of his age. These include gainful occupation that will enable him take up responsibilities as at when due, build a house, get married, raise children and contribute meaningfully to community development. Expectedly, Okolo has not confronted any of the above.

Conversely, Chidum returns after some years to discover that his family has remained the way he left it. Rather, his mother who should be enjoying the benefits of motherhood still supports the family. Inwardly, he nurses a fear that he could be like Okolo and he intends to confront that fear without delay. Again, before the community, he wants to cut a path and image clearly different

Chapter three | *John Iwuh, in*
Charles Nwadigwe, Molinta Enendu & Canice Nwosu (Eds.)
Metaphors and Climax, Reminiscences on the Drama and Theatre of Ogonna Agu
London, Adonis & Abbey Publishers

from his brother's, recover the pride of the family and be counted among worthy sons of the land. So, marriage is the first step, and the tonic that will support his aspirations and drive his efforts.

So it becomes a knotty case which the elders must approach with traditional logic to arrive at universal acceptance. Okolo's case is sheer irresponsibility and not lack of commonsense. So he is aware that the elders cannot deny the fact that a man must properly tend his homestead before bringing in a woman as his younger brother intends to do. He knows the custom as well as the tradition. Thus, if his brother is as mature and responsible as he claims to be, then he should see things from this perspective. With this hindsight, Okolo speaks like one guided by the family *ofor* (being the current bearer of the family symbol of justice), which smartly shields his own inadequacies.

While Chidum approaches issues with civility, caution and respect for human sensibilities, Okolo confronts issues with the mien of an unabashed, uncompromising and indifferent lout. This mindset made it possible to capitalize on the weakness of woman to consummate a relationship which his brother has systematically tried to build and nurture without recourse to conscience. For Chidum, it was like losing two battles: fighting for the empire with nothing but few trivial gifts to show for it; and singing all year round like a lovebird to a passerby whose attention for rhymes lasts no longer than a momentary fart.

Conclusion

War is a friction that wears the fulcrum of societies; the destruction of land and properties that take decades to rebuild are the more visible evidences among many. The slow gyre of economic life and the social progress of the people project another ugly picture. However, the most serious and devastating account so difficult to quantify is the multidimensional impact on the individual psyche.

Chapter three	*John Iwuh, in*
	Charles Nwadigwe, Molinta Enendu & Canice Nwosu (Eds.)
	Metaphors and Climax, Reminiscences on the Drama and
	Theatre of Ogonna Agu
	London, Adonis & Abbey Publishers

The collapse of hope and the doubtful aspiration of the youth results in mental de-assemblage, personality re-evaluation and spiritual deconstruction. This study examined the beagles of war, the ordeal of defeat and Biafra's dashed dream in Ogonna Agu's *Symbol of a Goddess and Cry of a Maiden*. It underscores Emenike's disparaged life owing to disillusionment from a lost war as a quintessential seed that fell on dry soil, among the millions of Igbo that withered in the Nigeria-Biafra War.

In *Symbol of a Goddess*, Emenike would have received sympathy from the community if not the brutal approach which he adopted for his course. From this point, evidence of his losses began to mount. He lost his father to the war, lost his reputation on return, with little or no flashes of reality that is obvious to anyone but him that his sea goddess could be a phantom. Emenike's downfall was his inability to drop the military force against a civilian community. He could not separate his paranoia against the enemies of Biafra from the commitment expected of a patriot who engaged in a fratricidal war as an ambassador of his community.

Although *Cry of a Maiden* and *Symbol of a goddess* are both anchored on postwar experiences, both of them exhibit different psychological impacts on their heroes. In *Cry of a Maiden*, Chidum returns from the war as a discharged soldier with the fulfillment of an accomplished war veteran along with presents for his family. The war ends, Chidum was happy to return because he was a mere mercenary, a combatant soldier drafted into the war as a citizen of the British colony. On the contrary, Emenike went to the war for a cause he believed in – Biafra. In this respect, losing the war means improper discharge with the burden of self-rediscovery. He is angry that he has no power to upturn the ceasefire declaration of the warlords.

Finally, Ogonna Agu's main concern in his two works has been to highlight the multiple losses in the life of young men who were

Chapter three | *John Iwuh, in*
Charles Nwadigwe, Molinta Enendu & Canice Nwosu (Eds.)
Metaphors and Climax, Reminiscences on the Drama and Theatre of Ogonna Agu
London, Adonis & Abbey Publishers

full of dreams and aspiration for the future before being whisked away by the beagle of war. For many who were privileged to be taught by the author, the experience of war as a dent on the psyche of men was not only familiar but memorable. The author indeed never lost focus in the choice of his protagonists in the two plays. The fates that befall them in the end thus become slaps on authorities that give rise to war with little consideration for soldiers that are mere pawns in a deadly game of winner takes all.

Notes

1. Follow link to "The Ten Best Books about...War" in the works cited section of this essay for all the listed books.
2. The 9th Annual Conference of the Igbo Studies Association, USA, April 2011.
3. The Reference is made to Ola Rotimi's *Ovonramwen Nogbaisi*, (Benin City: Ethiope Publishing, 1974).

Works Cited

Anaagudo-Agu, Ogonna. *Symbol of a Goddess*. Calabar: Wusen Publishers, 2005.

Anaagudo-Agu, Ogonna. *Cry of a Maiden*. Calabar: Wusen Publishers, 2000.

Forsythe, Frederick. *The Making of an African Legend*. London: Penguin Books, 1969.

Hastings, Max. "The Ten Best Books about War." 2010. Retrievedon Wednesday October 2, 2013. http://www.theguardian.com/culture/2010/mar/14/10-best-books-war-max-hastings

Chapter three | *John Iwuh, in*
Charles Nwadigwe, Molinta Enendu & Canice Nwosu (Eds.)
Metaphors and Climax, Reminiscences on the Drama and Theatre of Ogonna Agu
London, Adonis & Abbey Publishers

Iwuh, John. "Interrogating Vices in Southeastern Nigeria through Drama: The Image of Ndi-Igbo, Development and Political Relevance". Originally titled "Interrogating the incidences of Kidnapping and Murder: The Image of Ndi-Igbo, Development and Political Relevance". Paper presented at the 9th Annual Conference of the Igbo Studies Association, USA, April 2011.

Nwapa, Flora. *Never Again*. New Jersey: Africa World Press, 1992.

Obasanjo, Olusegun. *My Command*. Ibadan: Heinemann, 1981.

Ojukwu, Odumegwu E. *Because I am Involved*. Port Harcourt: Saros International Publishers, 1989.

Okoye, Chukwuma. *We the Beast*. Ibadan: Hope Publishers, 2002.

Wilder, Thornton. *Alcestiad*. New York: Avon, 1955.

Chapter three | *John Iwuh, in*
Charles Nwadigwe, Molinta Enendu & Canice Nwosu (Eds.)
Metaphors and Climax, Reminiscences on the Drama and Theatre of Ogonna Agu
London, Adonis & Abbey Publishers

Chapter Four

Meaning and Fragments: A Psychoanalytic Interpretation of Ogonna Agu's *Cry of a Maiden*

Uche-Chinemere Nwaozuzu

Preamble

Ogonna Agu can be classified among the group of Nigerian artists who are said to belong to the second generation of playwrights. The highlights of this group include, Femi Osofisan, Emeka Nwabueze, Bode Sowande, Esiaba Irobi, Tess Onwueme, Akanji Nasiru among others. Their plays articulated both cultural and political issues found in the Nigerian polity. Like most of his peers, Ogonna Agu taught in the University where his rich vein of creative output was crafted and produced. Among these include *Cry of a Maiden* which is the focus of this study. In any serious work of critical analysis, there is often the need to appropriate a fitting theoretical praxis in the polemical and evaluative explication. This reading of Agu's *Cry of a Maiden*, applies the psychoanalytical theoretical paradigm to probe meaning which are deemed fragmentary and putative in the play. In fact, the playwright himself alludes to this design in his introduction to the play where he attempted to highlight fleeting images, themes and characters that populate the text as follows:

> In writing *Cry of a Maiden,* my work is done. However, for the good midwife (the director) to deliver, I feel that there are aspects of experience which we have to share on the subject...It is on the basis of this understanding that I wish to underline some of the preoccupations that have prompted the writing of the play. . . *Cry of a Maiden* has a very strong cultural and symbolic interest . . . it is conceived as a domestic drama fashioned out of a fundamental human conflict. (i)

Chapter four | *Uche-Chinemere Nwaozuzu, in*
Charles Nwadigwe, Molinta Enendu & Canice Nwosu (Eds.)
Metaphors and Climax, Reminiscences on the Drama and Theatre of Ogonna Agu
London, Adonis & Abbey Publishers

In choosing the psychoanalytic paradigm to interrogate meaning in this play we feel that the fleeting nature of the characters and competing motives and actions clearly lend themselves to the lure of psychoanalytical investigation.

Theoretical Framework

Sigmund Freud's psychoanalytic theory is arguably one of the broadest theories that define human behaviour. This is because it seeks to explain not everyday behaviour but also abnormal behaviour, such as jealousy, war, prejudice, love and hate among others. Due to its breadth, it will be impossible to describe the theory in its entirety in this study. Rather we shall focus on the few highlights of particular relevance in this context. The highlights to be applied to our examination of *Cry of a Maiden* are the Psychic Conflict, the Unconscious Processes, the Mechanisms of Defence and Conservation of Energy. We shall briefly attempt to explain the terms above before showing how they apply to the main characters of the plays.

Psychic Conflict revolves around two models developed by Sigmund Freud; these are the evolutionary and the socio-cultural models. The evolutionary model argues that behaviour is often driven by deep-seated needs and ancestral desires. While the socio-cultural model underscores that the expression of these needs and desires is influenced by cultural contexts (Brown 59). This conflict between inner needs and external constraints plays a central role in Freudian theory. Furthermore, Freud maintains that behaviour represents a compromise between biological needs which reside in a psychological structure known as the id and social expectations, morals and values which are housed in a psychological structure classified as the superego (Brown 59). The third element, the ego, negotiates between the id and the superego

Chapter four | *Uche-Chinemere Nwaozuzu, in*
Charles Nwadigwe, Molinta Enendu & Canice Nwosu (Eds.)
Metaphors and Climax, Reminiscences on the Drama and Theatre of Ogonna Agu
London, Adonis & Abbey Publishers

while simultaneously avoiding danger in the external world. In fact, the ego according to Cherry, is engaged in a constant attempt to effect a compromise between what Freud calls "needs", "ought nots" and "better nots" (2-3). Societies help people balance these demands by providing them with socially benign ways to satisfy some of these animalistic needs and urges. In another vein this theory highlights the fact that social behaviour is often a disguised attempt to satisfy need for sexual gratification and the release of aggressive impulse.

The second aspect of Freud's theory that requires insight here is the Unconscious Process. The conflict Freud describes as psychic conflict is rarely one which we are consciously aware. He thus likened the mind to an iceberg (Horacio 24). The consciousness lies above the water. This is the part we see. The preconscious lies just below the surface. Although this part of the mind is ordinarily hidden, it can be accessed. For instance, Chidum in Agu's *Cry of a Maiden* tried to retrieve the memory of his boyhood before he went to war, while his brother Okolo remembered with sore-taste, his past relationship with the opposite sex. The largest part of the mind which is the unconscious, resides far below the surface and this is the most important part as it determines almost everything we do. It is this phenomenon that Freud terms the "unconscious process".

The third aspect of the psychoanalytic theory, the Mechanisms of Defence, highlights the idea that the unconscious is more than a repository of inaccessible materials. It also houses animal urges, painful memories we prefer not to recall and unflattering truths about ourselves we wish to avoid confronting. According to Freud, an active force called repression, keeps these forbidden thoughts and desires at bay (Brown 60). It is this repression that he calls the "mechanism of defense". Contemporary researchers often refer to these tendencies as self-enhancement biases generally used by

Chapter four | *Uche-Chinemere Nwaozuzu, in*
Charles Nwadigwe, Molinta Enendu & Canice Nwosu (Eds.)
Metaphors and Climax, Reminiscences on the Drama and
Theatre of Ogonna Agu
London, Adonis & Abbey Publishers

people to cast themselves in an overtly flattering light (Brown 59). For instance Okolo in Agu's *Cry of a Maiden* used the "mechanism of defense" to rationalize and avoid thinking of himself as someone who behaved in a negative manner or brought about a negative outcome in his family. His defence mechanism also led him to direct negative feelings he had towards his brother Chidum and greatly contributed to his prejudices.

Conservation of Energy which is the last aspect of the psychoanalytic theory being applied in this discourse holds that defending against psychological pain has an important cost. It uses up energy that could better be used for accomplishing more productive goals and tasks (Brown 60). This is the scenario that confronts Chidum in the play. To understand this aspect of Freudian theory better, it may be necessary to connect its root with the field of physics and the immutable but changeable nature of energy. The German scientist Hermann von Helmholtz proposed what is now known as the first law of thermodynamics. This principle states that energy is neither created nor destroyed, but is simply transferred from one state to another. Freud applied this principle to psychoanalysis, arguing that all psychological activity such as thinking, dreaming, perceiving, among others require psychic energy. He conceives of humans as closed energy in the sense that they were imbued with certain amount of energy such as that akin to physical energy that can neither be created nor destroyed, but can only be transferred from one state to another (Brown, 60). According to Freud, needs determine how much free energy exists. When a need arises, energy is invested in a desired object (Brown 60). This investment which he calls a cathexis, means that the energy is no longer available to perform other psychological work (this is what happened to Okolo). In some cases, a person can become fixated on a desired object thereby using up a great deal of psychic energy. For instance in Ogonna

Chapter four | *Uche-Chinemere Nwaozuzu, in*
Charles Nwadigwe, Molinta Enendu & Canice Nwosu (Eds.)
Metaphors and Climax, Reminiscences on the Drama and Theatre of Ogonna Agu
London, Adonis & Abbey Publishers

Agu's *Cry of a Maiden*, Okolo's longing for Ada produces this state of cathexis in him, because throughout the play he is not able to get his mind away from his love for the village belle.

Cry of a Maiden: Plot Design

The play, *Cry of a Maiden*, tells the story of two sons of Mgbochi, Chidum and Okolo who engage in a fratricidal quest for identity, self-assertion and filial conquest. The play opens with the noise of the pastoral African village environment. The plot unfolds with Chidum returning home having left years back to join the colonial forces of England in their war against the Japanese and the Germans during the Second World War. His return heralds an awakening in his elder brother who had remained indolent and laidback in terms of social and cultural responsibilities. Chidum triggers Okolo's indignation when he hints his intention to marry Ada and chart a family of his own. This disposition rubs off negatively on his older brother Okolo, who feels that the upstart should be made to understand how the traditional society he has left for years operates.

Hence, Okolo goes on to create obstacles for Chidum in his quest for self-actualization. He tells him to rebuild the family *Obi* as a prerequisite for any matrimonial ambitions. Okolo exploits the symbolic place of the *Obi* in traditional Igbo culture to complicate the task before his brother and stall his goal of settling down. Aided by his petulant and scheming friend Awili, Okolo succeeds in achieving his aim at the price of forcing his brother to run away after he challenges him to a mortal duel. The two brothers are reconciled at the end in an attempt to protect personal duty and family honour as well as soothe the bride's family. The Janus-faced Awili is also exposed as a interloper, gossip and womanizer.

Chapter four | *Uche-Chinemere Nwaozuzu, in*
Charles Nwadigwe, Molinta Enendu & Canice Nwosu (Eds.)
Metaphors and Climax, Reminiscences on the Drama and
Theatre of Ogonna Agu
London, Adonis & Abbey Publishers

Psychoanalytic Fragments of Meaning

The first insight into the psychological makeup of Okolo is given in Act One where the playwright cast him in the mold of a loser. First he laments the soured relationship with a girl he would have married as soon as his brother Chidum hints that he wants to settle down with a woman.

> OKOLO: Anyway, I've not given up the idea altogether; even though the girl I engaged gave me a rude shock. Maybe . . . Chidum can do as he pleases. But I must warn that a major task stares us in the face, the task of reconstructing this cottage. As you can see, the obi building has gone into ruins. And the shrine house has collapsed. (9)

The sentiment Okolo exhibits here can be explained by the Freudian evolutionary model as his remonstrations, appear to be driven by primordial personal desires anchored on ancestral tendencies. His recollection of past failed attempts to marry and the absence of an *obi* in his father's compound always have been with him in the subconscious. It only comes to the fore the moment his younger brother reveals his intention to find a wife and marry. The conflict between his inner needs and desires is reinforced by cultural fears which manifests as it dawns on him that probably he could be considered a failure by social and cultural standards. One can also say that his behaviour represents a compromise between biological needs which resides in his psychological structure. Thus he tries to rationalize his actions by drawing warped cognitive support from his friend Awili who ironically was already married.

> OKOLO: Thinks he's quick. He wants a settled life. Alas!
> AWILI: Young minds are infested with strange notions nowadays. Women! That's all they want- women!
> OKOLO: Ah! How did you know that? You're a prophet.

Chapter four | *Uche-Chinemere Nwaozuzu, in*
Charles Nwadigwe, Molinta Enendu & Canice Nwosu (Eds.)
Metaphors and Climax, Reminiscences on the Drama and Theatre of Ogonna Agu
London, Adonis & Abbey Publishers

AWILI: Exactly what is huddling in the boy's mind. And I am careless if he is a gangster; in a single combat I'll damage him and the whole crew of his tugs. . . (14)

AWILI: That's all they'll live and die for...

OKOLO: He's lucky. But sometimes I find a man should allow himself occasional wilderness. Life here is too drab. Dull. Uneventful. No excitements. No inspirations to achieve a higher goal. You find you need a woman. A woman to spur you to dance. A woman to make you sing. (14-15)

The inner battle between Okolo's biological needs and social expectations reaches a taut crescendo in the end and snaps, leading him to Ada, the girl Chidum had proposed to marry. The unconscious process manifests in the character of Okolo when Ada visits to give them Okpala's message that he was at the wineshed. Here the "emotional iceberg" as Freud terms it takes full reign of Okolo as he tries to chat up Ada. This unconscious nature which is unknown to his family rears up in form of a hitherto repressed romantic disposition towards the opposite sex and specifically Ada,

OKOLO: Be patient my dear. (*Patting her by the cheeks so that she turns her back, shy*). Who will do the carrying? It has always been the wish of Almighty God to send helpers at time of need.

ADA: (*Picking her fingernails*) What would you have me do for you now?

OKOLO: At least, play a second mother. Especially now that mother has gone to the waiting. And it's likely they'll stay long too.

ADA: I've told you I'm so busy. . . I have no time.

OKOLO: . . . my Ada (*Pause*) Ada a man must find time to relax . . . after all it is the same fun and laughter! (*Pause*). Now Ada look at that mirror on the wall. Can you see yourself? Don't you see you're beautiful? And what more does a man want? Ada since father died I've not had the peace of mind most men enjoy. . . (17-18)

Chapter four | *Uche-Chinemere Nwaozuzu, in*
Charles Nwadigwe, Molinta Enendu & Canice Nwosu (Eds.)
Metaphors and Climax, Reminiscences on the Drama and Theatre of Ogonna Agu
London, Adonis & Abbey Publishers

The above lines paint the image of a man at war with his inner self. Okolo traces this psychic turmoil to the time of his father's death. Thus, his psychic makeup has been one pool of conflicting emotions and needs which is about to be ventilated through his union with the village belle, Ada. The unconscious process, one may say, also highlights the fact that although Okolo has repressed his romantic or close association with the opposite sex, the desire has always remained there at the subconscious. At this stage of his development in the play, he exhibits features of the mechanism of defence. However, this seemingly inaccessible self soon yields to the unabashed persona of a flirt later in the play. The beginning of Act Two presents a totally changed Okolo who is brash, bold and very much in love as he attempts to woo Ada:

> OKOLO: You are a treasure to me. Ada, our love is at stake this way you do. Can't you see it? How long must you keep tottering on the scale? But this is the plight of one who must love. (19)

In another instance he boasts:

> OKOLO: Enough! Rise and don't cry. Stretch your tendrils to me, and trail on my body. . . You are the queen of the world! Tomorrow festival I shall parade a masquerade through the seven villages, drumming your name on housetops. In your name shall I challenge the demons, whoever dares to touch the maiden calabash of wine. On a roadside walk never, never will your toes kiss stone or wound the earth. Never will evil come to you. Or I'll have the world! (36)

As these tokens of romance progress, Okolo makes inroads, and begins to win the affection of Ada. However, some measure of doubt still tugs on his psyche, as confirmed by his reaction at the mere mention of Chidum's name by Ada. To this he retorts acerbically.

Chapter four | Uche-Chinemere Nwaozuzu, in
Charles Nwadigwe, Molinta Enendu & Canice Nwosu (Eds.)
Metaphors and Climax, Reminiscences on the Drama and Theatre of Ogonna Agu
London, Adonis & Abbey Publishers

> OKOLO: O well... that boy has things in his head. Mysterious acts in his head. He is itching to do that he'll be sorry for. Anyway... till he breaks that pot. Till he breaks my calabash of wine and I'll fizzle his strength. Ever seen such recklessness as he disposes? "Chidum, careful how you break that pot". And what was his reply? "You're telling me. I'm sober". (23)

The pot and the calabash here are quite significant. They both can stand as the signifier and the signified. They could allude to Ada as well as the institution of marriage or its consummation. In another vein, these lingering doubts on the part of Okolo leads him to expend his doubt and frustration by way of subtle threats at Ada if she dares mention the name of his brother.

> ADA: Where is Chidum?
> OKOLO: (With apparent jealousy) What about him? What do you want him for anyway?
> ADA: So I shouldn't ask...?
> OKOLO: What a hell you mean woman? I'm a dynamite! And I can't allow my moving spirit to be balked by your sentimentality.
> ADA: What?
> OKOLO: I said those sentiments you shed... You are sure I can't be touched by them (23).

Okolo's disposition above is a mere show of male bravado. Perhaps it may be more appropriate to see it as symptomatic of conserved psychic pain or energy being converted to personal and physical aggrandizement. Okolo's personality is not helped by the image of his friend Awili whom the playwright cast in the image of an easy-going, idle and jolly fellow. In fact the character himself offers us a graphic picture of his persona in the encounter with a woman in Act Two which goes thus:

> WOMAN: The thief you are. Do you know what you've done?
> AWILI: What is it I've done?
> WOMAN: Fox!
> AWILI: Enough woman. You're talking to a man.

Chapter four | Uche-Chinemere Nwaozuzu, in
Charles Nwadigwe, Molinta Enendu & Canice Nwosu (Eds.)
Metaphors and Climax, Reminiscences on the Drama and
Theatre of Ogonna Agu
London, Adonis & Abbey Publishers

WOMAN: Shut up! The man you are! If you don't know you are a blot in this village.

AWILI: Thank you.

WOMAN: By the way what do you think you are?

AWILI: Yours sincerely...

WOMAN: Ssssss. Don't talk. You think I'm those women with whom you frolic under dim lamps at night?

AWILI: My God! How this woman renders me valueless!

WOMAN: Thief! Thief! That's what you are! (*Picking the bone and throwing at him*) You wait! I'll see you executed in public. (*Exit Woman*)

AWILI: (*To audience*) Never mind her my good people. That's how she is. They say the thing is in her blood like . . . parasite. It eats her. Now something you don't know. Women are like flowers. I love them; and so pluck then in our play. At times I bruise them . . . (*lowers his voice*) . . . harlot. Now don't say I told you. I usually don't like women hanging beside me like handbag; and so first time she came near me I gave her a real slogging of my cane . . . I've finished her like a cigarette stick. Cigarette khaki, that's the word. Blow as you can you can't inflame her. (24-25)

We have gone at length to give this graphic illustration of the character of Awili so as to understand better the personality of Okolo before the return of his brother Chidum. As the saying often goes "birds of the same feather flock together" or "tell me who your friend is and I tell you who you are". If we were to use Awili as a foil for Okolo one can then postulate with some measure of objectivity that Okolo before the return of his brother was a seething psychological "bomb" that lived life as it came to him. The ideal of settling down with a woman was not priority in the scale of this character. It is instructive that in his pursuit of Ada he had conveniently forgotten that his father's *Obi* still remains in a state of disrepair. By the same token Awili's conscious attempt to cause friction and bring enmity between the two brothers is vividly captured by the playwright in the encounter he had with

Chapter four | Uche-Chinemere Nwaozuzu, in
Charles Nwadigwe, Molinta Enendu & Canice Nwosu (Eds.)
Metaphors and Climax, Reminiscences on the Drama and Theatre of Ogonna Agu
London, Adonis & Abbey Publishers

Chidum. He brazenly lies against Chidum to the brother claiming that the latter unwarrantedly insulted him whereas, the reverse was the case.

> AWILI: That brother of yours... No good. Ever heard a mad dog howling at a gentleman? Exactly what he did to me. For what? For something bad he was going to do and I cautioned him. What a foolish thought it was. (27)

A thorough reading of Awili's lines here betrays ambivalence. Two things come to the mind of any critic. First he talks of a wrong deed which Chidum was determined to carry out. However, he fails to mention it. We are thus left with the task of guessing what it was that Chidum was going to do. Subjecting the two views above to some level of analysis might yield the realization that Chidum's crime in the eyes of Awili was maybe his intention to marry and perhaps his designs for Ada.

Interpretation of Motif

Generally, motifs portend and express communicative values in creative works. It is pertinent at this juncture to consider how some of the motifs used in the play together with the psychological makeup of the main character yield various levels of meaning. The first is the motif of the calabash of wine. The symbolism of the calabash was given much visibility in the play. It helped in giving added psychological profile to the character of Chidum. Like his brother, Chidum also betrays some features of the Freudian model. Although he is presented as a simple and genial character at the beginning of the play, he evolves into a more complex and volatile one towards the climatic end. One could say that the motif of calabash of wine which is severally associated with Chidum can parallel the female. Here, it can be identified with Ada. The metaphor of breaking the calabash could also be likened to the act

Chapter four | *Uche-Chinemere Nwaozuzu, in*
Charles Nwadigwe, Molinta Enendu & Canice Nwosu (Eds.)
Metaphors and Climax, Reminiscences on the Drama and
Theatre of Ogonna Agu
London, Adonis & Abbey Publishers

of "knowing" a woman in the traditional society. At the point of his psychic evolution, Chidum exudes the Fruedian manifestation of psychic energy which is now converted from repressed frustration to anger and odium towards his brother. This channel becomes obvious given the fact that in the context of their battle for the attention of Ada, it appears that Chidum who makes the first bold attempt at indicating his interest loses out, or so it seems.

> OKOLO: Hea. Chidum, come here. Where's my calabash of wine? My beloved pot of wine?
>
> CHIDUM: Broke.
>
> OKOLO: What?
>
> CHIDUM: You broke it and you don't know. Your spirit followed me. I can't account for it. Yes, you followed me. The wine spilled. Burst the calabash.
>
> OKOLO: (*Reacts by landing him several blows on the belly*) You're a bum! A damned rascal! I'll have you battered for this (30).

The above exchange between Okolo and Chidum could be interpreted as centred on their competing interests in Ada. We could also argue that Chidum's reference such as, "you followed me" points to the fact that he expressed the first interest at settling with the girl. His defiance could also be said to be analogous to Okolo's initial attempts to obstruct his ambition with traditional issues such as lack of an *Obi* in the family and the visages of seniority. We see further use of the calabash to establish the delicate and irretrievable nature of broken bonds or affection. By resorting to fighting that eventually leads to the flight of Chidum from home, the playwright it would appear, seeks to orchestrate the intensity and seriousness of mores associated with conjugal relationship in the traditional society. We could also juxtapose this idea with the symbolism of the calabash as a fragile object that holds wine; a substance that is associated with goodwill, social bonds of various nature, good taste and tempered-revelry. We could see some of this in Anene's celebration of the tapster:

Chapter four | *Uche-Chinemere Nwaozuzu, in*
Charles Nwadigwe, Molinta Enendu & Canice Nwosu (Eds.)
Metaphors and Climax, Reminiscences on the Drama and
Theatre of Ogonna Agu
London, Adonis & Abbey Publishers

To tap? No. Only came to let you have a sip (*He hands the calabash . . . he gulps deeply and long*) A Little (*He hurries it from his mouth and most reluctantly hands it to Awili*) and if possible request for your small calabash! (*He grasps it again from Awili. He shakes it and is disappointed*) There's a well in your tummy. A bottomless well! (29).

Another element that gives us hints on the psychic state of the characters is the place of the character Ada in the evolution of Chidum and Okolo. The two brothers' interests in the same girl afford us the opportunity to chart their progression and development of their psychic selves. While Okolo presents a veritable personality template to appropriate the Freudian ideal Chidum serves more as an incidental character who is used to trigger the entire complex of psychoanalysis that Sigmund Freud talked about. The only time their psychological profile cohered appears to be when they had the quarrel before Chidum left the house. The texture of the coarse verbiages offers vivid insight into the unconscious process of psychoanalysis and the resultant mechanism of defence:

OKOLO: Better keep out this mother. I'll…

CHIDUM: …A snake. I want to slash. There's serpent lurking hereabout. Harassing. Dangerously lurking with the puff of the adder… Well then. Okolo here is yours! (*He tosses one of the machetes to him and he catches it*) Kill! And let thunder fall!

MGBOCHI: Ogbue! Ogbue! Ogbue… Nwike are you there..? Awili where are you? My God! These children! Always killing one another! (*Okpala rushes in*)

OKPALA: What's it woman? Okolo, what's it?

CHIDUM: I'll spill blood to wash his eyes…

OKOLO: That was no fight. You wait… (31-32).

Ada's disposition towards the two men at some point also became indeterminate. At the beginning, there was no hint of her preference for Okolo. As the play progressed however, Okolo, uses

Chapter four | *Uche-Chinemere Nwaozuzu, in*
Charles Nwadigwe, Molinta Enendu & Canice Nwosu (Eds.)
Metaphors and Climax, Reminiscences on the Drama and Theatre of Ogonna Agu
London, Adonis & Abbey Publishers

the lie of seniority to outwit his brother thus drawing closer to Ada. Despite this scenario, the girl still shows traces of interest in Chidume for which Okolo swiftly rebukes. It would appear the playwright used this design to orchestrate the depth of the human emotions when it comes to matters of relationship between the sexes. It also showed the superordinate image of the first born son in the traditional Igbo society. It is a state which confers on him advantages, such that he could have the first pick in matters such as marriage, inheritance and other issues involving the family; and in some instances, truncate those that he is opposed to even for selfish reasons. We can cite another instance of Okolo's show of repressed psychic pain in the aftermath of his first quarrel with his brother.

> OKOLO: The child that probes into the mystery of night thinks he's right. The stubborn he-goat has sought the storms, has also sunk with the blood. Stories have been told. Only yesterday a child crawled, too near the fire. In the dark, it crawled, till it received the relish of a burn. And warriors have bled before. They've spilled blood to wash our eyes. And we learn that dying they'd abhorred the smell of blood. So may they today when we have carried them shoulder-high. Chidum is the cog in my system. The headache in my stomach (27).

In the lines above Okolo clearly states his stand between him and his brother in their quest for Ada. We could see in his remonstration deep anger and pain. Pain at what he is going through and anger towards his younger brother who had the temerity to come out and claim a treasure he Okolo has fantasized over the years without being bold enough to stake a claim.

Conclusion

Agu's *Cry of a Maiden* could be said to use dramatic language that records both the immediate psychological tremors and the larger

Chapter four | *Uche-Chinemere Nwaozuzu, in*
Charles Nwadigwe, Molinta Enendu & Canice Nwosu (Eds.)
Metaphors and Climax, Reminiscences on the Drama and Theatre of Ogonna Agu
London, Adonis & Abbey Publishers

philosophical reverberations with a delicacy and precision that is almost seismographic. Ogonna Agu in this play, delighted in local puns, alliterations and verbal twists with the calabash and the palm wine as the central metaphors. The structure and theme develop primarily through a play and counter play of evolving dramatic images and symbolic actions in the household of Mgbochi and her two sons Okolo and Chidum. The play could be classified as "undramatic" but highly theatrical in terms of bold spectacular activity. This is because essential to drama, surely is not merely situation, but situation in movement. The playwright gave us several hints of the dramatic movement which were never followed up. A natural curve is the most usual symbol of dramatic action, as Aristotle puts it, "a beginning, a middle and an end", are three of its necessary features (38).

Nevertheless, Ogonna Agu's play captures the deep-rooted pain, ambition, disappointment, and joy that often define filial and conjugal relationships. In doing this, he plumbed the depths of the psychological makeup of two kinds of characters. The first kind conceals his ambitions and wants. The symptoms often manifest in personal pain and anger which most times turns antagonistic towards the assumed competitor. The second kind of character allows his ambition, instincts and desires to reign but in most cases encounter some form of the transferred aggression from the more psychologically reticent kind.

A careful look at human society today will highlight the existence of characters of both psychological provenance in virtually all social institutions but more particularly, within the nucleus family. Perhaps the most abiding reality or meaning which the *Cry of a Maiden* leaves us with is the knowledge that such conflicts may come but one must be abreast with the fact that they constitute part of the vagaries of existence within the template of human relations. Elsewhere, Nwaozuzu has articulated this design

Chapter four | Uche-Chinemere Nwaozuzu, in
Charles Nwadigwe, Molinta Enendu & Canice Nwosu (Eds.)
Metaphors and Climax, Reminiscences on the Drama and Theatre of Ogonna Agu
London, Adonis & Abbey Publishers

of absence of veracity when it comes to human behaviour (9). What determines the extent of the effect they have on human personality is the ability to see them for what they are; the dynamics of the complex psychic self.

Works Cited

Anaagudo-Agu, Ogonna. *Cry of a Maiden*. Calabar: Wusen Publishers, 2000.

Aristotle. "Poetics." *Dramatic Theory and Criticism: Greeks to Grotowski*. Ed. Benard F. Dukore. New York: Holt, Rinehart and Winston, 1974. 31-55.

Brown, Jonathan. *Social Psychology*. New York: McGraw-Hill, 2006.

Cherry, Kendra. "Psychoanalysis."*About.com, Psychology*. (pp. 2-4) Accessed 22 April, 2013.

Brown, Jonathon D. *Social Psychology*. New York: McGraw-Hill, 2006.

Horacio, Etchegoyen. *The Fundamentals of Psychoanalytic Technique*. New York: Karnac Books, 2005.

Nwaozuzu, Uche-Chinemere. "Perspective on Theme and Structure in Emeka Nwabueze's *Guardian of the Cosmos* and *When the Arrow Rebounds"*. *Castallia*, 9:1(2001): 1-9.

Chapter four | *Uche-Chinemere Nwaozuzu, in*
Charles Nwadigwe, Molinta Enendu & Canice Nwosu (Eds.)
Metaphors and Climax, Reminiscences on the Drama and Theatre of Ogonna Agu
London, Adonis & Abbey Publishers

Chapter Five

Ethnography, Gender and Self-Determination in the Drama of Ogonna Anaagudo-Agu

Ameh D. Akoh & Elizabeth Olayiwola

Introduction

Postcolonial African drama is a product of the angst-ridden socio-political environment. To state the obvious, therefore, is the fact that events either past or current supply materials for the dramatist's creation. It is not uncommon to see dramatists transforming historical materials into creative endeavours. In Africa, and Nigeria in particular, dramatists often recreate historical events for their audience's viewing pleasure and for documentation purposes. Historical events often recaptured by Nigeria dramatists include colonialism, coups d'état and military rule, monarchy, dictatorship, neocolonialism, ethnic war, riots, Nigerian Civil War, and so on. Issues raised in such plays are usually oppression, tyranny and the pain and hardship suffered by the citizenry as they lose lives and property.

Remy Oriaku mentions one of the ways through which historical materials can serve a dramatist: "Some historical playwrights borrow only ideas from events in history and then go on to create fresh actions, characters and events that has very little or no semblance to the original historical source" (135-136). He however states that these events must "be taken from the history of the primary audience of the play" because of the all-important fact that "for the playwright to succeed with his audience, it (the audience) must be made aware that what it is witnessing is the re-enactment of its own past" (129). Agu's *Symbol of a Goddess* and *Cry*

Chapter five | *Ameh D. Akoh & Elizabeth Olayiwola, in*
Charles Nwadigwe, Molinta Enendu & Canice Nwosu (Eds.)
Metaphors and Climax, Reminiscences on the Drama and Theatre of Ogonna Agu
London, Adonis & Abbey Publishers

of a Maiden fit into Oriaku's description of historical plays. First, Agu borrows from the events of the Nigerian Civil War, sometimes referred to as the Nigeria-Biafra War, as a premise for his artistic creation. He then, creates fresh actions and characters. Secondly, he has picked a familiar event, an event which belongs to his primary audience's past. The two plays were first produced in Nsukka and Calabar. These audiences must be quite familiar with the Nigeria- Biafra War. Seeing the actions of the plays unfold is to them a memento of their past.

In both plays, Agu narrates Igbo folkways while standing on a familiar premise (the Biafra War). In Bamidele's term we can say that Agu uses these historic plays to "perform ethnography" (56). We will get back to the issue of ethnography as we discuss critical issues raised in the plays under study.

Symbol of a Goddess

In *Symbol of a Goddess* Agu describes a post-war experience. The plot revolves around Emenike, a Biafra soldier who believes deeply in the Biafra cause. The Nigeria-Biafra war ends and both parties reunite again as one nation. Soldiers return to their homes to resume a normal life, but Emenike cannot settle into a normal life (war-free lifestyle). He refutes the fact that the war has ended. He terrorizes his community and prefers to marry a spirit than a human being. He rejects the wife married for him by his mother. At the end Emenike in an unusual manner settles into the community. We will anchor the analyses of this play on the theme of terror of war and self-transformation.

The Terror of War

The play begins with a prologue which immediately sets the mood of the drama. In the prologue, a war scene is enacted; the war songs also help in heightening the intensity of the scene. The

Chapter five | *Ameh D. Akoh & Elizabeth Olayiwola, in*
Charles Nwadigwe, Molinta Enendu & Canice Nwosu (Eds.)
Metaphors and Climax, Reminiscences on the Drama and
Theatre of Ogonna Agu
London, Adonis & Abbey Publishers

narrator speaks of the horrors that accompany war: "Here where I stand, I see desolation, grief and anguish among the children of men. At least that is what the civil war has brought gloom and hatred on the faces of men" (6). The war is ended but the anger and bitterness implanted by the war linger on. The experience of the brutal war makes Emenike a terror. Once again the narrator shares the experience of the Biafran soldiers:

> NARRATOR: Too bad, too bad. Those that could not run became prisoners in their own land. Some turned deaf and dump. Many died in the fields of battle . . . The sick, the hungry; they all came crowding into this one remaining place called Biafra. The maimed and deformed, they were all there, waiting to see when manna will fall from the sky. Waiting for the final end of the war whichever way it went-good or bad, for despair and misery haven taken their toll on them (8).

As the war comes to an end, Biafran soldiers are defeated, and in good faith the Nigerian army embraces the former. Yet Emenike remains with the terror of the war; thus it makes him a terror to himself, his family and community. He returns shooting gun into the air and terrifying the entire community. When he is reminded that the war is over, he rebuffs it. This is probably because the war continues on the inside of him. In an incident reported by Akudiri we see how the war has programmed his mind: "I heard it. He smashed it with his fist. Oh my God! He saw his image in it and thought it was his enemy, and so hit it with his fist..." (49).

Emenike's mother, Iluka, must have been giving kolanuts to her *Chi* each annual festival begging for her son to marry and procreate. Iluka also partakes of the pain inflicted by the war. Her only son has gone wild. The cord between mother and the only son is broken by war. Iluka awaits the day Emenike will get married and give birth to many children since she only has one. But Emenike refuses to grant her that pleasure. On his return from his

Chapter five | *Ameh D. Akoh & Elizabeth Olayiwola, in*
Charles Nwadigwe, Molinta Enendu & Canice Nwosu (Eds.)
Metaphors and Climax, Reminiscences on the Drama and
Theatre of Ogonna Agu
London, Adonis & Abbey Publishers

three-year absence as a result of the war, Iluka shares the emotional trauma his absence had exposed her to: "Three long years . . . Every day, I'm crying" (35). Emenike's response lacks sympathy of any form. He responds sharply "wipe your tears then" (35). The war has so hardened Emenike and taken all the love in him that he tells his mother: "If you want to know you are a dead tradition. Your types have all died. Die! So that we can cover you with sand"(37).

Akudiri, the "wife" of Emenike, shares from the bitter pills also. She is a maiden married to a man who refuses to acknowledge her as a wife. Emenike refuses to perform his conjugal obligations, when he eventually does so, he regrets his action. He sees it as a trap and refuses ownership of the pregnancy that results from his act. Akudiri appeals in vain to gain his love. She remains frustrated as Emenike chooses a goddess over her. The war offers her a bitter man for a husband. As Emenike dies "Akudiri, now visibly rounded with pregnancy cannot be consoled as sympathizers surround her" (67).

Self-Transformation

Agu does not only describe in detail the dilemma of war, he also offers a remedy in managing the trauma of a post-war situation. He proposes self-transformation as a means of managing the terror inflicted on the mind by war. Emenike who was already on the path of self-destruction, retraces his steps and rediscovers himself. In essence, despite all the horrifying experiences of wars, those involved can still achieve some self-induced transformation. Emenike re-orders his steps as he engages his mind in a creative venture. He is able to organize and direct a troupe:

> EMENIKE: Tell our men to come in, let them come in at once let them bring all those drums. All those skins and masks let them bring them (*Drummers start to enter .There is a general feeling of joy and merriment as they warm up their drums and generally*

Chapter five | *Ameh D. Akoh & Elizabeth Olayiwola, in*
Charles Nwadigwe, Molinta Enendu & Canice Nwosu (Eds.)
Metaphors and Climax, Reminiscences on the Drama and Theatre of Ogonna Agu
London, Adonis & Abbey Publishers

rump about) ...Space! Give them space! We are old soldier".
(22)

Emenike who had been a source of fear to the people becomes a source of joy. Although he still desires for Biafra to survive in the minds of his people, but his methodology is different, he replaces violence with diplomacy. He channels his energy to creative ends and becomes a man of the people. Thus, when Ide calls Emenike a beast the people protest until Emenike calms them. Igbonekwu attests to Emenike's transformation:

> The other issue to consider is how he has put his intellectual and emotional strength into great use. At first he came with guns. Now the guns are gone, and he is stirring the whole village with scenes of a magnificent masquerade. What a way to engage his mind and pull it from its destructive tendencies. (64)

Performing Ethnography in *Cry of a Maiden*

Ethnography is a means to represent graphically and in writing, the culture of a people. Although ethnography was pioneered in the biological, social and cultural branches of anthropology, it has also become popular in sociology.[1] Bamidele in his book *Literature and Sociology* defines performing ethnography "as the effort of the dramatist to present a play as an interface between the social and the aesthetic" (57). He establishes the nexus between drama and ethnography, recalling Gerald Wales's view that a play is a cultural artifact as well as an aesthetic object (56). Agu's plays pass for cultural artifacts as well as possessing aesthetic value. A reading of the plays unveils Igbo folk ways. The playwright employs a lot of folk music and dance, the display of masquerade and mask, the use of *Obi* and the exposure given to the goddess and other gods. He makes use of material and non-material aspects of the Igbo culture.

Cry of a Maiden tells the story of a young man, Chidum, who has just returned home from World War II. Chidum immediately

Chapter five | *Ameh D. Akoh & Elizabeth Olayiwola, in*
Charles Nwadigwe, Molinta Enendu & Canice Nwosu (Eds.)
Metaphors and Climax, Reminiscences on the Drama and Theatre of Ogonna Agu
London, Adonis & Abbey Publishers

declares his intention to settle the family way (get a wife). Okolo, his elder brother, objects pointing out that the *obi* should be mended before any marriage plans. His uncle, Udoka, agrees with Okolo. Chidum sees reasons with Okolo's idea and postpones his marriage plans.

The play tells the story of a traditional Igbo family. From Act One, the stage setting presents to us a typical Igbo cultural environment. In a compound, the men are seated on low stools with calabash of palm wine which is the way men from this part of the world relax. We can equate it with the Western ideal of seating by the bar. Then we see the women by the fireside, which seems to be a common locale of the traditional Igbo women but this time the women are taking care of their looks. Adego (Ada), a maiden, braids Mgbochi's hair. The playwright is concerned with how the folkway informs the vivid description of a fireplace in the Igbo context: "the fire place consists of mud-block, tripod for cooking, with a clay pot standing on it. A few light logs support the fire"(1). We see Ada singing as she makes Mgbochi's hair; a good example of African folkways. Africans virtually make melody out of every chore like singing while farming or pounding. In a traditional song, Ada eulogizes the hair oil as she applies it on Mgbochi's hair.

Although an allegorical reading of this play renders an account of the Nigeria-Biafra War (1967 – 1970), the playwright suggests this in the "Dramaturgist's Notes":

> In fact, *Cry of a Maiden* was written soon after the Nigerian Civil war in 1970. It has all the imprints of the war: the peace pact between the two brothers, the voluntary exile of the junior brother Chidum, and his return for a final settlement – all aspects of that war. (ii)

The playwright therefore engages in a form of "cultural politics" in the "stylization of historical material or historical reconstruction" in his play (Illah 118). However, the interest of this study is not to undertake a metaphoric reading of the play, rather

Chapter five | *Ameh D. Akoh & Elizabeth Olayiwola, in*
Charles Nwadigwe, Molinta Enendu & Canice Nwosu (Eds.)
Metaphors and Climax, Reminiscences on the Drama and Theatre of Ogonna Agu
London, Adonis & Abbey Publishers

the crux of the analysis is ethnography as employed in *Cry of a Maiden*. The play will be examined as a carrier of Igbo cultural values. First we will discuss the power held by the first son in Igbo culture and the place of music and dance. This will also necessitate a discussion of the intricate issue of sexuality and gender roles in Igbo culture as portrayed in the plays.

First Son Tradition

In Igbo society the first son is also known as *Okpala*. The first son is well regarded in the family and highly recognized in the clan. In *Cry of a Maiden*, the power wielded by the first son is both enormous and conspicuous. Chidum discusses his marriage plans with the men in the family; Okolo the first son thinks otherwise and that settles it. Chidum immediately dismisses his marriage plans. In Igbo society, and virtually all traditional African societies the first son is given considerable attention and scrutiny. In Achebe's *Things Fall Apart*, we see the deep attention Okonkwo gives his first son, Nwoye. Okonkwo raises him to control the household and represent his clan. Hence:

> Okonkwo was inwardly pleased at his son's development, and he knew it was due to Ikemefuna. He wanted Nwoye to grow into a tough young man capable of ruling his father's household . . . and so he (Okonkwo) was happy when he heard him grumbling about women. That showed that in time he would be able to control his women folk. No matter how prosperous a man was, if he was unable to rule his women and children, he was not really a man. (Achebe 37)

Okonkwo had earlier warned that he would not "have a son who cannot hold up his head in the gathering of the clan" (Achebe 24).

In some Igbo communities the *Okpala* solely inherits his father's *Obi* while other sons gradually leave to establish their own *Obi*. Okolo in the play under consideration is lazy and drinks palm wine all day. Yet he still has the final say on the affairs of the

Chapter five | *Ameh D. Akoh & Elizabeth Olayiwola, in*
Charles Nwadigwe, Molinta Enendu & Canice Nwosu (Eds.)
Metaphors and Climax, Reminiscences on the Drama and Theatre of Ogonna Agu
London, Adonis & Abbey Publishers

household. Agu writes in support of the first son tradition as he makes Chidum to accept Okolo's verdict. Despite Chidum's exposure and experience overseas he succumbs to Okolo's decision. Therefore, Okpala, Okolo's uncle speaks of Okolo's authority: "You are the elder . . . Without you this household is powerless. Chidum is powerless" (9-10). Okolo himself is aware of this. He parades his status as *Okpala* with pride: "Of course I'm the lord of this household" (22). Again he exercises his power as *Okpala* as he covets Ada (Chidum's love) for himself. In another instance, Okolo further demonstrates his power as first son as he briefs Chidum of happenings while the latter was away:

> I like Okafor and gave him Ekemma our sister. Like his father I discovered he's hard working. Has already extended his father's barns to accommodate another three-two hundred yams: Since I gave Ekema to that family, they've not failed to call me in for wine on big market days. (7)

As the first son, his in-law continually pays homage for releasing his sister in marriage. The power held by the first son in Igbo culture seems limitless.

Music and Dance

From an ethnographic viewpoint, "music accompanies and celebrates every rite of passage, birth, and christening, initiation into adulthood, and finally death and mourning" (Onwuekwe 171). Music and dance constitute a vital part of African cultural institutions, and the Igbo culture is no exemption. However, these dance and music vary. For instance, ritual dance and music differ in style and tone from that used for christening. Onwuekwe describes the ritual dance thus:

> As part of a spiritual ritual dance may be a symbolic form of communication with natural powers, or a trance-inducing movement enabling the dancer to communicate directly with the spirits. In some

Chapter five | *Ameh D. Akoh & Elizabeth Olayiwola, in*
Charles Nwadigwe, Molinta Enendu & Canice Nwosu (Eds.)
Metaphors and Climax, Reminiscences on the Drama and
Theatre of Ogonna Agu
London, Adonis & Abbey Publishers

masked dances the dancer assumes the temporary identity of a god or a powerful ancestral spirit. (175)

In *Symbol of the Goddess* Emenike takes "trance-inducing movement" and this needs elaborate citing:

(Emenike dances back on stage in retreating movement-first with his back. He raises a song . . .) There she comes...My egret! o! What a presence! Gold crop sinking . . . o! How can I gather you in my palms? Lady of the eyes. . . mother of the nation . . . Agboghommuo . . . God! Humbled am I by your majesty (the song rises till it fills the whole place. By now the spirit mask enters, escorted, dancing. Next it does a fast movement to the accompaniment of drums, and then collapses into a mass of cloth). (64-65)

Through ritual music and dance Emenike worships his goddess; a means of honouring, a way of propitiating, and a magical method of seeing his deity; the red-eyed goddess: "God! So brief... so brief her presence!" (65). Emenike sings on, until he transits to the world of his goddess: "Emenike collapses suddenly in all his height as song is stuck in his throat" (67). The song serves as the vehicle that transports him to the world beyond. This ritual enactment is reminiscent of Elesin's transitional prelude in Soyinka's *Death and the King's Horseman*.

Dirge is a type of music; it is music of lament or funeral. So, it is inseparable from mourning. Dirge differs in rhythm and tone; from the tone or type of dirge one can guess the occasion. In *Cry of a Maiden*, when Okpala hears the rhythm of the dirge in tribute to Adigwe he identifies that "a great man has died" (12). As part of the burial rites the youths announce the death of Adigwe according to the custom:

Make way for the thunder to howl! Way for lightning to flash! The lightning flash of the Sky! Let it sear the thickness of the night! Let the clouds rumble in their stomachs and echo Adigwe's name beyond the hills. Let it brush like pod and scatter in the distance for Adigwe is gone. O Adigwe! (12)

Chapter five | *Ameh D. Akoh & Elizabeth Olayiwola, in*
Charles Nwadigwe, Molinta Enendu & Canice Nwosu (Eds.)
Metaphors and Climax, Reminiscences on the Drama and Theatre of Ogonna Agu
London, Adonis & Abbey Publishers

As part of the rites the youths enact the good deed of Adigwe:

LEADER:	Threw the seven-eyed monster by the sacred stream, at night. And secured the maidens pots for drawing water. Who?
YOUTHS:	Adigwe!
LEADER:	Fought the bees empty handed on the palm tree. Who?
YOUTHS:	Adigwe!! (13)

The soloist keeps highlighting the good deeds of the deceased while the enactment continues. The inclusion of this scene is a deliberate craft by the playwright to unveil the nature of the burial rites of his people (Igbo). We also see music and dance serving social function as Okolo and Ada explore it on their romantic dates. The playwright speaks of the essence of the music and dance employed on the rendezvous: "The essence of the art of this dance is to evoke an emotion of love". (19)

OKOLO:	Adakego in town
ADA:	Yes!
OKOLO:	Adakego in town
ADA:	Yes
OKOLO:	You and I shall be friends by God's grace
ADA:	It's alright. (19)

The music and dance continue until the lovers become lost in their act. This reflects the nature of Igbo music and dance and perhaps Africa in general. As earlier said, there are dance and music for child birth, for marriage, for romance, for rituals, for farming, for burial and for virtually all human endeavours. Music and dance therefore permeate the life and living of the Igbo man as exemplified in the worlds of Agu's plays.

Gender and Sexuality

It is important to clear the mistiness over the usage of the two terms here – gender and sexuality – as they sometimes become

Chapter five | *Ameh D. Akoh & Elizabeth Olayiwola, in*
Charles Nwadigwe, Molinta Enendu & Canice Nwosu (Eds.)
Metaphors and Climax, Reminiscences on the Drama and Theatre of Ogonna Agu
London, Adonis & Abbey Publishers

more finicky in critical theory. The variegatedness in the usage, especially of gender, expresses a complication in both definition and representation which continues to "expose limitations and biases in our perspectives and to raise many questions" (Bridwell-Bowles 179). Thus, as we discuss in the following paragraphs, the issue of gender and sexuality in the Igbo culture as presented in the texts under study, we will align with Bridwell-Bowles to ask certain crucial questions as: Is gender learned or is it entirely socially constructed, or are there generic bases for some characteristics? How many genders are there? As it is evident in the plays, there seem to be an obscuration of knowledge, in our understanding, of gay, lesbian, bisexual, and transgender identities in delineating gender roles in the Igbo society. Our discussion of the plays, therefore, is based on the dramatist's avowed portrayal of the characters within the worldview they operate rather than this wide range of usage.

Sexuality in Igbo Worldview

Sexuality is derived from the word sex. Sex as an act involves the physical or psychological penetration. Sexuality is more embracive and revolves around human experience ranging from family relationships, dating, sexual behaviour, physical development, sensuality, reproduction, gender, body, and so on.[2] Lawal sheds more light on sexuality when he opines that "sexuality encompasses a set of ideas, meaning and social practices such as sexual behaviour like monogamy, polygamy, polyandry, etc.; sexual identity such as heterosexual, homosexual, bi-sexual, trans-sexual; sexual desire, sexual relations, sexual politics, etc." (273).

In this section, our discourse will focus on dating and sexual behaviour within Igbo worldview. In the Igbo tradition sexual relations are expected to transpire between the married. In *Cry of a Maiden*, Okolo and Ada engage in pre-marital sex but are accordingly reprimanded for it.

Chapter five | *Ameh D. Akoh & Elizabeth Olayiwola, in*
Charles Nwadigwe, Molinta Enendu & Canice Nwosu (Eds.)
Metaphors and Climax, Reminiscences on the Drama and
Theatre of Ogonna Agu
London, Adonis & Abbey Publishers

Okpala, you're a fellow man. And being a man, you happen to see a girl going to the stream you'd want to marry. A young maiden mind you, sweet and nubile. All you have to do is meet the parents. A traditional calabash of wine could have spoken for him (34).

The adverse consequence of a desecration of a material essence is abated by Agu when Okolo is made to marry Ada. Udoka affirms this "Well they will have to marry...after all that has happened" (40). The value of a girl within the traditional Igbo context revolves around her sexuality. After the sexual intercourse with Okolo, Ada is afraid of losing value. The table turns as Ada the 'wooed' becomes the 'wooer'. Initially, Okolo was the one trailing and imploring Ada but as soon as they begin to relate sexually which leads to her pregnancy, Ada takes turn wooing Okolo, to salvage what is left of her dignity.

Ada enters crying and pleading. She slowly walks up to Okolo and presents him with a piece of the broken pot, kneeling at his feet. Okolo gently takes it from her. Then, slowly the broken piece slips from his hand and breaks to pieces. Ada holds tight onto his leg and weeps...(36)

She weeps, begging for her honour; her fate is in Okolo's hands, having broken her pot of honour. If Okolo rejects her, she is doomed. No one will again look at her with dignity. The worth of a maiden in the Igbo society is tied to her virginity. If she is a virgin she is more respected and admired by suitors. On the other hand, the male is respected for hard work and number of yams in his barn. We shall return shortly to this issue of male-female dichotomy and society's gendered belief and categorization.

Polygamy is the sexual behaviour most practised in traditional Igbo society. The number of a man's wives was an indication of his wealth and affluence. Anene speaks of other reasons why polygamy is fashionable:

You see-I usually love my wives severally for one excellence or the other...but this one...hm...her waist is mortar. You're laughing? She's a

Chapter five | *Ameh D. Akoh & Elizabeth Olayiwola, in*
Charles Nwadigwe, Molinta Enendu & Canice Nwosu (Eds.)
Metaphors and Climax, Reminiscences on the Drama and Theatre of Ogonna Agu
London, Adonis & Abbey Publishers

real tobacco. Without delay, while the pot was still seething with fume, I tossed my pestle in the air and began to pound. I never knew she was trying my strength and I was determined to show her a bit of it. For hours on end I was lost pounding and pounding till the pot broke and the mortar . . .(28-29)

Anene's suggests a number of things about sexuality within the Igbo cosmology. One, men love to keep more than one wife because of their large appetite for sex. Two, men share their sexual experience with their friends. Three, sexual discussions are usually coded. Four, sexual relationships are to be discreetly discussed. Hence, Anene's speech strengthens the opinion that:

'The male gaze' appears to be the dominant construction of the female body where it operates to enslave, oppress, silence and distort female realities. Here the body functions as a figure of desire, and as a site for the domination of women. (Akwang 151-152)

Thus, men usually converse in proverbs or signs when handling matters of sexuality. The monopoly of signs-after all man himself is a sign-may be responsible for the continued seemingly impossible dismantling of the dominance of man in the Igbo society.[4] Signs dominate the universe, and it is logical that man sometimes operates his sexual power in codes as can be explained in Anene's position in this play.

Finally on sexuality is the issue of parenting. In the Igbo culture and most African settings, importance is attached to the family institution. A child is expected to grow under the roof of the father. A lot is attached to a child growing in his father's compound: sometimes when it becomes impossible for the child to grow in his father's house, the father is expected to at least claim ownership for the child. A child who cannot identify the father is usually stigmatized in the community. In the Igbo culture single parenting is not an option. It is therefore not surprising that Akudiri in *Symbol of the Goddess* begs tirelessly for Emenike's

Chapter five | *Ameh D. Akoh & Elizabeth Olayiwola, in*
Charles Nwadigwe, Molinta Enendu & Canice Nwosu (Eds.)
Metaphors and Climax, Reminiscences on the Drama and
Theatre of Ogonna Agu
London, Adonis & Abbey Publishers

acceptance. "Please don't throw me away. I ... I... am sorry for all that have happened. Take me and take my child". (49)

This takes us back to the issue we raised earlier on gendered categorization. While it is a stigma for a girl who becomes pregnant without full marital rites, it is not so for the boy or man. Thus in both plays the girl takes the shame, and even society's scorn, for an act committed by both-Okolo and Ada in *Cry of a Maiden*, and Emenike and Akudiri in *Symbol of a Goddess*-while the man is merely *persuaded* to marry the girl in order to take away the shame from the latter. This explains the reason why virginity becomes a central factor for a girl that is about to get married and no one bothers to ask if the man intending to marry such a girl is himself a virgin. This culture therefore gives the community the authority to vilify the female and make her bear the heavier brunt of an act jointly committed by both the male and female. It is a *machismo* of a tradition, akin to a Latin American culture which defines the basic traditional values affecting gender relations; an "explicit code" that sees the real man (*macho*) "to be courageous, sexually viral and aggressive, and superior to women. A woman, in contrast, is supposed to be passive, sexually conservative and faithful, obedient, and completely devoted to her mate" (Scupin 303-304).

Okolo's insatiable attraction to Ada in *Cry of a Maiden* seems to explain the above as he unleashes his "naked" energy on an inexperienced girl whom he takes from his younger brother by virtue of his being an *Okpala*. The masculinist society also seems to accept this state of affairs in favour of Okolo, again, "based on the 'common knowledge' that frigid women suffer from sexual hysteria" unlike other categories of women (Sharpe 223). The unprepared sexual encounter in this instance lays bare the cultural imaginary that privileges the man over the woman. Okolo's sexual volcano may however find explanation in the provision of culture or an ideological production of the dramatist to justify the

Chapter five | *Ameh D. Akoh & Elizabeth Olayiwola, in*
Charles Nwadigwe, Molinta Enendu & Canice Nwosu (Eds.)
Metaphors and Climax, Reminiscences on the Drama and Theatre of Ogonna Agu
London, Adonis & Abbey Publishers

104

sexual experience of both characters in search of social change. Again, this interpretation can find meaning only if we place it, especially the resolution of the crises generated by Okolo's attitude after the sexual encounter, within the context of the discourse of power in postcolonial and gender studies.

Gender Role

In cultural anthropology, a society sees gender in the light of specific behavioural traits that are assigned to each sex. From the reading of *Cry of a Maiden* gender roles are assigned along these cultural lines even though gender roles are socially constructed roles and such construction differs from one community to another. Since gender matters are common in today's society, the battle of the sexes also dominates almost every sphere of critical discourse. One of the factors responsible for this "war" can be traced to gender role differentiation. In African traditional societies, there exists the Keyssarian extension of what Akwang refers to as "stereotypic subject position" defining the perspectives and identity an individual assumes as predefined by the society.[3] The imposition of traditional gender roles in a modern society is a major aspect of the ongoing battle of the sexes (Akwang 150).

From the reading of *Cry of a Maiden* gender roles are established. But the focus of our discourse at this point is not actually an inspection of gender war but identification of gender roles as prescribed by the Igbo society. Ada speaks of her society's expectation of a female: "But I've finished all the household chores. I've scrubbed the floor and patterned the walls. Remaining only to press the oil from fibre" (4). In addition she is also expected to go to the stream with pots to fetch water. Patterning the walls seems to be what Okpara describes as *uli*, ostensibly the Igbo nomenclature for decorative wall patterns. Okpara explains that *uli* "is a creative exploration and expression of indigenous community ideas and forms in unique linear painting and drawing technique.

Chapter five | *Ameh D. Akoh & Elizabeth Olayiwola, in*
Charles Nwadigwe, Molinta Enendu & Canice Nwosu (Eds.)
Metaphors and Climax, Reminiscences on the Drama and Theatre of Ogonna Agu
London, Adonis & Abbey Publishers

These linear painting forms and drawings were originally painted on walls of Igbo traditional mud houses and human bodies" (92).

Okpala's definition of *uli* helps us to understand what Ada means by patterning the wall, a task conventionally performed by women. Thus, the women in the community depicted in *Cry of a Maiden* seem to be generally concerned with house chores. Chidum, the second son of Mgbochi orders Mgbochi, his mother to get him a tray. We are not sure of the rationale behind this; whether it was imbibed from his military training or culturally acceptable. Cooking for the married women is a socially constructed duty. Mgbochi rejoices at the thought of making soup for her family. However, it is not her role to be in the men's meeting even though they are her children. As Chidum commences the discussion with Okpala and his elder brother, Okolo, their mother Mgbochi exits. She is aware that staying out of that discussion is a role she has to play at the moment.

The males are not without a role, as society demands on them also in the Igbo community. As depicted by the playwright, the male is expected to go to war, defending the community from intruders. Chidum has just returned from war. This is one of the roles expected of a male in Igbo community and pre-colonial African setting at large. It is also expected of them to construct and mend their buildings. Okolo speaks of this male duty:

> ...a major task stares us in the face, the task of reconstructing this cottage. As you can see, the *obi* building has gone into ruins. And the shrine house has collapsed, thereby exposing the sacred goddess to [bad] weather and inhospitable rains. (10)

From this statement, the role of men as builders and spiritual leaders for the household is confirmed. In Igbo cosmology, an individual has a personal god *chi* and there are also household gods kept and maintained in the shrine house of the head of the house, usually the father or the oldest son. It is the male's role in

Chapter five | *Ameh D. Akoh & Elizabeth Olayiwola, in*
Charles Nwadigwe, Molinta Enendu & Canice Nwosu (Eds.)
Metaphors and Climax, Reminiscences on the Drama and Theatre of Ogonna Agu
London, Adonis & Abbey Publishers

the Igbo traditional norm to fulfill the spiritual obligations for his household. It is also their duty to farm major crops like yam (regarded as king of all crops in Igbo community).The bigger a man's yam barn the more respected he commands in the community. Okolo gives out his sister in marriage to Okafor because of the size of his barn: "I discovered he's hard working. Has already extended his father's barn to accommodate another three-two hundred yams" (7).

All of these render an account of the totality of the Igbo cultural heritage and some gender constructions inherent in daily existence and the social institutions. Individuals create an order in addition to societal order. But again, the playwright seems to approve the status quo as an Igbo normative culture which also explains a dualism in the cosmology depicted in the play. This dualism in dramatic representations "causes meaning to be contested, contradicted, and even challenged to yield its authenticity (Nwabueze 275).

Conclusion

A variety of issues are covered by the two plays discussed here; however, we have focused on three important areas that draw our attention. The beauty of literature is in its relevance through ages, its meta-textual nature and its flexibility to what Jonathan Culler describes as "modes of signification" (25). This is the reason why in New Criticism a classical Greek text can find bearing in modern day Nigeria.[4] Equally, Agu's plays situated in Igbo traditional society, some decades ago still find substance in today's discourse. Nigeria today faces enormous insecurity problems resulting from ethic wars, religious violence, kidnapping, militancy, bombing and all sorts of aggressive acts. Most of the perpetrators of these crimes seek to make one point or the other, violently seeking to expand and propagate their ideology. It is feasible that, like Emenike, in

Chapter five | *Ameh D. Akoh & Elizabeth Olayiwola, in*
Charles Nwadigwe, Molinta Enendu & Canice Nwosu (Eds.)
Metaphors and Climax, Reminiscences on the Drama and
Theatre of Ogonna Agu
London, Adonis & Abbey Publishers

Symbol of a Goddess the ex-militants can get involved in personal and socially transformative exercises; they can pull all their negative energies into productive ventures.

Another issue that can be generalized in Agu's writing is the responsibility woven around sexual relationship. Contrary to the West where sexual relationship is treated casually, Agu, influenced by his culture, ensures that Okolo and Ada bear the responsibility for their sexual activity. The baby is not aborted and Okolo does not bail out on Ada. They marry and together bear the responsibility resulting from sex. In *Cry of a Maiden*, the playwright preserves the Igbo cultural values on courtship; thus when Okolo and Ada break one, they are made to make amends. Here, consequence is attached to premarital sex unlike the Western world where sex is mostly seen as an expression of individual right and freedom; an act to appease the emotion and not the logic. Agu makes a recall to the traditional courtship pattern of his society. The two plays easily justify the existence of society-in-the-text and the text-in-the-society nexus.

Notes

1. See http://en.wikipedia.org/wiki/Ethnography. Accessed 27 Feb 2013

2. m.plannedparenthood psf/what- is-sexualityanyway2480.htm. Accessed 27 Feb. 2013.

3. Helene Keyssar discusses this with reference to the multiple subject positions of women of colour. She, however, pushes forward an apologia on plays that seek to replace this traditional thinking and redefine the subject position in the theatre; a position and discussion Akwang re-ignites here.

4. For details, see pp.25-26 of Jonathan Culler's *The Pursuit of Signs* where he appropriates Charles Sanders Peirce's idea

Chapter five | Ameh D. Akoh & Elizabeth Olayiwola, in
Charles Nwadigwe, Molinta Enendu & Canice Nwosu (Eds.)
Metaphors and Climax, Reminiscences on the Drama and Theatre of Ogonna Agu
London, Adonis & Abbey Publishers

of signs as suffusing the entire universe; an idea which Culler regards as being full of "taxonomic speculations".

Works Cited

Achebe Chinua. *Things Fall Apart*. London: Heinemann, 1958.

Akwang, Etop. "Shifting Contexts of Female Bodies: Slavery and Dissent in Nwamuo's *The Squeeze*." *The Dramaturgy of Liberation and Survival: Festschrift Essays on Chris Nwamuo's Scholarship*. Eds. Andrew Esekong and Babson Ajibade. Calabar: University of Calabar Press, 2009. 150-159.

Anaagudo-Agu, Ogonna. *Symbol of a Goddess*. Calabar: Wusen Press, 2005.

Anaagudo-Agu, Ogonna. *Cry of a Maiden*. Calabar: Wusen Press, 2000.

Bridwell-Bowles, Lillian. *Identity Matters: Rhetorics of Difference*. New Jersey: Prentice-Hall, 1998.

Culler, Jonathan. *The Pursuit of Signs: Semiotics, Literature, Deconstruction*.

Illah, Egwugwu. "Rotimi and the Drama of Culturalist Assertion: The Development of Cultural Elements in *Kurunmi* and Other Plays." *Cross Currents in African Theatre*. Ed. Austin Asagba. Benin: Osasu Publishers, 2001. 117-138.

Keyssar, Helene. "Introduction."*Feminist Theatre and Theory*. Ed. Helene Keyssar. London: Macmillan, 1996. 1-18.

London & New York: Routledge, 2001.

Lawal, A. A. "Sexuality, Religion and Spirituality." *Gender, Sexuality, and Mothering in Africa*. Eds. Toyin Falola and Bessie House-Soremekun. New Jersey: Africa World Press, 2011. 271-288.

Nwabueze, Emeka. *Visions and Re-visions: Selected Discourses on Literary Criticism*. 2nd Ed. Enugu: Abic Books, 2011.

Chapter five | *Ameh D. Akoh & Elizabeth Olayiwola, in*
Charles Nwadigwe, Molinta Enendu & Canice Nwosu (Eds.)
Metaphors and Climax, Reminiscences on the Drama and
Theatre of Ogonna Agu
London, Adonis & Abbey Publishers

Okpara, Chukwuemeka Vincent. "Traditional African Society: The Dynamics of Folk Art Language." *Journal of Black and African Arts and Civilization* 4.1(2010): 87-94.

Onwuekwe, Agatha I. "The Social-Cultural Implications of African Music and Dance." *The Creative Artist: A Journal of Theatre and Media Studies* 2:1 (2008): 171-185.

Oriaku, Remmy. "Historical Drama in Africa." *Papers in Honour of Professor Dapo Adelugba at 60. Ibadan:* End-Time, 1999. 129-137.

Scupin, Raymond. *Cultural Anthropology: A Global Perspective.* Englewood Cliffs, New Jersey: Prentice-Hall, 1992.

Sharpe, Jenny. "The Unspeakable Limits of Rape: Colonial Violence and Counter-Insurgency." *Colonial Discourse and Postcolonial Theory: A Reader.* Eds. Patrick Williams and Laura Chrisman. London: Harvester Wheatsheaf, 1993. 221-243.

Soyinka, Wole. *Death and the King's Horseman.* London: Methuen, 1975.

Chapter five | *Ameh D. Akoh & Elizabeth Olayiwola, in*
Charles Nwadigwe, Molinta Enendu & Canice Nwosu (Eds.)
Metaphors and Climax, Reminiscences on the Drama and
Theatre of Ogonna Agu
London, Adonis & Abbey Publishers

110

Chapter Six

Igbos and Modern Nigerian Nation-State: The Biafran War of Self-Determination in Ogonna Agu's *Symbol of a Goddess*

Canice C. Nwosu, Emeka Nwosu & Columba Apeh

Introduction

Historically, the traditional Igbo man like any other primordial man in most geographical enclaves of the world found himself in a hostile but nebulous environment, where he wrestled with the vicissitudes of life. Therefore, the theory of the origin and evolution of Igbo nation is not completely divorced from Marx and Engel's widely accepted "theory of historical forms of peoples' community by concrete material reasons." (The Institute of Social Sciences 231) Hence, the Igbo nation gradually developed from the zeal to live a settled life and cultivate the soil around presumed fertile and conducive geographical areas. According to the Institute of Social Sciences, "various forms of community- clan, tribe, nationality, nation- take shape, in the final analysis, under the impact of the production and reproduction of the material conditions of life and the objective requirements of social development"(231).

Thus, the formation trend of Modern Nigerian nation-state may be seen from a bottom to top progression: family-clan-community-tribe and finally the nation-state. Today the people referred to as the Igbo (Ndi Igbo) are the people occupying more than eighty percent of Eastern Nigeria's land mass, According to G.E.K Ofomata:

Chapter six | *Canice C. Nwosu, Emeka Nwosu & Columba Apeh, in*
Charles Nwadigwe, Molinta Enendu & Canice Nwosu (Eds.)
Metaphors and Climax, Reminiscences on the Drama and Theatre of Ogonna Agu
London, Adonis & Abbey Publishers

The land surface of Igboland lies between latitudes 4 '15' and 7 '05' North and longitudes 6 '00' and B '30' East. It covers a total surface area approximately 41,000 square kilometers. It has a total population of 3,818,208 (1963) census figures and a population density of 215 persons per square kilometer. Administratively it is made up of the entire Omambala (Anambra), Abia, Ebonyi, Enugu and Imo states, parts of Delta and Rivers States. (1)

However, recent studies submit that "the population of Anambra State alone by the 2006 disputed census was over 4million. The whole of the Southeast had over 15million inhabitants" (Nwadigwe 516).

There are many versions of occupation theory behind how the Igbo came to live in this part of the globe; some scholars say it was through migration, while others insist that, it was through creation. However, J.O. Ijeoma posits that; "theories of Igbo origins can be divided into three broad categories: Oriental, Niger/Benue, and Igbo homeland or independent origins" (40).

Despite divergent points among these three theories of Igbo origin, convergent points include that the Igbo nation was, prior to the colonial enigma, an independent and egalitarian tribe governed by the principles of equality and communalism. Igbo tradition, religion and culture are encapsulated in Igbo worldview which Canice Nwosu says "is one of the known worldviews in the African continent." Nwosu further explains that "the Igbo worldview is parallel to the worldviews of most African tribes. However, it is among the most egalitarian, responsive, dynamic and accommodating *worldviews*" ("Evolving a Performance . . ." 135). Unfortunately, the Igbo were among the last tribes to lose their independence during the colonial onslaught. Colonialism met stiff opposition in Igboland partly because the colonist failed to understand the Igbo political system of governance and partly because of the independent mindedness of the Igbo. Two important historical events led to the final loss of Igbo

Chapter six | *Canice C. Nwosu, Emeka Nwosu & Columba Apeh, in*
Charles Nwadigwe, Molinta Enendu & Canice Nwosu (Eds.)
Metaphors and Climax, Reminiscences on the Drama and
Theatre of Ogonna Agu
London, Adonis & Abbey Publishers

independence: the blackmail and final defeat of the Aros of Arochukwu by the British and the amalgamation of Northern and Southern Protectorates by Lord Lugard in 1914.

The amalgamation was a singular political and historical act by a British colonial officer that lumped over two hundred ethnic groups together in a geographical area referred today as Nigeria. Apart from the Igbo, other tribes affected by this forceful unification include Hausa, Fulani, Yoruba, Ibibio, Kanuri, Tiv, Efik, Igala, Edo, Ijaw, Nupe, and so on. The aim of the colonist was to govern this vast area of human and natural resources as an entity so that a nation-state to be likened to the United States or United Kingdom will evolve from the union.

Even though, the colonist forced the component units of the new nation-state to shed their residual characteristics and embrace the emergent culture; there was no attempt to study what these units had as pre-colonial institutions and develop them alongside the foreign ideals. Rather the British, blinded by their divide-and-rule policy introduced a dictatorial but centralized Indirect Rule system and tried to force it on all the constituent tribes including the Igbo that had a loose and egalitarian political system.

In addition to the above, British colonial policy always identified and aligned with a preferred ethnic group in almost all the colonies they ruled; this they also did in Nigeria. Hence, between 1914 and 1920 Lugard piloted the political affairs of Nigeria with his Hausa/Fulani allies and marginalized the Igbo and other progressives from the Yoruba tribe.

Consequently, the colonist's lack of sincerity of purpose further divided the component units rather than unify them. Therefore, contrary to the presumed expectation of the colonist and so-called founding fathers of the union, it failed to achieve true unity. The fragility of the Nigerian nation-state became obvious as it destroyed diversity, communalism and generated friction among

Chapter six | *Canice C. Nwosu, Emeka Nwosu & Columba Apeh, in*
Charles Nwadigwe, Molinta Enendu & Canice Nwosu (Eds.)
Metaphors and Climax, Reminiscences on the Drama and
Theatre of Ogonna Agu
London, Adonis & Abbey Publishers

the unequal component regions. Fear of domination of the minority by the majority ethnic groups increased and the leaders played dangerously on tribal and ethnic sentiments. Grievances of the founding fathers and leaders who presented the colonist as the nation's problems led to the struggle for independence which was won in 1960.

Unfortunately, the situation worsened after independence, bitterness and acrimony deepened because the political arrangement was stage-managed by the interest groups. Consequently the First Republic was hijacked in characteristic British colonial manner by a dominant political class favoured by the colonists. Hence, anti-social and dictatorial tendencies exhibited by this group marginalized and pauperized the people, especially the Igbo. Subsequently, as Nwosu observes "the nation is thrown into crises as component interest groups in the tilted federation call for the national question in a bid for self-determination and re-definition" ("The National Question . . ." 89)

The first among these bids for self-determination took place in 1953 when Northern Nigeria confronted Southern Nigerian over the date of independence. The North threatened to secede if the South refused her proposed date for independence. The Igbo bid for self-determination followed after the January 1966 coup, led by Major Kaduna Nzeogwu. The coup led to genocide against Igbos living in Northern Nigeria. In a critical analogy of the events that led to the Biafran war of self-determination, Raph Uwechue states:

> A misunderstanding of the motives behind the January coup led to the Northern revenge-or rather "over-revenge"-as witnessed by the May riots, the July counter-coup and the massacres of the September-October 1966. A similar misunderstanding of the intentions behind the actions of the Federal Government after these massacres led many Easterners, especially Ibos, to believe that what had happened was a planned attempt to exterminate them. (32)

Chapter six | *Canice C. Nwosu, Emeka Nwosu & Columba Apeh, in*
Charles Nwadigwe, Molinta Enendu & Canice Nwosu (Eds.)
Metaphors and Climax, Reminiscences on the Drama and
Theatre of Ogonna Agu
London, Adonis & Abbey Publishers

These events grievously affected the place of the Igbo in the fragile Nigerian nation-state. The Igbo perception of the Nigeria nation-state changed after the dramatic genocide meted against them and the Civil War that nearly annihilated the Igbo race.

Ogonna Agu is a playwright of Igbo origin, a true Biafran who was committed to the Biafran course-the war of survival and self-determination. Despite the "No Victor, No Vanquished" slogan that ended the Biafran War; like a true Biafran, Agu knows the truth. The war has not ended. Agu fought on and kept the Biafran spirit alive especially in his characterization of Emenike the hero of his *Symbol of a Goddess*. Therefore, the researchers in this study propose to critically examine the place of the Igbo in the present Nigerian socio-economic and political dispensation based on Ogonna Agu's recreation of this enigmatic historical event. In the research design, the Content Analysis approach and the qualitative research methodology are combined in this study to achieve set objectives.

Ndi Igbo and the Nigerian Nation-State

The Igbo (Ndi Igbo) are one of the major ethnic groups in Nigeria and among the well-known tribes across the globe. They are among the most travelled people of the world hence there is hardly any part of the globe you will visit without seeing the Igbos. Discussion on the place of the Igbo in the socio-political and economic dispensation of the Nigerian nation-state can be periodized into three: pre-Civil War, Civil War and post-Civil War periods. These broad demarcations stem from the fact that the Civil War had so much impact on the life of the Igbo people. The pre-colonial Igbo society was relatively peaceful and progressive. Since there were few monarchs mainly among the communities living close to the Western hemisphere, communal clashes were not as rampant as recorded in the areas with centralized system of

Chapter six | *Canice C. Nwosu, Emeka Nwosu & Columba Apeh, in*
Charles Nwadigwe, Molinta Enendu & Canice Nwosu (Eds.)
Metaphors and Climax, Reminiscences on the Drama and
Theatre of Ogonna Agu
London, Adonis & Abbey Publishers

government, where expansion of the kingdom and conquests usually resulted to frictions and wars. Therefore the Igbo co-existed peacefully with their neighbours before the colonial incursion.

Major crises, conflicts and communal clashes recorded in Igboland started with the colonial incursion. Most of them were motivated by resistance and revolts against colonialism and its allies. Hence, unlike some other tribes, the Igbo cherished their independence, fought for and defended it to the last. The pre-colonial Igbo political system was fragmentary, permissive and communal and therefore antipodal to the centralized, dictatorial and capitalist systems introduce by the colonist. Eteng posits that British colonization destroyed the:

> Kinship and extra kinship relationship embedded in the autochthonous community which previously tied the people inextricably to their most inclusive primary groups- family, peers, age-mates, neighbours, age-sets/grades, village groups, clans, and the group of dead ancestors. (196)

The Igbo are perhaps one of the most agitative groups during the colonial period; they participated actively in the nationalistic struggles and eventually played major roles in securing the nation's independence. However, events took a dramatic turn from the post-independent era when tribalism enthroned by the colonial masters mutated and hardened into an archetype that conditioned the distribution of values. When tribal goals supersede the overriding interest of the nation, there is the tendency that the collective objective of the nation-state may be thwarted. M.I.O. Ikejiani-Clark affirms that this scenario:

> . . . is particularly the case in Nigeria where ethnicity was highly politicized by the colonists, who came and institutionalized inter-ethnic rivalry and unhealthy competition. This was, however, sustained by the post-colonial state, whose actions and activities were a carry-over from colonial Nigeria. (629)

Chapter six | *Canice C. Nwosu, Emeka Nwosu & Columba Apeh, in*
Charles Nwadigwe, Molinta Enendu & Canice Nwosu (Eds.)
Metaphors and Climax, Reminiscences on the Drama and Theatre of Ogonna Agu
London, Adonis & Abbey Publishers

Hence,"political independence brought a new wave of colonialism, domination and intensive ethnic conflict" (Ikejiani-Clark 629). Thus, ethnic conflict and precarious political, social and economic situations that heralded the first Republic led to the betrayal and back-stabbing (*uta-azu*) of the Igbo that culminated in the Nigerian Civil War. Ikejiani-Clark observes that, "The Nigerian state, with very low autonomy is used by the Northern oligarchy to commit acts of ethnic suppression, subordination, deprivation and alienation . . . it was, in fact basically this that prompted the Nigerian-Biafran civil war (1967-1970)" (629).When the instruments and institutions of the state are coveted by a few, politicized and manipulated for inter-ethnic subjugation the outcome is usually catastrophic as evident in the Biafran war of self-determination.

The war and its aftermaths are devastating on "Ndi Igbo". The Igbos were consequently relegated to the background and excluded from participating in meaningful political and economic activities in their fatherland. They had no other option than to resort to buying and selling and community (self-help) development efforts. Ogonna Agu was not alone in this Biafran crusade and sustenance of the Biafran spirit; Catherine O. Acholonu's *Into the Heart of Biafra*, and Chukwuma Okoye's *We the Beast* also treated the experience of the Igbo during the Civil War.

Fragmentary Egalitarianism, Failed Nation-State and Self Determination

Agu's documentation of the Biafran war of self-determination in his play *Symbol of a Goddess* is reinforced by the scientific theory of classes and class struggle popularized by Lenin and Marx. Suffice it to say that this theory produced the national question and self-determination theories in exploiter societies of Arabic North and Sub-Saharan Africa. Prior to the colonial domination, the

Chapter six | Canice C. Nwosu, Emeka Nwosu & Columba Apeh, in
Charles Nwadigwe, Molinta Enendu & Canice Nwosu (Eds.)
Metaphors and Climax, Reminiscences on the Drama and Theatre of Ogonna Agu
London, Adonis & Abbey Publishers

independent Igbo nation was egalitarian, fragmentary and to some extent democratic. Given their colonial and post-colonial experiences in the Nigerian nation-state, many Igbo more or less have come to see the state as:

> ... an organization of the political power of the ruling class, the main instrument of class domination, an organ of suppression of one class by another. Previously, social power corresponded to the people themselves, express the community of socio-economic requirement and the interests of early human collectives. The class and state form of social power, while alienating itself from society, is called upon to defend the interests of the exploiters and keep the poor and exploited in submission. (The Institute of Social Sciences 268)

This level of antagonism among other component nationalities and the dominant bourgeoisie class raises national questions in national relations. According to the Institute of Social Sciences, the solution to national question is;

> ... indissolubly linked with the class character of the revolutionary process. Its essence lies in liquidating national oppression and national discrimination, in liberating the oppressed peoples and establishing social, that is economic and political equality of all nations and nationalities. (235)

This was what the Igbo set out to do in their war of self-determination based on the ". . . principles of self-determination of nations up to secession and the sovereign right of each nation to settle the national question..." (The Institute of Social Sciences 242) Agu's concretization of self-determination theory in *Symbol of a Goddess*, reveals his Marxist inclination and belief in the Biafran course. Unfortunately the Biafran revolution was sabotaged partly because of the over-zealousness of the leaders of the young Republic and partly because of:

Chapter six | *Canice C. Nwosu, Emeka Nwosu & Columba Apeh, in*
Charles Nwadigwe, Molinta Enendu & Canice Nwosu (Eds.)
Metaphors and Climax, Reminiscences on the Drama and Theatre of Ogonna Agu
London, Adonis & Abbey Publishers

Support rendered by industrial capitalist countries to racism and white chauvinism, racial discrimination, apartheid and state measures hampering the process of de-colonization and the national self-determination of peoples . . . (The Institute of Social Sciences 277)

The Biafrans were not as lucky as nations like Vietnam and Pakistan who adopted self-determination as a solution to the national question. The Igbo are not alone in this bid for self-determination, it happened in Ethiopia, Angola and even the defunct Soviet Union. At present, over thirty states are bidding for secession in the United States because of Obama's victory; therefore self-determination is becoming popular as a political instrument for conflict resolution.

Biafran War of Self-determination in Agu's *Symbol of a Goddess*

The expectations of the people from the playwright are high; as a historical repository he is not only charged with the responsibility of documenting history, re-enacting societal events and transmitting culture; he is also saddled with the task of keeping the peoples' dreams alive. As a playwright of Igbo extraction, Ogonna Agu did embrace these responsibilities bestowed on him by his professional calling. Ogonna hails from Nnobi in Idemmili South Local Government Area of Anambra State. He attended Dennis Memorial Grammar School (DMGS) Onitsha. He read English and Drama at the University of Nigeria, Nsukka and then proceeded to University of Leeds where he did his postgraduate studies. Agu came back from the U.K. and joined the University of Calabar. His Igbo nationalism and personality literature yielded fruits and made strong impression on his students in the Theatre Arts Department of the University of Calabar. In addition to *Symbol of a Goddess*, Agu's other creative works include, among others, *Cry of a Maiden, The Strong Boy of the Forest, Adiaha the Beauty Queen* and *Hunt for the Campus Guerillas*. He rose to the rank

Chapter six | *Canice C. Nwosu, Emeka Nwosu & Columba Apeh, in*
Charles Nwadigwe, Molinta Enendu & Canice Nwosu (Eds.)
Metaphors and Climax, Reminiscences on the Drama and
Theatre of Ogonna Agu
London, Adonis & Abbey Publishers

of Associate Professor before his untimely death on the 22nd November, 2011. This versatile artist of our time was a Poet, Director, Dancer, Choreographer, Actor, Cinematographer and Novelist. His simplicity, single-mindedness, artistic ingenuity and endurance spirit are artistic molecules scattered all over his literary creations. Among these intricacies and aspects of a Potter's fingerprints; single-mindedness, endurance spirit and simplicity of language are prominent in *Symbol of a Goddess*. The play revolves around a young Biafran war veteran-Emenike. The playwright's characterization and character exposition method reveals through Emenike's confrontation of other characters that doggedness, violence and romance with the supernatural are important requisites of self determination

Ogonna Agu's manipulation of Biafran war songs to the overall effect of the play is interesting. His reliance on artifacts and historical events vivifies the incidents that led to the total betrayal of the Igbo by some other component units of the Nigerian nation-state. Hence the playwright plays on the emotion of the reader making his mind's eyes see the Biafran war of self-determination as primarily an incident in history, a traumatic experiential issue ignited by ideological serfdom, brutality, animalistic tendency and calculated attempt to annihilate the Igbo race. Emenike's resistance symbolizes the Igbo struggle to ensure continuance of their race; it is sustained by cosmo-human beings; hence, a reflection of cosmic totality in communal struggle because Emenike draws his inspiration from the woman of deep waters.

Agu uses both audio and visual imageries to bring back feelings of the war for those who experienced it and make those who did not see the war to imagine what the Igbo passed through. He does not hide the fact that the play is set in Biafra, in his opening stage directions, he says:

Chapter six | *Canice C. Nwosu, Emeka Nwosu & Columba Apeh, in* Charles Nwadigwe, Molinta Enendu & Canice Nwosu (Eds.) *Metaphors and Climax, Reminiscences on the Drama and Theatre of Ogonna Agu* London, Adonis & Abbey Publishers

> . . . there is the need to contextually capture the action within the
> historical frame and period of the Nigerian civil war . . . At the
> background the Biafran flag of red, black, green with the rising sun is
> seen flying in the wind. (6)

Having established the milieu of the play, the playwright quickly introduces an important per-formative technique of the Igbo storytelling theatre-narration and uses it to heighten attention of the reader and audience. Hence the narrator uses the master storyteller's process to compress a four year historical event in three and half pages. Thus, the prologue becomes a window into the play, a miniaturized version of the entire play that captures the incursion of the Nigerian troops into Biafra and the crude Biafran resistance based on raw bravery and sheer determination. The Narrator not only captures the previous action but also recounts in emotion- laden rhythm and musical tone the predicament of the Igbo during the Civil War. Perhaps, the Civil War may be part of the Igbo man's destiny or it may be circumstantial as presented by some war historians. No matter the version, the narrator made reference to the 1966 crises that led to the blood-chilling massacre of the Igbo and Western Nigerian officers in the Nigerian army.

The killing of soldiers of Igbo origin by Northern Nigerian soldiers was one of the incidents in history that raises curiosity and beats the imagination of most radical theorists, historians and ta cti-cians. It is unusual for the army to throw their traditional *espirit de corps* solidarity to the dogs, rise against each other to the extent of slaughtering one another in cold blood. The awkwardness of this event made the world to view the Nigerian army with skepticism till the present time. Though one may argue that the January 1966 alleged Igbo coup led to the killing of Igbo officers by Northern Nigerian soldiers, the question that has not been answered is why the Northerners suddenly extended this crises that revolved around the leadership class to the ordinary Nigerian,

Chapter six | *Canice C. Nwosu, Emeka Nwosu & Columba Apeh, in*
Charles Nwadigwe, Molinta Enendu & Canice Nwosu (Eds.)
*Metaphors and Climax, Reminiscences on the Drama and
Theatre of Ogonna Agu*
London, Adonis & Abbey Publishers

killing children, pregnant women and helpless citizens. The pogrom was such that some Igbo were killed by their best friends who were Northerners. Thus betrayed, the Igbo decided to secede but the North and their allies could not let them go through negotiations and peaceful separation. The Narrator in the play affirms that "Biafra had no choice but to fight it out after all negotiations had failed. The grass, they said, would fight for them" (7).

The Biafran war was the last option for a people who faced great animosity, hatred and planned pogrom targeted at exterminating them. It was a war of self-determination born out of sheer willpower to ensure security of life and property for the Igbo of Eastern Nigeria. Based on the outcome of May 1966 Northern riots, the July counter-coup and the massacres of September-October, 1966, Igbo sovereignty was indeed the safest and surest way of guaranteeing her survival and existence. But more because of economic reasons, the Federal Government would not let the Eastern Nigeria (Biafra) secede. The two sides (Eastern Nigeria and Yakubu Gowon-Igboland led Federal Government) maintain their stands, no compromise whatsoever, war was imminent and the two forces clash. Agu in one of his scintillating stage directions paints the picture thus: Drums roll in the distance, the drums of war. The federal forces take positions. As this is happening the Biafran force move in and are ambushed. There is a fiery exchange of fire with smoke rising . . . (7).

Biafra suffered betrayal, sabotage and denial from neighbours, local and international communities including the world super powers. They clamped down on the young and ill-equipped republic, eventually on 16th January 1970 the thirty-month Civil War ended on a "no victor no vanquished" slogan. The impact of the war was devastating on the Igbo and the Narrator paints a sympathetic image of the effect of the Civil War below:

Chapter six | *Canice C. Nwosu, Emeka Nwosu & Columba Apeh, in*
Charles Nwadigwe, Molinta Enendu & Canice Nwosu (Eds.)
Metaphors and Climax, Reminiscences on the Drama and
Theatre of Ogonna Agu
London, Adonis & Abbey Publishers

NARRATOR: The sick, the hungry, they all came crowding into this one remaining place called Biafra. The maimed and deformed, they were all there, waiting to see when manna will fall from the sky. . . waiting for the final end of the war whichever way it went- good or bad; for despair or misery are taking their toll on them. (5)

When the war finally ended, there was no genuine effort or measures put in place to rehabilitate the Igbo and bring them back to the national fold. The "no victor no vanquished" crusade of the Yakubu Gowon-led Federal Government was mere lip service that never translated into action. Rather, there was general conspiracy to subjugate the Igbo, deprive and despoil Igboland. Policies like the "abandoned property" law, payment of twenty pounds flat rate to Igbos no matter the amount any Igbo man or woman had in the bank before the war and confiscation of deposits of those who had bank transactions during the war were oppressive policies targeted against the Igbo to continue the war beyond the battle field.

Therefore, the Biafrans learnt through the hard way that the war had not ended. The socio-political placing of the Igbo in the contemporary Nigerian society speaks volumes about the ongoing cold war against the Igbo; hence, one needs not be told that the war is still on. This unnecessary elongation of the war led to the sustenance of the Biafran war of self-determination which the playwright consummates in Emenike the hero of the play. This tough Biafran solider and hero of several Biafran battles at Ore, Otuocha and Abagana, affirms that the war has not ended as he confronts his kinsmen who in their suffering and misery surrendered to the Federal troops:

IGBONEKWU: (*moves closer*) No no no, Emenike keep that gun... don't shoot please, don't shoot. The war has ended.
EMENIKE: (*shouts*) it has not ended!

Chapter six | *Canice C. Nwosu, Emeka Nwosu & Columba Apeh, in* Charles Nwadigwe, Molinta Enendu & Canice Nwosu (Eds.) *Metaphors and Climax, Reminiscences on the Drama and Theatre of Ogonna Agu* London, Adonis & Abbey Publishers

IGBONEKWU: You have not come here to continue the war?
EMENIKE: I say it has not ended! We'll continue the fight! (12)

Not even the intimidating presence of Nigerian soldiers all over can stampede Emenike to surrender. Emenike whose alter-ego is the woman of deep waters refuses to be distracted by anything else: cry of his kinsmen, the wailings and fears of his mother, not even marriage could deter him, he fights on, because the Biafran course engulfed him like mental illness as pointed out by the commander of the Federal army. Ide a member of Emenike's family brings Emenike's fanatic love for Biafra to us; he calls him a runaway soldier and reports him to the Nigerian commander saying:

IDE: This is the place. Runaway solider number one . . . Biafran command. We tell him war has ended, he say war has not ended. He take gun. He shoot tatata everywhere. Look now the whole village is running . . . for one man with no sense. (13)

In reaction, the Commander queries:

COMMANDER: His father kwanu?
IGBONEKWU: He has died.
COMMANDER: Die? And lefam to craze? (13)

The Commander orders the soldiers to arrest Emenike's mother but they fail to take his eagle, his symbol of Biafra. However, events take a dramatic turn and Emenike realizes that the movement for the actualization of Biafra requires more than his solo effort, he joins his goddess to continue the struggle from the other part of the cosmos.

Chapter six | *Canice C. Nwosu, Emeka Nwosu & Columba Apeh, in*
Charles Nwadigwe, Molinta Enendu & Canice Nwosu (Eds.)
Metaphors and Climax, Reminiscences on the Drama and Theatre of Ogonna Agu
London, Adonis & Abbey Publishers

Conclusion

The place of the playwright in theatre practice and the general functioning of the society are of colossal importance to national relations theorists. Hence, the dramatist has been described as: "the conscience of the nation," "the watchdog of the society," "a historical repository", "a story-teller" and great observer of the incidents of history. Ogonna Agu fits into these diverse descriptions of the playwright. As a chronicler of events he captured the feelings of majority of the Igbo about the Nigerian/ Biafran Civil War. The Igbo race suffered genocide to near extinction and therefore resorted to a war of self-determination in order to remain in existence. Unfortunately, the Biafran vision was sabotaged and the war metaphorically terminated in a purported "no victor, no vanquished "slogan. But the Biafrans, and only the Biafrans know the truth; they tasted it and are still licking their wounds. The war has not ended. The struggle continues. The Biafran spirit lives on. These declarations are Agu's messages to the Igbo in *Symbol of a Goddess*.

Therefore, the researchers; preoccupation is to assess Ogonna Agu's re-enactment of the Nigerian/Biafran Civil War, its consequences and how it affects the Igbo in the Nigerian nation-state. The study was able to establish among other things that Ogonna Agu succeeded as a playwright. Through his war theatre he was able to participate actively in the struggle for the actualization of the sovereign state of Biafra. He believed in Biafra and therefore kept the Biafran spirit alive using his plays.

Through the analysis carried out by the researchers, it becomes obvious that the Igbos are not mere rebellious people, rather the study established that the Civil War was the last option for the Igbo given their experiences in the exploiter nation-state. The researchers therefore justify self-determination as a legitimate

Chapter six | *Canice C. Nwosu, Emeka Nwosu & Columba Apeh, in*
Charles Nwadigwe, Molinta Enendu & Canice Nwosu (Eds.)
Metaphors and Climax, Reminiscences on the Drama and
Theatre of Ogonna Agu
London, Adonis & Abbey Publishers

solution to the national question. Currently, Nigeria is a failed state which holds no future for the Igbo. Hence, if the feudal oligarchy in their political "jaywalking" demands that the Igbo must end the war, they must also embark on genuine, inclusive and people-oriented policies that will heal the wounds of the Igbo properly. So long as the Igbo remain marginalized in Nigerian state, the war of self-determination continues in more diverse and complex fronts.

Works Cited

Anaagudo-Agu, Ogonna. *Symbol of a Goddess*. Calabar: Wusen Press, 2005.

Eteng, I.A. "Community Development and Social Welfare." *A Survey of Igbo Nation*. Ed. G.E.K. Ofomata. Onitsha: Africana First Publishers, 2002.195-217.

Ijoma, J. C. "Historical Perspective." *A Survey of Igbo Nation*. Ed. G.E.K. Ofomata. Onitsha: Africana First Publishers, 2002. 39-54.

Ikejiani-Clark, M.I.O. "The Igbo in Contemporary Nigeria." *A Survey of Igbo Nation*. Ed. G.E.K. Ofomata. Onitsha: Africana First Publishers, 2002.628-643.

Nwadigwe, F. A. "Quality Assurance and Sustainable Cultural Promotion: Imperatives for Igbo Language Filmmakers." *Quality Assurance: Theatre, Media, and the Creative Enterprises*. Eds. Gowon Doki and Ted Anyebe. Makurdi: SONTA, 2013. 512-517.

Nwosu, Canice Chukwuma. "The National Question and Theatre of Relevance." *Nigerian Theatre Journal*. 7:1 (2004): 88-106.

Nwosu, Canice Chukwuma. "Evolving a Performance Oriented Critical Theory for African PostModern Theatre Practice."

Chapter six | *Canice C. Nwosu, Emeka Nwosu & Columba Apeh, in*
Charles Nwadigwe, Molinta Enendu & Canice Nwosu (Eds.)
Metaphors and Climax, Reminiscences on the Drama and Theatre of Ogonna Agu
London, Adonis & Abbey Publishers

Ph.D. Dissertation. Department of Theatre and Film Studies, University of   Nigeria, Nsukka. 2011.

Ofomata, G.E.K "Introduction." *A Survey of Igbo Nation.* Ed. G.E.K. Ofomata. Onitsha: Africana First Publishers, 2002.1-12.

The Institute of Social Science. *Philosophical Foundations of Scientific Socialism.* Eds. F.I. Zakharov, V.V. Sushinky and A.V Shestopal. Moscow: Progress Publishers, 1985.

Uwechue, Raph. *Reflections on the Nigeria Civil War: Facing the Future.* New York: Africana Publishers, 1971.

Chapter six | *Canice C. Nwosu, Emeka Nwosu & Columba Apeh, in*
Charles Nwadigwe, Molinta Enendu & Canice Nwosu (Eds.)
Metaphors and Climax, Reminiscences on the Drama and
Theatre of Ogonna Agu
London, Adonis & Abbey Publishers

Chapter Seven

Troubled State and National Development in Ogonna Anaagudo-Agu's *Cry of a Maiden*

Ofonime Inyang

Background

There is certainly a lot to worry about when we encounter *Cry of a Maiden*, Ogonna Anaagudo-Agu's commentary on failed relational dynamics and what it imposes on the prospects of an emerging nationhood. This play parades the troubling scenario of a house against itself. In a paradigmatic dramatization where culture forms the structure of realization and expression, in open consort with the Aguian temperament, the troubling mismanagement of diversity and ethnic differences in a nation stares one in the face. The metaphoric allusion to the "cry of a maiden" can therefore be considered a deliberate juxtaposition of national distress resulting from massive dislocations in the life of a nation. Traditionally, a maiden cannot cry unless something is wrong. Maidenhood is configured as a season of joy and conviviality. There is nothing but beauty and effervescence about the maiden as maidenhood is the breaking forth season into womanhood. When a maiden desists from singing, dancing and sharing fun moments with her peers in preparation for transition into the direction of every woman's dream, her home, then there is more to worry about.

Enuda like Nigeria, can be likened to a society wandering about in search of lost rhythm as "one whose ancestral exhalations stubbornly overwhelmed its merely convenient administrative identity" (Soyinka 54). It is not sure if it is one nation or a "union

Chapter seven | *Ofonime Inyang, in*
Charles Nwadigwe, Molinta Enendu & Canice Nwosu (Eds.)
Metaphors and Climax, Reminiscences on the Drama and Theatre of Ogonna Agu
London, Adonis & Abbey Publishers

of incompatible" mates. It is beaten by the seditious powerplay between its siblings and portrays scars of several fights and interregnum. The lacerative tendencies of the various units that make up the nation are uncomfortably animated boldly in the dramatization. At another level, this is another drama of deceit, back-stabbing and national distortion for the benefit of a few. It is set in a traditional environment and the play depicts what Hope Eghagha, in the foreword to Leke Ogunfeyimi's *Sacrifice the King*, describes as "timeless lessons about power, about dictatorship and the need for consciousness of its antecedents" (Ogunfeyimi viii). The situational demonstration of the stark realities of modern socio-political setup where betrayal and dictatorship are lifted to the level of stagecraft even in contexts of close relational make-up resonates in vivid terms in this play.

One brother uses his age and *local wisdom* to the advantage of the other while the other acts in self-defence but with little or no restraint. Both of them still exhibit a war mentality. They are victims of a war or wars they did not cause. It is a tale of betrayal and dislocation at home on return from abroad. The home cheats the young and they find solace in a retreat back to the "jungle" in readiness for another round of endless battles of survival. It is also a tale of lust in the absence of love, of greed and struggle in the heart of a race. It is the story of a home thorn between the past and the present. Peace becomes elusive as anger reigns supreme. The nation is yet to find peace from its sins; the freedman has not actually found freedom in the Promised Land (Dubois 11). Post-independence Nigeria was conjectured as a land of promise for her citizenry yet more than fifty years after British rule, Nigeria is yet to actualize that promise of bliss for Nigerians in the land of their birth. Awhefeada reasons that "the promising disposition of independence was like a meteor which did not last" (59). Consequently, remnants of shattered hopes hang in wanton

Chapter seven | *Ofonime Inyang, in*
Charles Nwadigwe, Molinta Enendu & Canice Nwosu (Eds.)
Metaphors and Climax, Reminiscences on the Drama and Theatre of Ogonna Agu
London, Adonis & Abbey Publishers

despair and desperation as men fail to heed the voice of wisdom. The home boils with ripple effects on the nation.

The Dramatic Plot

Agu's *Cry of a Maiden* is a straight and simple story of two brothers emerging out of the shackles and brutality of a post-war era with different perspectives to reconstruction and resettlement. Set in Igboland, southeastern Nigeria in 1945 after World War II, the play captures the barefaced realities of a post-conflict existentialism urgently needing genuine reconciliation and rehabilitation before pursuing reconstruction and sustainable development. This post-conflict environment woven around the experiences of "Hitler's war" (8) interlinks succinctly with the "Biafran war" at home as the play had its own dramatic life in 1973 after the Nigerian Civil War that left scary aftermath in the heart of the land especially in the East. Chidum returns from the Second World War with a mind to settle down to reclaim lost years and define his personal rhythm in life but meets opposition in the action of an elder brother who stayed back home and did not see the "need to settle down to regular family life" (ii).

The traditional requirement for an elder brother's permission before a young man marries or engages in any venture of substance as is common in Igbo society and most part of Africa is exploited to the disadvantage of a an aspiring young person bent on redefining his life. Okolo finds his younger brother's gut as a personal affront and he, in the words of Awili, "must be taught to respect his elders" (21). He works on his youthful ignorance and exuberance and uses it as a stumbling block to his desire and a vehicle of his grand usurpation scheme. The kernel of the situation is broken when Okolo seduces Ada, the girl Chidum intends to marry and Ada finds herself muddled up in a domestic triangular conflict where she loses out as the pawn. A dangerous conflict

Chapter seven | *Ofonime Inyang, in*
Charles Nwadigwe, Molinta Enendu & Canice Nwosu (Eds.)
Metaphors and Climax, Reminiscences on the Drama and Theatre of Ogonna Agu
London, Adonis & Abbey Publishers

brews in the heart of the family and further shatters the *Obi* which badly needed repairs.

The *spirit* of the family gets thrown out into the cold as a fight that threatens to claim lives breaks out in a season that should have naturally heralded celebrations and spring joy in the heart of a maiden. Instead of having the environment serenaded by the lilting voice of a maiden rendering sweet song of hope and progress, a debilitating cry by a maiden whose pot is broken in a careless exchange of emotions rather disturbs the peace of the community and of the race. The story captures in virtual forms the interconnecting tendons of filial relations in the African society and how they constitute the ingredients of social and political development as well as underdevelopment. The evident mitigating scheme of this system is also questioned in a tone that is however not critical but probing and suggestive. It is therefore a story of domestic politics and its implication on the national landscape.

Nigeria, Conflict and National Survival

Nigeria is a large nation in West Africa covering about 356,668 square miles with an estimated population figure of 140 million people as indicated in the 2006 Census Report. The country's border to the south is the Bight of Benin and Biafra, which are located on the Gulf of Guinea in the Atlantic Ocean. Nigeria's border on the West is Benin, on the north by Niger, and on the east by Cameroon. Nigeria stretches roughly 700 miles from west to east and 650 miles from south to north, covering an area of between 30 and 150 E longitudes and between 40 and 140 N latitude (Falola and Heaton 36). The country is rich in beautiful vegetation and flora and fauna consisting of dense forests, vast farming settlements and forest reserves, free-flowing rivers, waterfalls, river basins, natural wetlands, creeks, and game

Chapter seven | *Ofonime Inyang, in*
Charles Nwadigwe, Molinta Enendu & Canice Nwosu (Eds.)
Metaphors and Climax, Reminiscences on the Drama and Theatre of Ogonna Agu
London, Adonis & Abbey Publishers

reserves, giving the country a total coastline length of 800km (500 miles).

The major rivers in Nigeria are the River Niger, considered the third longest river in Africa and Benue where the country derives its water sources (Udo 225). Nigeria comprises of more than 200 different tribes and ethno-linguistic groups namely Hausa-Fulani, Yoruba, Igbo, Ibibio, Kanuri, Ijaw, Tiv, Idoma, Urhobo, Itshekiri and Jukun (Falola and Heaton 61). The country gained independence from British colonial rule on October 1, 1960. Over the years, there has been creation of states and regional reconfiguration in the country for political and socio-economic administration, giving the country a thirty-six-state structure located in six geopolitical regions.

The lustre of Nigeria painted in its massive and diverse population and the sheer beauty and inviting allure of its vegetation stands in stark contradiction to the many political problems of the nation. In fact, Nigeria is an immensely blessed nation with lots of challenges. Achebe is of the view that the trouble with Nigeria is clearly and squarely a failure in leadership (1). Shaba writing in the foreword to *Nigeria: Years Eaten by the Locust* affirms Achebe's observation and particularly directs a great chunk of the blame for Nigeria's political problems on military incursion into the politics of the nation: According to Shaba:

> Nigeria today practices civil rule, that is, a government by civilians. Though the evils of the years of military rule are not completely gone; though Nigerians cannot boast of having as yet, the calibre of persons they wish to have at the helm of affairs; and though she is yet to transform to the land of our dream; the vast majority of Nigerians-those who have seen the military (with the collaboration of civilians and traditional rulers) devastate and literally, bring down the country on her knees – agree that the worst of civilian governments is better than and be preferred to the most benevolent military government. For as many

Chapter seven | *Ofonime Inyang, in*
Charles Nwadigwe, Molinta Enendu & Canice Nwosu (Eds.)
Metaphors and Climax, Reminiscences on the Drama and
Theatre of Ogonna Agu
London, Adonis & Abbey Publishers

133

remember too well, the passage to the present political dispensation was one long, arduous and tortuous one (Ehusani v).

The military claimed righteous intentions each time it aimed for power only to perform worse than those it sacked from office. Femi Osofisan, foremost Nigerian dramatist and political commentator in an interview in *Voices Offstage: Nigerian Dramatists on Drama and Politics* throws his own voice in support of the position advanced above. To Osofisan, "...the military was very much the obstacle to any kind of social order that is progressive" (33). The tendons of militaristic adventure in the political space can be traced to the Civil War in Nigeria and how that became the anchor of political dominance and injected war-like and violent thinking into the national psyche. People gradually became more inclined to "fight" for their right or to be heard after the war. The polity became heated by several shades of ambition as loud protestations with occasional ugly consequences became the norm in the country.

The above represents the Nigerian experience in the leadership sphere .This is to say that there is something wrong with the Nigerian system which gives concern to the citizens and keen watchers of development in the country. Many books have been written to highlight the Nigerian question however most opinions concerning Nigeria marvel at the dramatic way the nation survives as an entity in the face of many challenges. Nigeria is often seen as a cat with nine lives in reference to her survival capacity in the face of many political turbulence including a Civil War that devastated the nation and left it severely battered, disintegrated and disunited.

That particular war incidentally also features as a sub-thematic premise of Agu's *Cry of a Maiden* and is taken to represent the critical situation of Nigeria's collective development and especially how the scars of the war has taken so long to disappear from the

Chapter seven	*Ofonime Inyang, in* Charles Nwadigwe, Molinta Enendu & Canice Nwosu (Eds.) *Metaphors and Climax, Reminiscences on the Drama and Theatre of Ogonna Agu* London, Adonis & Abbey Publishers

national landscape. The feeling of distrust and alienation still appear to linger in the collective national consciousness leading sometime to agitation and tension by parties that feel inadequately accommodated in the scheme of things as can be seen in the relational infractions between Okolo and Chidum.

Beyond the Nigerian Civil War, other conflicts have challenged the country's prospects of stable nationhood and further expand the base of disagreement in the country. These include inter-ethnic uprisings, religious conflicts, tumultuous political crises especially the June 12, 1993 election crisis and internecine socio-religious militancy including the current Boko Haram attacks. The nation has seen a lot of disturbing developments in its lifetime and has survived to the surprise of her watchers. At the root of most of these conflicts is the issue of the foundational context of the Nigerian federation itself which some consider as a forced coalition of different people and tribes instituted by the British, Nigeria's former colonial master, to their advantage and for the gains of their political interest in the country.

This argument seems to play out from time to time as most Nigerian crisis always erupts out of a feeling of being marginalized and denied access to the national cake by a particular ethnic or interest group. The incipient cry for self-rule by the Movement for Actualization of Sovereign State of Biafra (MASSOB) and other ethnic-based interest groups or *resource control* agitators like the case of the Niger Delta region are echoes of this age-old feeling. It therefore appears as if Nigeria is truly a "convenient administrative" set up, an umbrella of governance and not a nation as some Nigerian citizens seem to maintain stronger allegiance to their ethnic roots than to the national symbols of the union. This position is already not in want of contextualization as the play in focus also idealizes on the issues of relationship and how it affects the development and fortunes of a nation.

Chapter seven	*Ofonime Inyang, in*
	Charles Nwadigwe, Molinta Enendu & Canice Nwosu (Eds.)
	Metaphors and Climax, Reminiscences on the Drama and
	Theatre of Ogonna Agu
	London, Adonis & Abbey Publishers

The anchoring of a people's drive for development and reconstruction on an ethnic (Igbo in this case) rather than a national canvass explains the true character of the complex rendering of the Nigerian experience and the common dynamics of development discourse in the country. Therefore to the Nigerian or the people who belong to the Nigerian federation, identity is fostered by ethnic dictates rather than a national consciousness. Most Nigerians see themselves first as Ibibio, Yoruba, Kanuri, Ijaw, Hausa, Afemai, Efik before thinking of being Nigerians. This cast of ethnic loyalty cuts across all strata of the society and acts as the basis of the various expression of partial involvement or outright lack of commitment by Nigerians in the national project. The drive for development therefore gets stifled in the process as development becomes defined and contextualized along ethnic lines leaving the nation, the *Obi* in this context in ruins.

The Symbolism of *Obi*

The story of *Cry of a Maiden* takes off from the need for national development in a post-war society that bears all the characteristics of modern day Nigeria. The totem of that national landscape is the *Obi*, the representative symbol of manhood and stability in spiritual and environmental terms. Nigeria is the *Obi* that is requiring urgent national reconstruction because it is currently in a bad state. This classification has been justified by the observation that Nigeria is a culturally diverse nation-state that is beset by ethnic agitations that have made the country constantly unstable right from independence (Ugolo 41). National instability in Nigeria is portrayed in the failed state of the *Obi*. The ethnic conflict and tensions can also be seen in the state of mistrust between the two brothers portrayed in the play. The *Obi* as a symbolic signifier of Nigeria's national landscape with all the instability that works against her development draws our attention to the need to

Chapter seven | *Ofonime Inyang, in*
Charles Nwadigwe, Molinta Enendu & Canice Nwosu (Eds.)
Metaphors and Climax, Reminiscences on the Drama and Theatre of Ogonna Agu
London, Adonis & Abbey Publishers

rebuild and reposition the nation for posterity and also to enable it get her right place in the comity of nations.

The significance of the *Obi* in Igbo cosmology is reflective of the heart and soul of a nation in an enlarged context. To a great extent, a man's worth is measured by the stability in his *Obi* and so every right-thinking man works hard to put it in order as it is not only the primary dwelling place for members of a household but also holds a multi-utilitarian significance that connects all facets of life in the family. The "Dramaturgist's Note" in *Cry of a Maiden* captures this essence:

> First, it is like a temple in every sense. There, the ancestral symbols of religious observances are kept. The altar of the ancestors is also arranged here. It is a cultural centre, a museum of antiquities, and a social meeting place all lumped into one. The point therefore is that a homestead without an *Obi* is a dead place, since it is the hub of activities of the household. The early morning kolanut invocation takes place here. The *Chi* shrine is located just outside the *Obi*. The collapse of one's *obi* under whatever circumstance portends danger for the family. It literally spells death for the head of the household. And as it is said, when the right hand of a deity falls to the ground, then tragedy has befallen the entire household. (iv)

The description of the *Obi* extracted out of the playwright's note gives in details the importance that is attached to the place. The *Obi* is like an embodiment of all the internal dynamics that make up a nation and failure to put it in order is considered an invitation to crisis. It contains all the departments that make up the operational organs of the nation. The cultural resources and relics of value in the society are stored there. The economic engine of the society is controlled from there as the health and wellbeing of the members of the society emanates from there thus ensuring productivity in the land. Seen within this perspective, the *Obi* we meet in Agu's play is in a state of complete decay. It is in a decrepit

Chapter seven | *Ofonime Inyang, in*
Charles Nwadigwe, Molinta Enendu & Canice Nwosu (Eds.)
Metaphors and Climax, Reminiscences on the Drama and
Theatre of Ogonna Agu
London, Adonis & Abbey Publishers

form and needs urgent reconstruction. The picture is that of a national crisis that requires urgent attention. Okolo raises serious concerns:

> But I must warn that a major task stares us in the face, the task of reconstructing this cottage. As you can see, the obi building has gone into ruins. And the shrine house has collapsed, thereby exposing the sacred goddess to [bad] weather and inhospitable rains (10).

No additional words are required to paint the gory picture of a nation in crisis. The state of the *Obi*, clearly in ruins, and that of the "shrine house" gives us a lucid idea of the state of the household (nation). The use of the word "collapse" is indicative of a massive spoilage or decay that has bedevilled the national landscape. This state of affairs gives clear indication of a society that finds itself at the threshold of systemic failure. Structures have decayed and there is evidence of desperation for change by the citizenry to steer the nation out of its downward slide (Inyang 126). Even the spiritual state of the nation is not spared thereby creating a scenario of national catastrophe that needs reformation and transformation and not mere political rhetorics. It is a "task" that stares the nation in the face and there is requirement for someone to take up the responsibility. The one being looked upon in this case is Chidum, a younger member of the family who in a larger context represent the youth of the nation.

But this is where the contradictions in the society become manifest. How can a nation wait for its young ones to shoulder the responsibility of rebuilding what was destroyed in the first instance by the negligence of their elders? Why did Okolo wait all those years with his two hands in-between his legs for the younger brother to return from the war front in Burma to raise an *Obi* for the family? Why are the elders only interested in manning leadership positions, sitting tight, renewing their tenures and

Chapter seven | *Ofonime Inyang, in*
Charles Nwadigwe, Molinta Enendu & Canice Nwosu (Eds.)
Metaphors and Climax, Reminiscences on the Drama and
Theatre of Ogonna Agu
London, Adonis & Abbey Publishers

pushing the youth to the front once there is need for people to pay the supreme sacrifice that will ensure the survival of the nation? Why are the young ones always made the scapegoats of national development aspirations? These are questions yearning for answers if the nation is truly desirous of sustainable development.

The Context of Dramatization

The play *Cry of a Maiden* opens on a note of optimism and the promise of development but ends on a note of betrayal, despair, crisis and underdevelopment. In a rather emblematic portrayal, Nigeria is mirrored in its mal-functional fluctuating state after years of self-rule. The coming of independence promised a future of stability and advancement yet many years after the flag ceremonies, the nation is yet to understand itself. This is in direct correlation with the situation in Mgbochi's household where the return of Chidum marks a new day of hope and rebuilding and yet ends in a shattering hopelessness that is midwifed by the ambition and jealousy of Okolo, a belligerent and lazy elder brother that usurps that which belongs to the younger brother. Okolo, like the average Nigerian old politician is afraid of losing power, authority and influence to the diligent and more vibrant youth. It is the case of the elder waiting at home while the young one battles it out in the field yet sits to watch his effort being usurped by another.

The opening scene (in the directorial remarks) in Act One shows a family coming together after years of pains and near thought of losing a beloved brother in the warfront forever. There is evident joy and peace woven in the ambience of a long-awaited homecoming replete with the strengthening of family ties:

> In an out-house. Chidum and Okolo are sitting on low stools in front. A calabash of wine stands on the floor between them. Mgbochi their mother is sitting quite apart near the fireplace, which is set just a few

Chapter seven | *Ofonime Inyang, in*
Charles Nwadigwe, Molinta Enendu & Canice Nwosu (Eds.)
Metaphors and Climax, Reminiscences on the Drama and
Theatre of Ogonna Agu
London, Adonis & Abbey Publishers

steps beside her. Adaego is plaiting Mgbochi's hair as she admires in the mirror(1).

The picture of the family exudes a home in silent recollection of the past and the urge to rebuild for the future. Developments in the family are assessed especially since the departure of Chidum and there is evident lack of rest and succour for years. Mgbochi reminiscences about her absolute lack of "sleep since [their] father died" (9). The past is now sent off in this quiet family ceremony of welcome and reunion. Wine is woven within the nostalgic setting to establish the celebratory mood as wine is common in such scenes of reunion in the African community.

Ada is the harbinger of a future that is to be formed out of the nascent dreams of Chidum while Mgbochi and Okolo represent the stabilizing presence of the ancestry and the backing of the elders. The scenery establishes a significant moment in the life of this family as they await the arrival of the Okpala, the Custodian. What happens after this meeting will generate the prism through which development is to be pursued in the family nay the society generally.

The direction of development is voiced in Ada's song as the play opens. The set path of national development is beginning to admit distortions. In this song, the prime issues of the nation are raised in ironic questions that require sincere answers:

> I asked Nwadike at
> his home:
> Nwadike, who will lead
> This great nation?
> And he stood up fine fine
> he is also in the dance.
> Be quick, Nwadike, be quick
> racing, walking and with
> your staff of office. . .

Chapter seven | *Ofonime Inyang, in*
Charles Nwadigwe, Molinta Enendu & Canice Nwosu (Eds.)
Metaphors and Climax, Reminiscences on the Drama and
Theatre of Ogonna Agu
London, Adonis & Abbey Publishers

At the core of the song is the search for a new direction, leadership and unity in the nation. The nation is seriously in need of a new direction and appears to be lacking the men that are willing to take up the task of rebuilding the land. Obviously, people in the mold of Okolo and Awili his friend could not provide such leadership. The need for sincerity and commitment at the helm of affairs of the nation becomes imminent. Thematically, the perennial leadership problem that has remained the bane of African development rises again. Researchers and commentators on African development insist that the main reason why Africa's people remain in the quandary of poverty and underdevelopment is as a result of poor quality of leadership (Mills 1). What is needed is apparently transformative leadership that can engineer growth and development and lead the people into prosperity. However, this appear elusive as the old leadership seems bent on sitting on the way of the emergence of that new leadership. In the case of this play, Okolo sits in the middle of the whole process and works surreptitiously to truncate the emergent leadership that is encapsulated in Chidum's return. Chidum acts in his innocence not knowing there is a conspiracy of the elders to stop him from attaining his desired status of a "man poised between love and ownership" (4). He has dreams yet does not know that his dreams constitute a threat to his elder brother who has vowed to "damage him and the whole crew of his tug" (14).

Local Aesthetics and Nuances

The tragicomic manifestations in the Nigerian society especially in the political arena are replicated in characters like Awili and Ebere. Their conniving and negative meddlesomeness as a means of political and economic survival play out in nuanced sequences. The story runs in cyclic momentum offering a spectacle of indigenous thought, music, dance and movement. It is almost an

Chapter seven | *Ofonime Inyang, in*
Charles Nwadigwe, Molinta Enendu & Canice Nwosu (Eds.)
Metaphors and Climax, Reminiscences on the Drama and Theatre of Ogonna Agu
London, Adonis & Abbey Publishers

archetypal situation of "movement of transitions" to use Oyin Ogunba's popular phrase. Traditional poetry mixes with mythopoeic rituals to create a play rich in local idiom, colour and finesse. The dramatic action is crafted as a continuous chain in tune with the African total theatre style. Though broken into acts and scenes, dramatically its realization is suited to the playing context in an arena setting. The playwright in his authorial comment suggests, "one continuous uninterrupted flow" (v).

The cultural universe of the play is African and Igbo in context and flavour. Songs, proverbs, wise sayings, mores, incantations, body adornment, hair plaiting, palm wine tapping, masquerading are given prominence in actions and dialogue. The festival idiom assumes the creative space of traditional African expression resonating in a characteristic fervour of the immediate locale of action. Mgbochi affirms: "Your thought fell quite to the purpose. Today is a market festival. When peasants all over the land take rest after the hard and long planting season"(3). The community's celebration of harvest is complemented with generous feasting and merrymaking that is often extended to the contracting of marriages as is expected to be the case between Chidum and Ada though unfortunately aborted by unforeseen circumstances. There is traditional presentation of gift of items like tobacco, gin, loincloth, onions by young ones to their parent on return from abroad as a mark of appreciation for raising them up:

> CHIDUM: Fetch me a tray, mother...
> Here-some of the things I brought back
> from India, Palestine and Burma. It was
> indeed a tedious thing battling in the white
> sands of Jerusalem and the jungles of Burma.
> Here they are-this aluminum pot, given me
> by the quartermaster of my contingent. Here,
> a jack-knife which I seized from a mortal enemy.
> Can you see the blood-stained edge? Here, the

Chapter seven | *Ofonime Inyang, in*
Charles Nwadigwe, Molinta Enendu & Canice Nwosu (Eds.)
*Metaphors and Climax, Reminiscences on the Drama and
Theatre of Ogonna Agu*
London, Adonis & Abbey Publishers

> shell of an Ostrich egg. This roll of tobacco,
> loincloth and onions . . . (6)

Parental appreciation of gifts with blessing completes the ritual and festival of life. The imposing presence of the shrine in each household and in the community further consolidates the traditional African cosmo-human space of the environment. There is constant mention of the ancestors and the need to rebuild the *Obi* in their honour and as a measure of manliness and ancestral self-worth.

The trend of discourse tilts to the local political situation and how that affects the development of the society. Local industry is commended as in the case of Anene, the palm wine tapper. Local institutions like marriage and polygamy is talked about in the play in reference to the existence of the practice in the community as in most African societies. The play generally exudes the interplay of traditional society as it gradually begins to engage the modern and globalized tenets. The conflict that ensues can also be partially credited to that unexpected meeting between the old and the new, the local and global, the conservative and the liberal and the dawn of new ways of doing things pitted in contest with the old ways of the ancestors.

Conclusion

Some critical questions are raised by Ogonna Agu's *Cry of a Maiden*. For examples: how does a nation develop in the environment of constant ethnic tensions erupting out of relational mistrust? What keeps a nation's youthful energy abroad? Why do young ones fear to go back home? Is it so that they are not deprived of what they fought and built for years by usurping elder siblings? In *Cry of a Maiden*, tears roll out of the broken dreams of a nation where lies and manipulations are used in submerging development possibilities in a post-war society. The study has

Chapter seven | *Ofonime Inyang, in*
Charles Nwadigwe, Molinta Enendu & Canice Nwosu (Eds.)
Metaphors and Climax, Reminiscences on the Drama and
Theatre of Ogonna Agu
London, Adonis & Abbey Publishers

examined the conflict and crisis in this drama of politics and tradition which is unarguably a dramatic depiction of the Nigerian experience.

Agu's *Cry of a Maiden* is a timeless play which significantly engages the paradoxes and contradictions of a nation in search of lost relational self in a complex environment ruled by ambition, usurpation and mistrust. It is a play that offers a strong portrayal of the national distortions that work against Nigeria's drive towards unity and sustainable development. The virulent voice of the playwright as not only a commentator but a creator of national images is fostered by Agu's striking engagement with the problematic of a post-war society constantly in development transitions held captive by a "decadent philosophy in the conduct of societal affairs in the country generally" (Nzewi 7). The dramatic representation is not merely an attempt at aesthetic orchestration but a necessary development intervention using the instrument of the dramatist. The aim is to see how the wrongs in the society can be corrected and the society put on a fresh path of embrace of ethnic and cultural diversity, value-based leadership and productive governance.

Ogonna Anaagudo-Agu can therefore be applauded as a contributor to national development and conflict resolution discourse in Nigeria as his play generates fresh thoughts on the constants of Nigeria's threatened federacy and the imminent tensions instigated by ethnic-based and violent religious groups such as Boko Haram currently witnessed in the country. The survival of the nation as an entity-a nation that has gone through war, several political turbulences, coups and yet still survives-are already re-tested in the new challenges that appear to threaten the very foundation of nationhood. Fiscal inequity, prevalent corruption, economic hardship, unemployment, terrorism, environmental degradation, insecurity, disease, hunger and poverty now confront the

Chapter seven | *Ofonime Inyang, in*
Charles Nwadigwe, Molinta Enendu & Canice Nwosu (Eds.)
Metaphors and Climax, Reminiscences on the Drama and Theatre of Ogonna Agu
London, Adonis & Abbey Publishers

nation in ways that also threaten its foundation. These appear to be the current war of survival that Nigeria must fight and win.

As a nation, Nigeria is endowed with abundant human and material resources that should enable her survive and mature into a stable democracy and viable nation thereby become a good example to other countries in Africa. The management of the ethnic diversity that the nation is blessed with should adopt models that can tap from that diversity because the diversity is an important factor of national development which have been put to good use in the development of other nations. The need for Nigerians to maintain and celebrate their ethnic identity while working hard to protect the collective national interest is the direction that the playwright wants the nation to face. The deliberate attempt at reconciliation between Okolo and Chidum at the end of the play signals these intentions.

Works Cited

Achebe, Chinua. *The Trouble with Nigeria*. London: Heinemann Publishers, 1984.

Agu-Anaagudo, Ogonna. 2000. *Cry of a Maiden*. Calabar: Wusen Press Ltd.

Awhefeada, S. "Rethinking J.P.Clark's *Ozidi* in the Light of Contemporary Nigerian Experience."*Songs of Gold: Fresh Perspectives on Clark*. Eds. Sunday Ododo and Greg Mbajiorgu. Ibadan: Kraft Books Ltd. 2011. 58-70.

Adeoti, Gbemisola. "Femi Osofisan." *Voices Offstage: Nigerian Dramatists on Drama and Politics*. Ed. Gbemisola Adeoti. Ibadan: Kraft Books Ltd. 28-38.

Chapter seven | *Ofonime Inyang, in*
Charles Nwadigwe, Molinta Enendu & Canice Nwosu (Eds.)
Metaphors and Climax, Reminiscences on the Drama and Theatre of Ogonna Agu
London, Adonis & Abbey Publishers

Dubois, W. E. B. *The Soul of Black Folk*. New York: Signet Classic, 1995.

Ehusani, George. *Nigeria: Years Eaten by the Locust*. Ibadan: Kraft Books Ltd. 2002.

Falola, Toyin and Heaton, M. M. *A History of Nigeria.* Cambridge: Cambridge University Press, 2008.

Inyang, O. 2007. "Sick Characters in Search of a Healer: Ahmed Yerima's *The Angel* and the Search for Political Reforms in Nigeria."*Making Images, Re-making Life: Art and Life in Ahmed Yerima*. Eds. Uwemedimo Atakpo and Stephen Inegbe. Uyo: Modern Business Press. 125-138.

Mills, G. *Why Africa is Poor and What Africans Can do About It.* Johannesburg: Penguin Books, 2010.

Nzewi, Meki. *Brain Rot*. Pretoria: African Minds, 2012.

Ogunba, Oyin. *Movement of Transition*. Ibadan: Ibadan University Press, 1975.

Ogunfeyimi, Leke. *Sacrifice the King*. Lagos: Wealthsmith Global Services. 2004.

Soyinka, Wole. *You Must Set Forth at Dawn.*Ibadan: Bookcraft/London: Ayebia Clarke Publishing Company, 2006.

Udo, R. K.*A Comprehensive Geography of West Africa*. Ibadan: Heinemann Educational Books, 1978.

Ugolo, Christopher E. "Ogunde's Dance Choreography and the Quest for National Unity in Nigeria."*African Performance Review*, 4:2 (2010):41-53.

Chapter seven | *Ofonime Inyang, in*
Charles Nwadigwe, Molinta Enendu & Canice Nwosu (Eds.)
Metaphors and Climax, Reminiscences on the Drama and
Theatre of Ogonna Agu
London, Adonis & Abbey Publishers

Chapter Eight

Appearance is Deceptive: Conceptualizing Costume Design for Ogonna Agu's *Symbol of a Goddess*

Francisca A. Nwadigwe

Introduction

Costumes are essential in achieving believability in a theatrical production because of its intimate connection with the actor's physical appearance and human experience. The use of costumes in performance is basically to help the audience understand a theatrical event through characterization. Fundamentally, costume is used to identify the gender, culture, social and economic status, occupation, age, relationships and moods of characters. It equally contributes in establishing the period and style of the production thereby giving it the desired identity. Drama is action expressed in audio-visual forms. Hence, Dare Owolabi explains the power of costumes as expressive dramatic actions conveyed in visual format:

> While you may not utter a word, by way of spoken language your dress is an action in itself that is capable of communicating volume. Don't forget that action is said to speak louder than words. Your dress can therefore say much about you and your personality. (4)

In practice, there is a pronounced difference between a performance that is properly costumed and the one that is not. The former provides a richer spectacle with a significantly higher verisimilitude than the latter. Thus, the audience tends to accept what they see as realistic when the characters are recognizably human and their actions probable and credible. Costume has been

Chapter eight | *Francisca A. Nwadigwe, in*
Charles Nwadigwe, Molinta Enendu & Canice Nwosu (Eds.)
Metaphors and Climax, Reminiscences on the Drama and Theatre of Ogonna Agu
London, Adonis & Abbey Publishers

identified as a complementary resource for performance scenography because it is a kind of moving scenery that controls stage spectacle and influences the audience focus of attention. Adegbite affirms that, "when other arts of the theatre, such as costume and make-up are incorporated" then scenography "becomes exclusively a complete process . . . without which a play becomes naked, bare, boring and even less understandable" (39).

The communicative essence of costume in human relations is not only recognized by theatre artists but by linguistic anthropologists as well. According to Olaoye, semiotics, a branch of linguistic anthropology "is the science of signs and signification which has influenced anthropologists to view dress culture as a system of communication" (6). Similarly, Lyndersay suggests that dress culture goes far beyond the identification of race, tribe and ethnicity to indicate age, social and economic class. Thus, through dress and make-up styles, more detailed information like marital status of a person can be communicated and recognized (426). Furthermore C.S. Peirce and the Swiss Linguist, Ferdinand de Saussure also see dress (costume) as both symbolic and iconic. For instance, flamboyant dressing symbolizes festive mood or joyous occasion, while black or dark dress is a sign of sorrow, sadness or mournful occasion (qtd. in Olaoye 6). Costuming creates and heightens aesthetics in performance because it assists the actor to assume the desired gait, carriage and movement that are vital in role interpretation. This is illustrated by Edwin Wilson using a production of Shaw's play, *Caesar and Cleopatra* where Cleopatra was costumed in a long flowing gown of the Egyptian nobility with bright colours. The costume helped the actor to extensively portray the character (262).

To explore the potentials of using costumes to enhance the production of a play for better understanding and aesthetic appreciation, Ogonna Agu's *Symbol of a Goddess* will be used as a case study. The play *Symbol of a Goddess*, is relatively complex, and

Chapter eight | *Francisca A. Nwadigwe, in*
Charles Nwadigwe, Molinta Enendu & Canice Nwosu (Eds.)
Metaphors and Climax, Reminiscences on the Drama and
Theatre of Ogonna Agu
London, Adonis & Abbey Publishers

features many characters. These characters belong to different social stratifications; they also identify with different ideologies and social groups and are equally interwoven or webbed into different distinct subcultures and belief systems. This complexity in the characterization of the play *Symbol of a Goddess* poses challenges to the costume designer. The costumier needs to be down-to-earth but cautiously selective in creating the costumes to achieve the optimum design that could portray the characters to the audience without ambiguity.

Significance and Methodology

This study is essential because it seeks to provide a functional design concept for costuming the production of *Symbol of a Goddess* for effective communication to the audience. The concept can equally be used to visually interpret similar modern African plays for the audience through the agency of costume design. The method adopted by the research is the content analysis approach to data collection which entails the scrutiny and interpretation of the chosen text. The units of analysis include character, setting, costumes, dramatic action, theme, dialogue, period, time, society and culture depicted in the plot. Additional or secondary data were obtained from published texts, journals, magazines and personal observations. The analyses of the data were descriptive, critical and interpretative with the objective of finding the optimum approach for visually expressing the play through costume. Efforts were made to eliminate threats to the validity of the study and hence make the findings generalizable.

The playwright, Ogonna Anaagudo-Agu, born October 15, 1948 attended the Dennis Memorial Grammar School (DMGS) Onitsha and later the University of Nigeria Nsukka (UNN) where he obtained a B.A. Degree in English and Drama. He proceeded to Leeds and later London where he did his postgraduate studies in

Chapter eight | *Francisca A. Nwadigwe, in*
Charles Nwadigwe, Molinta Enendu & Canice Nwosu (Eds.)
Metaphors and Climax, Reminiscences on the Drama and
Theatre of Ogonna Agu
London, Adonis & Abbey Publishers

drama and theatre and obtained his Masters and Ph.D. respectively. He lectured in the University of Calabar and became an Associate Professor of Theatre Arts until 2011 when he died. He has published and produced many creative works which include novels, poetry and plays. His works often reflect his identity as a true Igbo man who creates from his Igbo cosmology. In 1971, he won a prize on poetry in an all-African competition in the University of California Los Angeles. Ogonna was married with children. A play is meant to be put on stage; hence this study is significant because it will highlight the artistic contributions of Ogonna Agu to the African stage throughout his career as summarized above. The study will also enrich the available literature on Agu's works and provide a technical resource to designers, directors, researchers and theatre practitioners working on the play and modern African drama in general.

Dramatic Action and the Plot Sequence

The choice of the play *Symbol of a Goddess* among many other works by the author was purposive. Though the play has been produced on stage, a comprehensive study and conceptualization of its costume design for the modern African stage has not been done by scholars and practitioners. Thematically, *Symbol of a Goddess* is about a young Biafran veteran, Emenike, who returns from the Civil War between Biafra and the Nigerian Federal forces frustrated and vengeful because of his bitter experience. He decides to continue his war on different planes and battlefronts of his existence. To effectively costume any play, it is vital to understand its storyline as embedded in the characterization and dramatic actions. The play, *Symbol of a Goddess*, opens with a prologue where the narrator recounts the historical situation of the Nigerian Civil War as a background to the plot. He begins thus:

Chapter eight | *Francisca A. Nwadigwe, in*
Charles Nwadigwe, Molinta Enendu & Canice Nwosu (Eds.)
Metaphors and Climax, Reminiscences on the Drama and Theatre of Ogonna Agu
London, Adonis & Abbey Publishers

> NARRATOR: . . .Here where I stand, I see desolation, grief and
> anguish among the children of men. At least that is
> what the Civil War has brought. Gloom and hatred on
> the faces of men. (5)

The narrator goes further to introduce us to the hero of *Symbol of a Goddess* Emenike, his exploits and present state of mind.

> NARRATOR: Emenike was the hero of that twilight battle that day
> at Abagana. He has seen action at Gekem, he has seen
> it all at Ore, he had seen it at Otuocha. What
> happened to this boy at last I cannot tell, but he was
> one of the brave men Biafra ever had. Yet Biafra
> collapsed. (6)

Narrator also reflects on the present situation of the people. There was hunger, sickness and other terrible things associated with war. Thus, "Ojukwu the war hero of the battle left in search of everlasting peace" and the war ended (8). Then, the real problem of a typical post-war society started when young freedom fighters like Emenike came back from battle dissatisfied and refused to accept that the war has ended. This desolation often gives rise to many vices such as armed robbery and violence.

Emenike a young Biafran veteran returns home highly frustrated and dissatisfied with his experiences in the war. His father was brutally killed by the Federal forces. The ideology which led to his fighting the war was not actualized and he is angry and wants vengeance. Emenike becomes violent and hostile to even his kith and kin. But instead of the family to assuage his feelings and rehabilitate him, they match his hostility with hostility. This is evident in Ide his cousin, as well as Iluka and Igbonekwu who try to confront him by using different tactics. Ide constantly calls the army commander and his soldiers to arrest Emenike. The commander and his soldiers drive Emenike's prized bird away and bring down the cage from the Iroko tree. His

Chapter eight | *Francisca A. Nwadigwe, in*
Charles Nwadigwe, Molinta Enendu & Canice Nwosu (Eds.)
Metaphors and Climax, Reminiscences on the Drama and
Theatre of Ogonna Agu
London, Adonis & Abbey Publishers

151

mother Iluka is arrested when Emenike was not found. In another occasion the commander and his soldiers destroy his homestead.

Even when he tries to develop the masquerade cult, Emenike is called all sorts of derogatory names suggesting he was a lunatic and homosexual. Emenike leaves the village but Iluka, Igbonekwu and Ide plan and marry for him in his absence despite his objection that he does not want to marry. They call a native doctor to concoct some talisman to bring Emenike back to the village using the wife (Akudiri) as part of the ritual.

Three years later when Emenike comes back to the village Iluka introduces Akudiri to him. He still rejects her but his mother Iluka implants the girl in his bed chamber. Emenike could not resist Akudiri and she becomes pregnant. But he refuses to marry Akudiri; thus the family tries to force him to marry the girl. Ide comes to fight Emenike in his house in a bid to force him to marry Akudiri. They also propose a church wedding even though Emenike is not a Christian. They involve the whole community and invite the Council of Elders, with Ezeala presiding, to try and force Emenike to marry Akudiri. Emenike being a strong-willed man is able to surmount these forces and refuse to be distracted from his water goddess who came as *Agboghommuo*.

Along the line, Igbonekwu begins to understand Emenike's personality. He cautions Ide to stop bringing the army commander into the family feud, arguing that they can solve their problems on their own. He admits being a convert of Emenike and admires his vision in creating the masquerade cult. In search of lasting peace away from a troubled world full of hostilities, Emenike joins the Goddess to swim into the deep waters. Finally, Okobe loosens Emenike's anklets, signalling his freedom from the turbulent physical world, and thereafter leads the procession with incantation as Emenike is taken out for burial as he transits to the Other world.

Chapter eight | *Francisca A. Nwadigwe, in*
Charles Nwadigwe, Molinta Enendu & Canice Nwosu (Eds.)
Metaphors and Climax, Reminiscences on the Drama and
Theatre of Ogonna Agu
London, Adonis & Abbey Publishers

Characterization in Symbol of a Goddess

A clear understanding of characters in *Symbol of a Goddess* will provide an insight into their personalities and highlight what makes each character different from the other. Characterization is a primary factor upon which costume design is anchored in a play production. Therefore to justify the choice of costumes for the characters in *Symbol of a Goddess*, it is essential to underscore what the key characters represent.

Emenike

Emenike, the hero of *Symbol of a Goddess* is a brave solider who fought for Biafra. He believes in the ideology of Biafra and thus becomes frustrated, angry and violent when the Biafran dream could not materialize. He refuses to accept that the war has ended. Instead, he tries to immortalize Biafra by being artistic about it. He sacrifices himself by forming the masquerade cult personified by the *Agboghommuo* or *Egbe Eyi-Ugo* the River Goddess and getting married to her. A determined man, he is not deterred by any opposition despite their size or strength. A stubborn character, Emenike refuses to yield to external pressures. He stands his ground to fight all opposition and still marries the Goddess. He is a traditionalist to the core and believes in charms, spirits and ancestral powers.

Ide

A vengeful character that believes in matching force with force. He calls the Commander to arrest Emenike who tried to shoot him. He drives Emenike out of the village using the commander. He also leads the Commander to destroy Emenike's house. Ide is however respectful and protective of his people. He listens to Igbonekwu and relents when he is asked to stop bringing the Commander into

Chapter eight | *Francisca A. Nwadigwe, in*
Charles Nwadigwe, Molinta Enendu & Canice Nwosu (Eds.)
Metaphors and Climax, Reminiscences on the Drama and
Theatre of Ogonna Agu
London, Adonis & Abbey Publishers

their family conflicts. He withdraws the improper word he used after calling Emenike a beast. He is a man who adapts to changes easily. Immediately the war ended, he quickly mingles with the Federal forces. Ide is a Christian and against the traditional worship adored by Emenike. Nevertheless, he strongly believes in constituted authority in both the traditional and modern societies. Hence he reports Emenike to the Ezeala and the Elders to force him to marry Akudiri and claim her pregnancy.

Igbonekwu

Igbonekwu is a dynamic character; a man who lives up to his position as a village organizer. He is gentle and able to steer a middle course in most situations. He intervenes and intercedes for Emenike and Iluka in times of crisis. He is able to curtail Ide's vengeful disposition towards Emenike and also prevents Emenike from shooting Ide. He is the second person in the play who understands Emenike's creativity of keeping Biafra alive through the masquerade cult. He publicly pronounced his regrets in trying to impose Akudiri on Emenike. Igbonekwu strikes a balance on issues and he is neither a pronounced Christian nor traditionalist.

Okobe

Okobe is the head of the masquerade cult. He is a true traditionalist with good leadership qualities as well. This is exemplified in the way he patiently gives a listening ear to Emenike and is able to understand his intention for establishing a masquerade cult personified by the Goddess of the River, *Egbe Eyi Ugo*. He thus helps Emenike to achieve his ambition of establishing the masquerade cult. He also gives Emenike ankle strings when he realizes the anklet he needs is to be applied differently from that of the *Ozo* titled men. A gentle and respectful man, he avoids confrontation even when he is insulted. When Emenike died, it

Chapter eight | *Francisca A. Nwadigwe, in*
Charles Nwadigwe, Molinta Enendu & Canice Nwosu (Eds.)
Metaphors and Climax, Reminiscences on the Drama and
Theatre of Ogonna Agu
London, Adonis & Abbey Publishers

was Okobe who gave him the last honour by coming to carry his body for burial in a solemn procession while reciting traditional prayers.

Iluka

A mother who has sincere love for her son Emenike and feels genuinely concerned for his well-being. When the war ended, she was anxious to know if Emenike survived. Igbonekwu and Ide had to reassure her of his safety. Even after her arrest by Commander, her concern for Emenike grew even more. Iluka reacted and defended her son Emenike when Nneaku rained abuses on Emenike calling him a lunatic and homosexual. She believes marrying for Emenike will make him calm and more responsible. Hence she sought the support of Igbonekwu and Ide to get a wife for Emenike. Iluka is also a forceful character. She was able to impose Akudiri on Emenike even when he rejected her on the night of his return. She still implanted her in his bed chamber which led to the pregnancy. She believes in tradition and the efficacy of charms. She brought a medicine man and used Akudiri as part of the ritual to bring Emenike back. When Emenike returned, she openly rejoiced that her ritual had worked. Despite Emenike's aggression, Iluka is not deterred from pursuing the goals she believes in. Her opposition to Okobe and some other characters is borne out of her love and concern for Emenike's welfare.

Akudiri

Akudiri is the wife married for Emenike. She is an epitome of traditional African womanhood. Akudiri truly loves Emenike even without knowing him. She married Emenike against the advice of her mother, Nneaku. In addition, she presented herself to be used

Chapter eight | *Francisca A. Nwadigwe, in*
Charles Nwadigwe, Molinta Enendu & Canice Nwosu (Eds.)
Metaphors and Climax, Reminiscences on the Drama and
Theatre of Ogonna Agu
London, Adonis & Abbey Publishers

in a ritual to bring Emenike back home and waited patiently for three years for Emenike's return. Akudiri is humble, patient and docile even when Emenike scolds, neglects and taunts her. But she is not weak. She studied Emenike's personality and warmed herself into his heart. Akudiri has inner strength as well. Despite being heavily pregnant, she was ready to contest with the *Agboghommuo* for Emenike though she lost. She also believes in traditional religion. When Emenike broke the mirror, she knew the charm is destroyed but still tried all she could to keep Emenike. She still stands for the future because she was pregnant for Emenike, a symbolic assurance of continuity after Emenike's death.

Commander

He is a well-trained Federal solider, who does his job with seriousness. He believes every opposition must be crushed. He responds promptly to calls by Ide to crush Emenike's purported violent behaviour. Commander is an aggressive solider. When he could not get Emenike, he arrested his mother and made sure she was taken to the barracks. He scared Emenike out of the village and went ahead to destroy his homestead. As much as he believes in the power of the gun, he also recognizes the potency of indigenous charms and medicine. Emenike considers him a threat to Biafra ideals and philosophy.

Nneaku

The mother of Akudiri, she has the welfare of her daughter at heart. She initially gave Akudiri to Iluka on trust and charged Iluka to take care of her daughter. She is weak and lacks control of her daughter. Nneaku could not convince Akudiri to leave Emenike on realizing that Emenike was a violent man. Even when Akudiri became pregnant and Emenike rejected her, she could not

Chapter eight | *Francisca A. Nwadigwe, in*
Charles Nwadigwe, Molinta Enendu & Canice Nwosu (Eds.)
Metaphors and Climax, Reminiscences on the Drama and
Theatre of Ogonna Agu
London, Adonis & Abbey Publishers

stand firm and mount pressure as Iluka, Ide and others did so that Emenike marries Akudiri. Instead, she resorts to empty threats against her daughter and verbal abuse of Emenike.

Ugonne

Ugonne is a village gossip, a friend of Iluka, and a jolly good fellow who has her friend's welfare at heart. Ugonne is happy to see the romance being enkindled between Emenike and Akudiri. She believes that the romance will refute the gossip in the village that Emenike was a homosexual. A great supporter of Iluka, Ugonne helped to assure Nneaku that Akudiri was in good hands under the care of her friend Iluka. Finally, Ugonne is also a traditionalist like her friend Iluka.

Costume Design for Symbol of a Goddess

James Thomas asserts that script analysis is fundamental to theatrical design (3). Based on this reality, the study has attempted to present the plot and characterization of the chosen play. In fact, character analysis which is an aspect of script analysis is indispensable in producing an effective costume design for a production. This is because costumes are personal to the actor who assumes the role. In most cases, the costumes are regarded as part of the character and extensions of each character's identity and personality. Theatrical costumes are practically inactive and hardly valuable without the actor to adorn it and interpret character. Between the actor and the audience, appearance becomes deceptive. To the audience imagination, the actor is what the costume presents him to be. The actor is first *seen* to be what he visually represents before the performer executes the role (character) in action to complete the communication and enhance meaning.

Chapter eight | *Francisca A. Nwadigwe, in*
Charles Nwadigwe, Molinta Enendu & Canice Nwosu (Eds.)
Metaphors and Climax, Reminiscences on the Drama and
Theatre of Ogonna Agu
London, Adonis & Abbey Publishers

157

In planning and designing the costumes for *Symbol of a Goddess*, the chosen concept in this study is anchored on the five key determinants of character. This approach is quite useful to a costumier in making vital decisions concerning character associations, physical and psychological attributes and their predictable behaviour. Furthermore, since the costumier usually works with other artists in the production team, a "working collaboration with chosen concept, especially for theatrical production" becomes imperative (Adegbite 39). The character determinants that significantly informed the costume design concept include will, desire, moral stance, decorum and mood-intensity.

Will is the inner strength, the tenacity, or otherwise of the character to pursue and accomplish goals. The desire is what the character wants most. In addition, it is what the character stands for or believes in. It is the prize to be won or lost. The ability to accomplish a desire is dependent on the strength of will. Moral stance concerns the morality of the character; the conscience that justifies the pursuit of a desire. The character's moral uprightness or depravity can influence his will and ultimately determine his desire. Character decorum is the same as his or her density. It includes the physical appearance, gait, manners, outward behavior and comportment of the character. The character mood in tensity concerns the composure, poise, and energy of the character at the beginning of a scene or units of action and their ability to sustain it to the end.

The character determinants are somehow connected and they combine with allied factors such as conflicts, subtext, cultural norms, given circumstances, polar attitudes and previous action. All these are generally expressed through the design concept and ultimately influence the choice of costumes for the play. Indeed, Gillette argues that the dividing line between fashion and costume design is the application of production concept (385). Hence, in

Chapter eight | *Francisca A. Nwadigwe, in*
Charles Nwadigwe, Molinta Enendu & Canice Nwosu (Eds.)
Metaphors and Climax, Reminiscences on the Drama and Theatre of Ogonna Agu
London, Adonis & Abbey Publishers

fashion design "primary attention is given to creating visual design that gives little, if any, thought to the personality or character of the person who ultimately will wear the clothes". Furthermore, "the fashion designer may follow the fashion currently in vogue" and in the process show "little, if any, stylistic consistency from one design to the next". But "costume design is different. To be effective, the costume designs for a production need to (1) reflect the production design team's agreed upon interpretation of the production concept … (2) exhibit a unity of style among all costume designs for that production; (3) provide a visual reflection of the personality and nature of each character at a given time in the play" (Gillette 385).

Similarly, Nwadigwe explains that "though design may create aesthetic beauty, it need not be beautiful as long as it satisfies the intention of the creator". Hence, unlike fashion, the theatrical costume's core objective is "the imaginative and harmonious combination or juxtaposition of diverse elements by the artist so as to project a central idea" (91). In the conceptualization of costuming for a production of Agu's *Symbol of a Goddess*, these factors will certainly affect the elements of colour, line, texture, and mass chosen for the costumes, their transitions, motifs and the principles applied in designing each costume in order to suit the characterization. After a careful textual analysis and consideration of other relevant factors including periodization without prejudice to the directorial concept, the following Costume Chart is recommended for the play:

Chapter eight | *Francisca A. Nwadigwe, in*
Charles Nwadigwe, Molinta Enendu & Canice Nwosu (Eds.)
Metaphors and Climax, Reminiscences on the Drama and Theatre of Ogonna Agu
London, Adonis & Abbey Publishers

Costume Chart

Characters	1st Appearance	2nd Appearance	3rd Appearance	4th Appearance	5th Appearance	6th Appearance	7th Appearance	8th Appearance	9th Appearance	10th Appeara
NARRATOR Age-About 60 years	Free styled Igbo traditional chieftaincy gown with side slit (*Isi-Agu*) with a red cap attached with eagle feather. Beads for the neck and wrists									
EMENIKE Age 25-28	A variegated khaki green army uniform (Camouflage), green stockings, black boots and a red beret	Same as in first appearance	Knee length shorts and green T-shirt. black military boots and green stockings	Same as 3rd appearance but now added with raffia (*Aju*) and anklet	Brown trousers, light green shirt with diagonal lines, a pair of brown shoes	Shorts, bare-chested (topless), bare foot	Same as in sixth appearance	Same as in sixth appearance but now added is a black military boot	White wrapper, raffia on waist, arms and anklet, bare chest, bare foot and white head band	Multi-co *Abada* trousers shirt wit sandals anklet
GBONEKWU Age 58-62	Grey colour trousers, grey colour jumper, made with plain material	Same as in first appearance	Same as in first appearance	Igbo chieftaincy attire, red cap and leather sandals	A free-style *Abada* shirt, woolen Igbo cap, wrapper knotted in male fashion and leather slippers	*Abada* jumper and trouser with leather slippers and striped woolen Igbo cap	Same as in sixth appearance			
DE Age 29 -32	Dark red or ox-blood safari suit with brown leather shoes, no stockings	Same as in first appearance	Same as in first appearance	A velvet jumper and trousers with matching shoes	Plain trousers and shirt with sandals or shoes	Knee length knicker and jumper shirt with sandals	Same as in fourth appearance			
LUKA Age 60-65	*Abada* wrapper (slightly faded) and blouse. Simple scarf and slippers, no jewelry	Same as in first appearance	*Intorika* George wrapper and lace blouse, big head tie, jewelry and leather slippers	Faded wrapper and a casual blouse (may be of the same wrapper material)	Same as in fourth appearance or a different set of *Abada* wrapper and blouse	*Abada* wrapper and blouse with plain scarf and slippers	A multi-coloured *Abada* wrapper with blouse, slippers, and earrings.			

Chapter eight | *Francisca A. Nwadigwe*, in
Charles Nwadigwe, Molinta Enendu & Canice Nwosu (Eds.)
Metaphors and Climax, Reminiscences on the Drama and Theatre of Ogonna Agu
London, Adonis & Abbey Publishers

DBE 45 years	Knee-length knickers, bare- chested, raffia on waist, arms, and forehead. Bare foot with anklets	Same as in first appearance	Same as in first appearance						
DIRI 4 years	A blue *Intorika* George wrapper, big head scarf, lace blouse, leather slippers and jewelry	Slightly faded *Abada* wrapper and blouse. Slippers, no jewelry	*Abada* wrapper tied above her breast and above the knee to expose her laps. Topless	A short-sleeved *Abada* gown, slippers, dangling earrings only	Olive green maternity gown, slippers and small earrings.				
MANDER 0 years	Plain khaki green army trousers, short sleeved army safari shirt with pips, red beret, thick green stockings and black military boots	Dark green army camouflage, uniform, red beret, thick green stockings and black military boots.							
NNE years	A rich multi coloured *Abada* wrapper, lace blouse, big scarf, leather slippers and jewelry	A casual *Abada* wrapper (slightly faded), blouse, plain scarf and slippers							
AKU years	A bright multi-coloured *Abada* wrapper, light blue lace blouse, big scarf, leather slippers and jewelry	A short *Abada* wrapper and blouse, scarf made of the same material, slippers							
YTE years	Brown shorts (swimming trunks can serve), topless, barefoot								
MAN rs and	A white sleeveless jumper shirt, white wrapper tied on the waist, cowry-								

Chapter eight | Francisca A. Nwadigwe, in
Charles Nwadigwe, Molinta Enendu & Canice Nwosu (Eds.)
Metaphors and Climax, Reminiscences on the Drama and Theatre of Ogonna Agu
London, Adonis & Abbey Publishers

	beaded head band on a red cap with feathers, raffia bag, ankle strings, cowry-stringed neck lace with snail shells and bare foot.								
ZEALA 0 years and bove	A golden chieftaincy cap with eagle feathers. A chieftaincy Igbo velvet shirt (*Isi Agu*), jumper and Akwete wrapper, beaded leather slippers, heavy neck beads, ankle strings and ivory beads on wrists								
HORUS Different ges)	Assorted attires reflecting their ages and social status								
AMUSU/ OLIDERS	Plain khaki green military uniforms, beret and black military boots respectively								
RUMMERS	Knickers with singlet and raffia (*Aju*) on waist and arms with rattles on legs.								
MAIDENS 0-24 Years	Assorted colours of simple George wrappers, topless, beads on neck, waist and foreheads, leather slippers and								

Chapter eight | Francisca A. Nwadigwe, in
Charles Nwadigwe, Molinta Enendu & Canice Nwosu (Eds.)
Metaphors and Climax, Reminiscences on the Drama and Theatre of Ogonna Agu
London, Adonis & Abbey Publishers

	light jewelry									
RAL ES	Green camouflage military uniform, combat helmets, military stockings and black boots.									
RAN ES	Brownish khaki military camouflage outfit, black jungle boots, red beret with emblem of rising sun, thick stockings									
NERS AR	Assorted, trousers, singlet, shirts, knickers, loin cloth, traditional wears, slippers, bare foot, no caps									
GEES us Ages)	Assorted attires reflecting different ages, gender and social status.									
D us Ages)	Assorted attires reflecting different ages, gender and social status									

Conclusion

From the findings and observations, it can be stated that an effective design of costumes cannot be isolated from the play's given circumstances and the five major determinants of character. This study is based on an artistic and technical appraisal of Ogonna Agu's *Symbol of a Goddess* for stage production. As an

Chapter eight | Francisca A. Nwadigwe, in
Charles Nwadigwe, Molinta Enendu & Canice Nwosu (Eds.)
Metaphors and Climax, Reminiscences on the Drama and Theatre of Ogonna Agu
London, Adonis & Abbey Publishers

interpretative work of art, this costume design serves as a guide and provides essential information to future designers intending to produce *Symbol of a Goddess* for the stage. The suggested costume schemes are practicable recommendations for a production of the play founded on a given concept. However, other conceptual, stylistic and contextual factors and variables may lead to the choice of a different costume approach.

In a discourse on culture and visual communication, Agu maintains that items of adornment in the Igbo tradition such as the "Uli essence" are expressive of diverse and deeper meanings. They constitute "signs on the bodies of the women, on compound walls and on shrine murals" ("Uli Essence. . ."153). Although Uli is not a practicable make-up material for the modern Western-oriented African theatre due to its difficulty in removal for change of make-up between scenes, but its essence can be represented or simulated using liners, acrylic, kajal and other removable substances and make-up materials. In its elaborate application, make-up can also become the costume as evident in some cultures in Africa and Asia. The point being stressed here is that visual appearance of the performer in every performance is a basic responsibility of the costume designer who must anchor the interpretation on some workable concept using motifs and design elements and principles to actualize the intended objectives. Therefore, the diverse metaphors and highly symbolic essence of Agu's *Symbol of a Goddess* opens a door of potentials for visually interpreting the text through costumes and allied accessories.

Works Cited

Adegbite, Adesina. "Scenography and Conceptual Interpretation of Joe de Graft's *Muntu*."*Contemporary Discourses on Media and*

Chapter eight | *Francisca A. Nwadigwe, in*
Charles Nwadigwe, Molinta Enendu & Canice Nwosu (Eds.)
Metaphors and Climax, Reminiscences on the Drama and
Theatre of Ogonna Agu
London, Adonis & Abbey Publishers

Theatre Arts in Nigeria. Eds. Hyginus Ekwuazi, Charles Aluede and Osakue Omoera. Delhi: Kamla-Raj, 2012. 39-44.

Anaagudo-Agu, Ogonna. "Aka Umuagbara: Uli Essence and Symbols in the Development of an Indigenous Igbo Script." *The Parnassus: University of Uyo Journal of Cultural Research.* 2 (2005): 152-162.

Anaagudo-Agu, Ogonna C. *Symbol of Goddess.* Calabar: University of Calabar Press, 2005.

Gillette, Michael J. *Theatrical Design and Production: An Introduction to Scene Design and Construction, Lighting, Sound, Costume, and Makeup.* (4th Edition). Boston: McGraw-Hill, 2000.

Lyndersay, Dani. "Traditional Kanuri Dress: An Overview of its Origins and Unique Styles." *A Gazelle of the Savannah.* Eds. Omoera Osakue, Sola Adeyemi and Benedict Binebai. Kent: Alpha Crownes Publishers, 2012. 413-434.

Nwadigwe, Charles. "Art and Attitude: Imperatives for Design in Contemporary Nigerian Theatre." *The Performer: Ilorin Journal of the Performing Arts.* 4(2002): 91-104.

Olaoye, A. A. "Nigerian Dress Culture in Corporate Institutions: A Linguistic and Anthropological Perspective." Paper Presented at the National Workshop on "Promoting Nigerian Dress Culture for National Identity". Cyprian Ekwensi Cultural Centre, Abuja, April 7-9, 2010.

Owolabi, Dare. "What is Your Language: Speech or Dress?". Paper Presented at the National Workshop on "Promoting Nigerian Dress Culture for National Identity." Cyprian Ekwensi Cultural Centre, Abuja, April 7-9, 2010.

Thomas, James. *Script Analysis for Actors, Directors, and Designers.* Boston: Focal Press, 1992.

Wilson, Edwin. *The Theater Experience.* (9th Edition). Boston: McGraw-Hill, 2004.

Chapter eight | *Francisca A. Nwadigwe, in*
Charles Nwadigwe, Molinta Enendu & Canice Nwosu (Eds.)
Metaphors and Climax, Reminiscences on the Drama and Theatre of Ogonna Agu
London, Adonis & Abbey Publishers

Chapter Nine

Culture, Tradition and Conflict Resolution: Issues in Ogonna Agu's *Cry of a Maiden*

Emeka Ofora

Introduction

Studies in the fields of sociology and anthropology have identified culture and tradition as human phenomena that have universal application. There is no society in the world that does not have one form of cultural identity or the other. Since culture is divergent in nature, one society can easily be distinguished from the other because of its cultural practices. Culture has been defined as "the way of life of a group of people" (Olaoba 11). This includes the establishment of a legal system which is fundamental to the maintenance of peace and harmony in order to obtain meaningful existence in the society. This definition hinges on the fact that without culture having certain elements that can be used to institute order in the society, the achievement of any meaningful development in any society will be difficult, if not impossible.

Similarly, tradition is described as "any habit or event, whether individual or group, which is sustained over a considerable stretch of time" (Umukoro 25). Culture and tradition share symbiotic relationship. The similarity of culture and tradition always permits their interchangeable usages. Hence, Umukoro is of the view that for a tradition to transform into culture, it must be deeply rooted in the lives of the people. But for Oyedepo, there is no remarkable difference between culture and tradition. This is reflected in her definition of culture as synonymous with "tradition, customs or

Chapter nine | *Emeka Ofora, in*
Charles Nwadigwe, Molinta Enendu & Canice Nwosu (Eds.)
Metaphors and Climax, Reminiscences on the Drama and
Theatre of Ogonna Agu
London, Adonis & Abbey Publishers

ethics" (21).The expression of culture and observance of tradition in human society sometimes creates conflict or disagreement among people or groups. According to Onigu Otite, conflict is usually caused when people in a community begin to pursue divergent interests, goals or aspirations (154).Furthermore, Otite explains that conflict is a social problem that can be addressed through the formulation of a workable strategy, competent enough to bring it under control. Cultural norms and traditional approaches can be deployed in conflict resolution.

In essence, traditional or cultural conflict resolution, is the systematic way of using traditional means to mediate between two or more disagreeing people or groups in a given situation so that peace and order can be attained in the society. This chapter examines how Ogonna Agu artistically applied this instrument and technique to contend with the domestic dissension which arose between Okolo and his younger brother Chidum in the play, *Cry of a Maiden*. This is important considering the recent quest for African writers to always incorporate in their creative works the cultures of the environment from which they write. Writers such as Cyprian Ekwensi, Chinua Achebe, Ngugi wa Thiong'o, Wole Soyinka and Ola Rotimi have so far been singled out for their dogged efforts in ensuring that the culture of their various environments are adequately alluded to in most of their literary creation (Ibrahim 340).

The reason is for them to use the literary medium to project aspects of African values to other parts of the world in order to correct the long-standing Western impression that Africans have no history. The Nigerian postmodern writers have been urged to adopt this pattern of writing in creating Nigerian literatures. This is important because considering the large population of the country and its various ethnic groups, such method of writing will help to explore and harness the diverse cultures in the country for the purpose of national development To buttresses this view,

Chapter nine | *Emeka Ofora, in*
Charles Nwadigwe, Molinta Enendu & Canice Nwosu (Eds.)
Metaphors and Climax, Reminiscences on the Drama and Theatre of Ogonna Agu
London, Adonis & Abbey Publishers

Ernest Emenyonu opines that Nigeria as a country is endowed with both ethnic and cultural differences, which when properly harnessed, would engender a sense of oneness in the country. He therefore urged the Nigerian writers to always give full attention to the cultural practices of the people in their creative works and by that help to establish a premise upon which national solidarity could be built (Ibrahim 340). Emmanuel Obiechina also argues that it is in this manner that "the writings can be referred to as Nigerian writings" (qtd. in Ibrahim 341). Ogonna Agu distinguished himself through his various works as a true Igbo (Nigerian) creative writer. Most of his works reflected the daily lives and common beliefs of the ordinary people of his environment and culture area. This ideology and practice are clearly manifest in his creative works.

Cry of a Maiden: The Synopsis

Cry of a Maiden addresses domestic issues that have universal appeal. It can be categorized under the melodramatic genre of drama. Oscar Brockett and Robert Ball describe melodrama as a "form of literature which relates both to tragedy and comedy . . . it relates to tragedy through its serious action and to comedy, through its happy ending"(49). It relates to tragedy through its serious action and to comedy, through its happy ending. The play therefore tells a story of two brothers, Okolo and Chidum who engage in a type of conflict that can split their brotherhood and therefore set bad precedent in their family. Chidum, an ex-service man having returned home after the Second World War decides to get married in order to settle down to family life. But Okolo whose consent is needed before this can be done refuses to approve the idea on the basis that Chidum should first rebuild the family *Obi* that is in a state of ruin before thinking of getting married. But with the conceited influence of Awili, Okolo outwits Chidum and

Chapter nine | *Emeka Ofora, in*
Charles Nwadigwe, Molinta Enendu & Canice Nwosu (Eds.)
Metaphors and Climax, Reminiscences on the Drama and
Theatre of Ogonna Agu
London, Adonis & Abbey Publishers

covets his lover Ada. The resultant conflict and tension constitute the climax of the play. But afterward, peace is negotiated by their uncles, Okpala and Udoka and normalcy is restored.

Cultural Indices in the Play

The play begins in a family celebration over the return of Chidum, one of the family members after long separation owing to the war. This mood transmutes into tense moment when Chidum in the presence of his paternal uncle, Okpala, formally requests the consent of Okolo to get married and begin to raise his own family. This move is in keeping with the Igbo tradition. In Igbo traditional society, it is seen as abnormal when a second son in a family gets married while the first born is yet to do so. In such cases, the second son who wants to marry should first sponsor a marriage ceremony for his elder brother (this applies where the elder brother is financially incapacitated) or make passionate appeal to his elder brother to allow him marry. The other reason why Chidum must appeal to the conscience of Okolo to permit him to get a wife is because of the position tradition places him (Okolo) as the first son of the family. What this means is that since their father is deceased, Okolo is in charge of the entire family and his interests represent the wishes of the ancestors. Okpala affirms: "Okolo, you are the elder (in this family). Without you, this household is powerless. Chidum is powerless" (10).

This position makes any blessing given under the threshold of the ancestral domain most relevant. It would as well be interpreted as the ancestors' blessings because Okolo is traditionally deemed to represent and defend their interests. The reason is that the Igbo man from inception is a religious being, who always believes in the existence of the ancestors and their wholesome influence in virtually all human activities (Adewoye 7). The fear of these ancestors and the punishment they inflict on those who disobey

Chapter nine | *Emeka Ofora, in*
Charles Nwadigwe, Molinta Enendu & Canice Nwosu (Eds.)
Metaphors and Climax, Reminiscences on the Drama and
Theatre of Ogonna Agu
London, Adonis & Abbey Publishers

the laws of the land has continued to be a guiding principle to the conduct of individuals in the society (Adewoye 14). A dialogue between two characters in the play, Mgbochi and Chidum provides insight in this direction:

MGBOCHI: I ask again, what are you doing?
CHIDUM: A snake I want to slash. There's serpent lurking here about. Harassing. Dangerously lurking with the puff of the adder.
MGBOCHI: You are sure it's not the . . .
CHIDUM: Python? Not the python. I know it's sacred and respect it. I fear Agbala and his curse. (31)

This same ancestral fear is presumed to be responsible for Chidum's compliance to Okolo's directive to rebuild the dilapidating family *Obi* (homestead), a condition Okolo insists must be fulfilled before he can give consent to Chidum's marriage proposal:

OKOLO; ... Chidum can do as he pleases. But I must warn that a major task stares us in the face, the task of reconstructing this cottage. As you can see, the Obi building has gone into ruins. And the shrine house has collapsed, thereby exposing the sacred goddess to [bad] weather and inhospitable rains (10).

The *Obi* in question is the rightful inheritance of Okolo by virtue of his being the first born of the family. The Igbo reserve much respect for the traditional *Obi* because of its cultural relevance. It is a symbol of the homestead and family survival. It serves as a place where ancestral symbols of religious observances are displayed. As the playwright informs in his preliminary notes to the play, the *Obi* also serves as a "cultural centre, a museum of antiquities, a social meeting place and a place where early morning kolanut invocation takes place" (i). Consequently, he emphasized that:

Chapter nine | *Emeka Ofora, in*
Charles Nwadigwe, Molinta Enendu & Canice Nwosu (Eds.)
Metaphors and Climax, Reminiscences on the Drama and
Theatre of Ogonna Agu
London, Adonis & Abbey Publishers

The collapse of one's Obi under whatever circumstance portends danger for the family. It literally spells death for the head of household. And as it is said, when the right hand of a deity falls to the ground, then tragedy has befallen the entire household (iv).

Therefore, any family in the Igbo traditional society that does not have the *Obi* is like a dead zone where nothing happens, which often implies the absence of a head in the household. Chidum's acceptance to bring back the glory of the family by rebuilding the *Obi* can be argued from two angles: first, he does not want to attract the anger of the gods whose shrines and sacred objects are exposed to harsh weather. Second, Chidum agrees to repair the *Obi* in order to keep himself away from public ridicule. This is because a man's worth in Igbo society is usually judged not with the edifice he built for himself but on the state of his ancestral *Obi*, which is generally believed to be the "hub of activities" for the household ancestors (Agu iv).

It is against this background that every Igbo man works hard in life to survive. This is not basically for his self-interest alone but that of the entire family. Charles Nnolim alludes to this when he states that; "the usual question which confronts every Igbo man in life is to succeed or not to succeed" (146). This tradition of diligence is encouraged in Igbo traditional communities by the manner the society is structured according to class usually determined by economic or material achievement. In an analysis of class structure and social relations in a typical Igbo setting as represented in Achebe's Umuofia community, Udenta states that:

To be able to participate effectively in the creation and dissemination of ideas in Umuofia community, one has to take titles. Title-taking in this context is a material "property" and not a status symbol. It guarantees one limitless accolades, respect, influence and authority; they become a corporate body of the wishes and commands of the ruling class (92).

Chapter nine | *Emeka Ofora, in*
Charles Nwadigwe, Molinta Enendu & Canice Nwosu (Eds.)
Metaphors and Climax, Reminiscences on the Drama and
Theatre of Ogonna Agu
London, Adonis & Abbey Publishers

Laziness in any way is completely discouraged in Igbo communities. It is usually seen as leprosy which is infectious and must therefore be avoided. Ogonna Agu succinctly recreates this tradition in his *Cry of a Maiden*. Anene is seen in the play as symbolic of every hardworking Igbo man who never allowed anything to derail his sense of commitment to duty:

OKPALA: Anene works hard. At thirty he has tethered another sheep (9).

AWILI: Already he's built a zinc house in his father's obi. Next year, he tells me, he will buy a bicycle. (14)

A man of this quality is usually the target of every maiden in the community. Every parent aspires to have him as a son in-law. Okolo and Chidum, through the following dialogue confirm this view:

OKOLO: I like Okafo and gave him Ekemma our sister. Like his father. I discovered he's hard working. Has already extended his father's barns to accommodate another three-two hundred yams . . .

CHIDUM: The family is stable, what's more, of a noble birth.

OKOLO: God forbid my sister going where she will ever suffer in life . . . (7)

Language is also another aspect of Igbo culture which Ogonna Agu gives adequate representation in *Cry of a Maiden*. Umukoro asserts that among ". . . all the aspects of culture that we have, speech or language is the most articulate index of cultural identification and the most profound element of social unification" (26). The Igbo spoken language is not isolated from the culture of the people because it finds meanings in their daily lives. Wardhaugh explains that "the culture of a people finds reflection in the language they employ: because they value certain things and do them in a certain way, they come to use their language in

Chapter nine | *Emeka Ofora, in*
Charles Nwadigwe, Molinta Enendu & Canice Nwosu (Eds.)
Metaphors and Climax, Reminiscences on the Drama and
Theatre of Ogonna Agu
London, Adonis & Abbey Publishers

ways that reflect what they value and what they do" (qtd. in Weje 164).

The misunderstanding which breaks out between Okolo and Chidum in the play is usually found in the daily saying of the people that "Ofu nne na-amu, ofu chi anaghi eke " which translates to mean: "born of one parents; forged by different creative powers". This originates the belief by the Igbo that every man has his personal god (*chi*) which helps him to realize his life destiny. However, being that Okolo and Chidum have different creative powers, they are bound to pursue divergent goals and aspirations. This same supernatural belief also extends and finds meanings in the daily songs of the people:

> Adakego n'obodo
> Ayi!
> Adakego n'Obodo
> Ayi!
> Okwa mu na gi geme nwanne Ma Chukwu kwe
> Ayi!.
> Ma Chukwu ekweghi,
> Odiba n'uwa ozo kwa
> Ayi!

Meaning: "Adakego in town, yes! You and I shall be friends by Gods grace. If not in this world, in the next". Ogonna Agu in this context underscores the Igbo belief in life after death.

Among the Igbo, physical death does not end the existence of a human being as a member of the society. Therefore, every individual regulates his conduct to conform with the moral standard of the society since it is believed that "The onye metara n'uwa ka eji ala mmuo" (whatever one sows in this world, the same is what he will reap in the world to come). Other language codes which are exploited in the play include adage, idioms and proverbs. For instance: "when the right hand of a deity falls to the

Chapter nine	*Emeka Ofora, in*
	Charles Nwadigwe, Molinta Enendu & Canice Nwosu (Eds.)
	Metaphors and Climax, Reminiscences on the Drama and
	Theatre of Ogonna Agu
	London, Adonis & Abbey Publishers

ground, then tragedy has befallen the entire household (iv); "A vulture's head does not make lather with soap" (32).

Culture and Conflict Resolution in *Cry of a Maiden*

Ogonna Agu's philosophy as reflected in this play suggests that there are reliable qualities in Igbo tradition and culture than they are in militancy and militia which can be tapped to contend with and mediate among the conflicting members of the society. In buttressing this, Onigu Otite maintains that "the Africans do not need a judge of western type before justice can be dispensed" (12). The nature of African traditional system which permits an individual sin or offence to contaminate the entire society encourages collective efforts of members of the community to intervene in individual or group conflict which as envisaged, may disrupt the peaceful life of the people. Such intervention is made through the representatives of the community, usually the elders, who ensures that the conflicting members of the community are reconciled so that peace and order will be maintained in the community. According to Kopytoff, these elders are regarded as ancestors by the people. Because having lived long and encountered a lot of experiences, the elders become endowed with the wisdom of the ancestors with which they administered justice and fair play (Olaoba 33).

Ogonna Agu applied this principle in resolving the conflict between Okolo and Chidum in *Cry of a Maiden*. Udoka, Okolo's maternal uncle becomes enraged at the crisis that is engulfing his sister's sons and becomes determined to see peace returned to that family. He insists: "I refuse [your kola] not till you tell me, what has been boiling in this compound (39). The timely intervention and mediation of these elders (Udoka and Okpala) is intended to purge away the evil which begins to encroach into the family. The elders whose wisdom in this context must be contested begin with

Chapter nine | *Emeka Ofora, in*
Charles Nwadigwe, Molinta Enendu & Canice Nwosu (Eds.)
Metaphors and Climax, Reminiscences on the Drama and
Theatre of Ogonna Agu
London, Adonis & Abbey Publishers

questioning Okolo to determine his readiness for settlement "Now are you ready to make peace and break this pot of evil?" Okolo who has no option than to accept, further reveals his efforts so far to ensure that Chidum is searched for and brought home: "He [Chidum] broke fence three months ago. Till now he hasn't returned. But I have sent some armed men to look for him and force him back home" (39).

As Chidum is forced home by a group of young men, the elders re-unite them by allowing them make solemn promise:

UDOKA:	Swear to me-both of you-that henceforth, you will not fight again.
OKOLO:	I swear
CHIDUM:	I swear
UDOKA:	Bear witness . . . spirits of our fathers! Earth and sky bear witness. . . (4)

After giving them a pot of concoction to drink from, Udoka requests for kolanut to seal the oath. The oath-taking and the communion eating of kolanuts by Okolo and Chidum mark the high point of the reconciliation. It binds with strong force the oath each has made. In Igbo traditional society, the violation of such oath is usually punished with ignoble death such as swollen stomach.

Conclusion

In the various themes highlighted by Ogonna Agu in *Cry of a Maiden* the issue of cultural resonance takes a central position. This is hinged on the importance of adopting the traditional heritage of a people in resolving conflicts among them. In this play, the writer seems to be calling for a rethink and change of attitude. While condemning indirectly the recent developments in most African countries where militancy, militia and suicide bombing have become options for registering grievances, the dramatist suggests

Chapter nine | *Emeka Ofora, in*
Charles Nwadigwe, Molinta Enendu & Canice Nwosu (Eds.)
Metaphors and Climax, Reminiscences on the Drama and Theatre of Ogonna Agu
London, Adonis & Abbey Publishers

the use of the peaceful traditional arbitration and dispute resolution methods as veritable means to contend with crisis situations in the society.

Ogonna exposes clearly the normal family feud, the type that creates deep disharmony and breeds dangerous enmity between brothers and kinsmen as depicted in Okolo and Chidum's case. The ugly effect of this is that it can create opportunity for other members of the community to begin to get involved in the crisis and thereby help to escalate it as Awili tried to do in *Cry of a Maiden*. Once this happens, the traditional laws and order stand to be violated and disrespected, a situation that can attract the anger of the gods and ancestors against the entire society. Ogonna Agu seems to be calling the society to order. While condemning the attitude of using war and extra-judicial process to pursue one's demands and grievances, the writer encourages the peaceful traditional systematic method as a veritable means to mediate between warring individuals, or groups in order to restore normalcy in the society.

Works Cited

Adewoye, O. *The Judicial System in Southern Nigeria*. London: Longman Group Ltd. 1977.

Anaagudo-Agu, Ogonna. *Cry of a Maiden* Calabar: Wusen Press. 2000.

Brockett Oscar, G. & Ball, Robert, J. *The Essential Theatre*. 8th Edition. New York: Wadsworth, 2004.

Ibrahim, Binta.F. "Oral Traditional Performance and its Implication for Nigerian Literature in English."*Nigerian Literature in English: Emerging Critical Perspectives*. Ed.

Chapter nine | *Emeka Ofora, in*
Charles Nwadigwe, Molinta Enendu & Canice Nwosu (Eds.)
Metaphors and Climax, Reminiscences on the Drama and
Theatre of Ogonna Agu
London, Adonis & Abbey Publishers

Onyemaechi Udumukwu. Port Harcourt: M & J Grand Orbit Communication Ltd. 2007. 340-357.

Nnolim, Charles. *Approaches to the African Novel: Essays in Analysis.* 3rd Edition. Port Harcourt: Malthouse Press Limited. 2010.

Olaoba, O. B. *An Introduction to African Legal Culture.* Ibadan: Hope Publications, 2002.

Otite, Onigu. *Ethnic Pluralism, Ethnicity and Ethnic Conflicts in Nigeria.* Ibadan: Shaneson Publishers. 2000.

Oyedepo, E. I. "Women in Culture and Democracy: Conservative and Progressive Opinions." *Nigerian Women and the Challenges of Our Time.* Eds. Dora O. Chizea and Juliet Njoku. Lagos: Malthouse Press Ltd. 1991. 21-25.

Udenta O. Udenta. *Revolutionary Aesthetics and the African Literary Process.* Enugu: Fourth Dimension Publishing Co. Ltd. 1993.

Umukoro Matthew. *The Performing Arts in Academia and Other Essays on Drama, Theatre and Media Arts,* Ibadan: Evans Brothers (Nigeria Publishers) Limited. 2010.

Weje Annette. "Language and Gender: A reflection of Ikwerre Culture in Amadi's *The Concubine.*" *Critical Perspectives on Elechi Amadi.* Ed. Seiyifa Koroye. Port Harcourt: Pearl Publishers. 2008. 164-169.

Chapter nine | *Emeka Ofora, in*
Charles Nwadigwe, Molinta Enendu & Canice Nwosu (Eds.)
Metaphors and Climax, Reminiscences on the Drama and Theatre of Ogonna Agu
London, Adonis & Abbey Publishers

Chapter Ten

Of Dreams and Wakefulness: Re-Reading Reality and Illusions in Ogonna Agu's *Symbol of a Goddess*

Tochukwu Okeke

Introduction

Dreams and wakefulness are direct opposites. Where dreams can be said to be mere illusions, as they occur in sleep, wakefulness presupposes reality. In other words, events that occur in dreams are seldom tangible or coherent though some people who claim to interpret dreams would want others believe that events in dreams are often what exist in the human subconscious mind in times of wakefulness. Some dreams are known to come in opposites and some in metaphors. An example is the biblical account of Pharaoh's dream where seven fat cows represented seven years of plenty and abundance of food and seven thin cows represented seven years of famine (Gen 41: 51-2). On the other hand, wakefulness is consciousness; events that occur in this period are those that happen in real life and in real time. Dreams are purely personal. A person can be held accountable for events that happen in his period of wakefulness but no one can actually be held liable for the events he recounts as having taken place in a dream. Making a distinction between dream and reality Jacob Agaku posits that:

> Reality consists of the natural living and the ability to see it thus, in its most naked or unrefined form. This entails spontaneity, barrenness, vulgarity and the ability to see and present things the way they are, and not how they ought to be. . . The dream world actually has no subjection to moral, cultural or religious ethics. Therefore it flows free without inhibition or censorship. (73)

Chapter ten | *Tochukwu Okeke, in*
Charles Nwadigwe, Molinta Enendu & Canice Nwosu (Eds.)
Metaphors and Climax, Reminiscences on the Drama and Theatre of Ogonna Agu
London, Adonis & Abbey Publishers

The above assertion buttresses the Encarta dictionary definition of dream as "a sequence of images that appear involuntarily to the mind of somebody who is sleeping, often a mixture of real and imaginary characters, places and events" (np). However, it is a fact that certain dreams affect reality as with the biblical example of Joseph, Pharaoh and the cows. Since dreams affect reality, playwrights have used drama to put forward their dreams and visions about their society.

Drama, according to Emma Uzoji, is a 'medium of artistic expression where all aspects of human experience are mirrored in a dynamic form" (49). This goes to prove that "dramatists, like other serious artists, are involved in tackling the problems inherent in their society" (Nwabueze 163). Hence, what a playwright presents in his play is essentially a personal vision of his society since dramatists as artists are believed to possess "deep and studied insight into human nature and the affairs of man, coupled with an acute sensibility" (Umukoro 23). Even in instances where the playwright draws his artistic source materials from actual events in a society's history, he can exercise his artistic license by recreating the event(s) to suit his artistic vision. Nevertheless, he makes decisions about handling certain factual details and ensures that he manipulates the events skillfully without losing the original story. Thus, Echebiri argues that:

> The central consideration of an African writer who expresses historical event in his work should be the message he intends to convey and not the accuracy of his fact. This implies that the writer can freely alter or distort or manipulate historical facts to suit his dramatic purpose. (qtd. in Nweke 12-13).

It follows therefore, that vision or dream-where dream is something hoped for or something that could exist or happen in real life-is a central source of artistic creation. This is an integral ingredient of what is regarded as creative imagination. The

Chapter ten | *Tochukwu Okeke, in*
Charles Nwadigwe, Molinta Enendu & Canice Nwosu (Eds.)
Metaphors and Climax, Reminiscences on the Drama and Theatre of Ogonna Agu
London, Adonis & Abbey Publishers

playwright thus creates characters and situations out of this dream, a fictitious world of characters that would ultimately represent his social reality. These characters and situations in turn become a microcosm through which the artist (playwright), as an individual, addresses society because, as Umukoro explains, "the ultimate goal of art is social communication which presupposes a message and an audience" (23). Consequently, within a dramatic work are encoded messages which society decodes either through the reading of the work as a play text or watching its dramatization in a theatre.

The messages encoded in plays always reflect the artist's vision and level of commitment towards the good of the society. This commitment is anchored on the fact that the ultimate concern of a playwright is to admonish society of her past mistakes and navigate ways of avoiding the pitfalls of the past in order to achieve a truly humane society in their present and future existence. Hence, the welfare of the society albeit through a projection into the future or a recreation of past events is the paramount objective of devoted dramatists. This therefore projects the playwright as a committed artist; one who uses his creation as a means of "advancing certain ideas for the liberation of society. . ." (Nwabueze 44). Using Ogonna Agu's *Symbol of a Goddess*, this chapter interrogates the use of dreams in advancing certain ideas that could help in the liberation of societies that have experienced wars and civil strife.

Symbol of a Goddess: A Brief Synopsis

Symbol of a Goddess tells the story of Emenike, a veteran of the Nigerian Civil War who fought on the Biafran side, and his attempt at adapting to the new Nigeria after the fall of Biafra. He is portrayed as being too patriotic to the Biafran cause that he fails to come to terms with the obvious fact that the quest for Biafra has

Chapter ten | *Tochukwu Okeke, in*
Charles Nwadigwe, Molinta Enendu & Canice Nwosu (Eds.)
Metaphors and Climax, Reminiscences on the Drama and Theatre of Ogonna Agu
London, Adonis & Abbey Publishers

been lost and that what is left is to readjust to the reality of a war that has been fought and lost. Emenike pits himself against society, defying tradition by wearing the *Ozo* anklet even when he is not married and has not taken the *Ozo* title. As the play progresses, we see Emenike refusing to be reintegrated into the post-civil war Nigeria. He sees some traditional institutions like marriage as a hindrance not minding the fact that he fell to the seductions of Akudiri, his supposed wife. Emenike finds pleasure in the surreal world of dreams and the illusions of an eventual manifestation of Biafra which he sees in the woman of deep waters and represents in his creation of the magnificent masquerade, *Egbe Eyi Ugo*. In the end, he is overwhelmed by his inability to adapt to contemporary realities and the pressure from his family and community.

Dream and Wakefulness in *Symbol of a Goddess*

Every playwright is committed towards the enlightenment of his society and thus pricks the conscience of the people through his works. In each play, the playwright sets out to tackle a problem which directly affects his immediate environment. Such problems could be political, religious, cultural, social or psychological; in some instances, a play may deal with most if not all of these problems in various dimensions. Plays like Wole Soyinka's *The Road*, Femi Osofisan's *Arigindin and the Night Watchmen*, Emeka Nwabueze's *Guardian of the Cosmos*, Charles Nwadigwe's *Udoji* among others fall into this category. Such plays present us with the complexities of life such that "when we watch a tragedy, we gain insight into the motivations and sufferings of a man of flesh and blood whose insightful experiences are portrayed before us" (Nwabueze 163).

Symbol of a Goddess presents such a situation where the reader is given an insight into the psychological problem of socio-economic integration and cultural adaptation of "a man of flesh

Chapter ten | *Tochukwu Okeke, in*
Charles Nwadigwe, Molinta Enendu & Canice Nwosu (Eds.)
Metaphors and Climax, Reminiscences on the Drama and Theatre of Ogonna Agu
London, Adonis & Abbey Publishers

182

and blood" in a society emerging out of a Civil War. Though written less than a decade ago, the play is set in the early 1970s. The location is Biafra, the present day southeastern Nigeria. This is evident in the names of the characters, their costumes, properties and setting as well as the songs used to buttress the theme of the play. As the play opens, we behold the Narrator who is regaled in the full chieftaincy outfit of the southeasterners of Nigeria (jumper, red cap to which is stuck two eagle feathers). This narrator sets the audience on an empathic journey through the play:

> NARRATOR: It is by streak of chance that man is born to carry his cross in this great wide world, more so, if he is a man of destiny. Here we stand, I see desolation, grief, anguish among the children of men. At least, that is what the civil war has brought. Gloom and hatred on the faces of men. (6)

The play is about war and the after effect of war on the individual in particular and the society at large. Emenike, the hero of the play, has adamantly refused to end the war. To him, the war has extended beyond the battle between two warring nations to include the devastations caused by the war; the economic downturn of the society; the neglect of the government on the supposed losers of the war not minding the fact that it was said that there was "no victor; no vanquished"; and the psychological trauma of those that witnessed the war. Thus, Emenike brings the war home after surviving the "twilight battle at Abagana" (7). Every person becomes a perceived enemy as he has failed to rise from the illusions of his dream nation, Biafra. He refuses to lay down his arms and settle into a normal life:

> IGBONEKWU: No, no, no, Emenike keep that gun... don't shoot please, don't shoot. The war has ended.
> EMENIKE: (*shouts*) It has not ended!
> IGBONEKWU: You have not come here to continue the war?
> EMENIKE: I say it has not ended! We'll continue to fight! (12)

Chapter ten | *Tochukwu Okeke, in*
Charles Nwadigwe, Molinta Enendu & Canice Nwosu (Eds.)
Metaphors and Climax, Reminiscences on the Drama and Theatre of Ogonna Agu
London, Adonis & Abbey Publishers

Emenike feels cheated; his vision of a new world (if Biafra had succeeded), has in reality eluded him. The war had raised his hopes of a very bright future in the new nation. He risked his life, forfeited all pleasures and put in thirty months of his youthful energy and vision towards the realization of a new nation state. But in the end, that dream turned into a nightmare. He finds himself faced with the harsh realities of the devastations of war; of children becoming orphans; of women becoming widows and the men losing their wives to Nigerian soldiers; of children with acute malnutrition (*kwashiokor*); of education terminated; of job opportunities lost and properties forfeited; of genocide and war crimes committed but ignored by the international community. However, rather than settling down into this obvious reality and try to pick up the pieces of his life as common in war-torn communities, Emenike resorts to illusions and a false life:

ILUKA: Tell me, tell me what we shall tell her. That Emenike is not man enough to cater for her daughter.
EMENIKE: As you wish...
ILUKA: I thought you had always wanted to live like a soldier?
EMENIKE: How does . . .
ILUKA: You should accept everything you have done, on your honour.
EMENIKE: Telling me!
ILUKA: You are afraid you would lose your darling Biafra... woman with the red eyes... you fought till the plumes on her body pulled and scattered in the fields. But you never thought of the child... what it might mean to you... your own very blood! (52)

Emenike represents the vast majority of Igbo youths who lost their identity in the thirty-month Civil War. These were men in the prime of their youth, cajoled or compelled into the war on the philosophy of an independent nation with unlimited opportunities for the economic, social, educational and psychological

Chapter ten | *Tochukwu Okeke, in*
Charles Nwadigwe, Molinta Enendu & Canice Nwosu (Eds.)
Metaphors and Climax, Reminiscences on the Drama and Theatre of Ogonna Agu
London, Adonis & Abbey Publishers

development of the individual. As presented in the play, Emenike must have been an enterprising youth; industrious and creative, hence the reason why the effects of the war were too hard for him to bear. This is also seen in the fact that he commands respect among the youths and is able to channel his energy, amidst the skepticisms of his kinsmen into creating one of traditions age long icon, a masquerade, *Egbe Eyi Ugo*:

IGBONEKWU: Elders of our land, I am not in support of any one, but you have seen for yourselves. Emenike is like a ram-headed one with crooked horns... he retreats before he strikes. Biafra is alive in him. Who am I to impose a woman on him. Sometimes, I regret that action. The other issue to consider is how he has put his intellectual and emotional strength into great use. At first he came with guns. Now the guns are gone, and he is stirring the whole village with scenes of a magnificent masquerade. What a way to engage his mind, and pull it from destructive tendencies. I myself have become his convert. He is asking other converts to come and join in relieving an experience... the experience of a nation in turmoil... (64)

Emenike retreats into the dream world where he creates fantasies of a perfect society with the most beautiful wife and a serene life filled with music and feasting. This is evident in the dialogue between him and Okobe, the traditional priest, when Emenike in his euphoria, requested for the anklet, the insignia of *Ozo* title; the highest title taken by men in Igbo land:

OKOBE: Emenike, you have not married. Wait, when you-
EMENIKE: Why should I marry?
OKOBE: Aah! You are *akomogeri* then?...
EMENIKE: (laughs). Is that what they say of Emenike? Nonsense! What do they know of Emenike? Do they know that I keep a date?
OKOBE: With who?
EMENIKE: *Agbogho oke ego*

Chapter ten | *Tochukwu Okeke, in*
Charles Nwadigwe, Molinta Enendu & Canice Nwosu (Eds.)
Metaphors and Climax, Reminiscences on the Drama and Theatre of Ogonna Agu
London, Adonis & Abbey Publishers

OKOBE:	Who? Who, Emenike?
EMENIKE:	The lady of the red eyes... I go to see her every day. I call her on the drums... but, she is lost, lost in the clouds... A lost dream (*laughter*).... I will invoke her again, I will sing to her always, chant her poetry to her, my song will give her body... she will come back to me, divine goddess incarnate.
OKOBE:	Aha! I get you now. You don't want Biafra to die? This is dangerous you know.
EMENIKE:	I live for her and she for me. (18)

We have cited this passage extensively in order to show the magnitude of the psychological trauma an average person undergoes as a result of war. The playwright has thus shown how brave men can lose touch with reality and descend into the psychic world of dreams and delusion as a consequence of war. In *Symbol of a Goddess*, the psychological effect of war is made evident as Emenike is presented as a renegade:

IGBONEKWU:	Commander, Commander-the young man is angry.
COMMANDER:	Angry?
IGBONEKWU:	With everybody. From the white man to Gowon. Whiteman bring church. Emenike no wan' go. Gowon bring one Nigeria, Emenike no want hear. (16)

Here, the play has advanced a case for the conflict and confusion that arise out of a new order especially if that new order comes at the wake of a war. Though Emenike is used as a symbol of that confusion, it is a fact that his actions were necessitated by the environment. Emenike can therefore be said to be the embodiment of tradition if he would hate the white man for bringing 'church', a symbol of Western civilization that in actual fact chattered the course of life of the colonized people of southeastern Nigeria. This fact has earlier been given a voice by Chinua Achebe through the character of Obierika in his *Things Fall Apart* thus:

Chapter ten | *Tochukwu Okeke, in*
Charles Nwadigwe, Molinta Enendu & Canice Nwosu (Eds.)
Metaphors and Climax, Reminiscences on the Drama and Theatre of Ogonna Agu
London, Adonis & Abbey Publishers

The white man is very clever; he came quietly and peaceably with his religion. We were amused at his foolishness and allowed him to stay. Now he has won our brothers and our clan can no longer act as one. He has put a knife on the thing that held us together and we have fallen apart. (124-5)

It follows therefore that Emenike's problems like those of war stricken individuals in the society arose out of circumstances they could not control and Ogonna Agu has succeeded in his dramatization of this conflict because as Ngugi wa Thiong'o observes, "drama encapsulates within itself the principle of opposites which generates movement. There is in drama a movement from apparent harmony, a kind of rest, through conflict to a comic or tragic resolution of that conflict..." (54). The opposites in *Symbol of a Goddess* is between the vague state of Emenike's dream of something he sincerely longs for though difficult to attain (as seen in his desire for Biafra and the maiden of the deep waters) and the real state of something that has concrete existence and must be confronted in full consciousness (like the marriage to Akudiri and getting a job). This is exemplified in the fact that at his moments of wakefulness when he is able to come to terms with reality, Emenike showed love and care to a woman betrothed for him by his mother:

EMENIKE:	Let me see your face (*lifts her face*).
AKUDIRI:	My fear is gone.
EMENIKE:	Let me see your legs.
AKUDIRI:	The same old legs (*pause as he admires her*) But when the moon rises you prey on my lust... (41).

However, in his moments of dream; in his flight from reality, he relives moments that are far removed from present circumstances:

EMENIKE:	Wait, what am I doing? (*starts to moan*). Iluka! Iluka! You have killed me. Who is this girl that you brought to sleep

Chapter ten | *Tochukwu Okeke, in*
Charles Nwadigwe, Molinta Enendu & Canice Nwosu (Eds.)
Metaphors and Climax, Reminiscences on the Drama and Theatre of Ogonna Agu
London, Adonis & Abbey Publishers

> with me in this house. Who told you that she is my wife?
> Let me tell you, when my goddess rises from the river,
> the waves will escort her... the clouds hold the rain...
> when she comes there will be light on the river bed. (44)

So, all through the play Emenike consciously or unconsciously realizes and also doubts his identity, he continually battles with this intrapersonal conflict, a surrealistic struggle between dream and reality.

> EMENIKE: She's my legitimate wife... what are you telling me! You are not my wife, not even my mistress... my mother is only using you to fight her... but wait for her, wait till I rise from my sleep, carrying a load of sacrifice to the water's edge... (45)

Emenike can therefore be said to be remotely aware of the realities around him but because of the conflict of opposing forces seeking to be made manifest through him, he could not face reality squarely. Through this the playwright made a bold statement about the lasting nature of the traumatic effect of war on the psychology of the individual and the collective psyche of the society. Thus Emenike laments his loss:

> EMENIKE: The right hand of my deity has fallen . . . Here I will sit and weep for my darling goddess-my beloved country lost in the clouds. The pain of loss... my anguish in the battle front . . . blood in my eyes... but I'll keep calling her on this drum till she hears me and comes . . . (56-7)

Thus, Emenike, like most victims of society, is aware of certain realities but becomes a victim of fate because of the cosmic forces beyond his control.

Ogonna Agu in *Symbol of a Goddess* has tried to re-establish tradition as a potent force against the maladies of modernity through the actions of Iluka, Emenike's mother, who has tried to

Chapter ten | *Tochukwu Okeke, in*
Charles Nwadigwe, Molinta Enendu & Canice Nwosu (Eds.)
Metaphors and Climax, Reminiscences on the Drama and Theatre of Ogonna Agu
London, Adonis & Abbey Publishers

use the marriage institution as a silent force to bring Emenike down to reality:

> ILUKA: You know Emenike has ... Agwu in his head. Force, that's what he wants!

As Iluka rejects brutal force as seen in the characters of Ide and Commander, she adopts a subtle but potent coercive force which she finds in Akudiri. Yet, in spite of all these tactics to rehabilitate Emenike from the effects of war, he seems too far gone in an idle hope that the seeming realities of his dream world will materialize someday. He pursues this hope to the extent that even when he seem to be winning the case brought against him by his kinsman, Ide, as a vagrant and jobless man, the lure of the dream poses a greater force:

> EMENIKE: Emenike has come again! Fire that burns the forest! That's what they call me. He said I was not married, now he has admitted that I am married to the daughter of the sea. What is wrong with that? Very soon they will be calling me! Very soon I will carry my sacrifice to the river, and invoke her, and sing for her... very soon she will be here my darling woman of the sea... I'm hearing you! I am *Egbeyiugo*- the eagle stronger than the kite! When I see you, my world is filled with wonder. All the people come to see you. All the market stalls are shut... you become *obialu ka ahia mma* . . . dancing mask that compels attention . . . bystanders stand and mope... *enenebe eje olu* . . . workers go on holidays to behold you! (*Drums repeat, Emenike dances a few dignified steps, jumps up*) Off I go to behold the queen of the depths . . . lady of red eyes . . . mother of nation . . . egret lost in the clouds . . . (63-4)

It is this unrealizable dream that consumed Emenike. Torn between reality and dreams, he fell for the "safer" world of illusion and fantasy thereby making it obvious that war, in whatever form,

Chapter ten | *Tochukwu Okeke, in*
Charles Nwadigwe, Molinta Enendu & Canice Nwosu (Eds.)
Metaphors and Climax, Reminiscences on the Drama and Theatre of Ogonna Agu
London, Adonis & Abbey Publishers

has more negative than positive (if any) impact on humanity and society.

Conclusion

A playwright is considered the conscience of the society and plays are avenues through which the subconscious and conscious thoughts of the artist are expressed. Through the artistic work of the playwright, individuals are called to question on the happenings in society. From the resolution of conflicts in the play, the consequences of the dramatic action that have direct bearing on real life existence are brought to the society's consciousness. This study has attempted an analysis of Ogonna Agu's *Symbol of a Goddess* as a journey between dreams and realities with the aim of bringing out the psychology of socio-economic integration in a society that has experienced a war and armed conflict.

Ogonna Agu, in *Symbol of a Goddess*, has presented us with a type of drama where, as Nwabueze puts it, "the issue revolves around domestic problems and the effect of society on those problems". This is the type of plot wherein most of the characters are victims of society and its institutions. In this type of "bourgeois drama", the hero does not fight "their conditions like the heroes of classical tragedy", instead they "succumb to their fate whimpering in resignation and self-pity" (Nwabueze 178–179). Emenike is an example of such characters because as he is unable to adapt to the "new" Nigeria after the fall of Biafra, he becomes disillusioned into some societal ills like arrogance, violence and vagrancy.

The playwright has tried to present a realistic picture of an Igbo community in the 1970s after the Civil War with its attendant confusion and unease. Being himself a veteran of the said war and like most Igbo youths at that time led into the war with grandiose dreams of an ordered Biafran nation, but disillusioned at the fall of Biafra, the playwright must have crafted the drama out of history

Chapter ten | *Tochukwu Okeke, in*
Charles Nwadigwe, Molinta Enendu & Canice Nwosu (Eds.)
Metaphors and Climax, Reminiscences on the Drama and Theatre of Ogonna Agu
London, Adonis & Abbey Publishers

and personal experience. It can therefore be said that, though the characters are fictitious, they may remotely pose some realities to some individuals who have experienced war and armed conflict.

In Emenike, the playwright has combined the forces of arrogance, psychology and euphoria as the hero's Achilles' heel. These were the factors that led to his fall despite his ingenuity at recreating tradition and redirecting his energies towards productive vision as exemplified in the appearance of the magnificent masquerade, *Egbe Eyi Ugo*. The masquerade institution itself, one of the most cherished traditions of the Igbo, appears to have been eclipsed by the Civil War and modernity; hence Emenike's newfound vision seemed to have had minimal impact on his people.

In *Symbol of a Goddess* therefore, Agu can be said to have made a clear statement on the distinction between illusions of dreams and realities of wakefulness through a clear presentation of the events that happen in real life and the occurrences in dream which are simply ideas in the mind of an individual that are seldom realizable.

Works Cited

Achebe, Chinua. *Things Fall Apart*. Ibadan: Heinemann, 2002.

Agaku, Jacob. M. "Reality and Realism of Poverty in Nigeria: A Cultural Reading of MDG 1 Towards a Transformative Development." *Nigerian Theatre Journal*. 10:1 (2010): 73-82.

Anaagudo-Agu, Ogonna. *Symbol of a Goddess*. Calabar: Wusen Publishers. 2005.

Encarta Dictionary.www.encarta.brothersoft.com/encartadictionar y.html. Accessed 02/10/2012

Chapter ten | *Tochukwu Okeke, in*
Charles Nwadigwe, Molinta Enendu & Canice Nwosu (Eds.)
Metaphors and Climax, Reminiscences on the Drama and Theatre of Ogonna Agu
London, Adonis & Abbey Publishers

Good News Bible with Deuterocanonicals/Apocrypha. New York: American Bible Society. 1993.

Nwabueze, Emeka. *Visions and Re-Visions: Selected Discourses on Literary Criticism.* 2nd Edition. Enugu. Abic Books. 2011.

Nweke, Damian. "The Playwright as a Re-creator of History: A Study of Ola Rotimi's *Hopes of the Living Dead* and Canice Nwosu's *Hopes of the Living.*" B. A. Long Essay Submitted to the Theatre Arts Department, Nnamdi Azikiwe University, Awka. August, 2012.

Umukoro, Matthew, M. *The Performing Arts in Academia and Other Essays on Drama, Theatre and Media Arts.* Ibadan. Evans Brothers. 2010.

Uzoji, E. E., "The Prophetic Power of Drama: Nigeria's Elections and Soyinka's *Beatification of Area Boy*". *Nigerian Theatre Journal.* 11:1 (2011): 49-64.

Wa Thiong'o, Ngugi. *Decolonizing the Mind: The Politics of Language in African Literature.* Nairobi: Heinemann. 1988.

Chapter ten | *Tochukwu Okeke, in*
Charles Nwadigwe, Molinta Enendu & Canice Nwosu (Eds.)
Metaphors and Climax, Reminiscences on the Drama and Theatre of Ogonna Agu
London, Adonis & Abbey Publishers

Chapter Eleven

Symbolic Archetype and Family Conflict in Selected Plays of Ogonna Agu: *Cry of a Maiden* and *Symbol of a Goddess* as Paradigms

Chidiebere S. Ekweariri

Introduction

Playwriting is a complex art. In writing a play, the dramatist needs to make a number of critical decisions. Consequently, "the playwright must ultimately come to decisions about the overall meaning, social and political he wishes his plays to express and how best he could effectively convey it" (Euba 381). In the process of weaving the dramatic piece together and finding ways of conveying the message(s), some meanings are sometimes subsumed in ambiguity and symbolism which require the intellectual insights of the reader to demystify. Most times, things that stand for another are usually employed to communicate meaning. In African plays, the use of symbolic archetype and discussion of family conflicts run through. This is because they are everyday occurrence. *Symbol of a Goddess* and *Cry of a Maiden*, two modern African plays written by a traditionalist, Ogonna Anaagudo-Agu, fall into this category. Other creative works by the playwright include *Adiaha the Beauty Queen*, *The Strong Boy of the Forest* (novels); and *Hunt for Campus Guerrillas* (a play) and *Odu Okike* (poetry) among others. Therefore, the basic preoccupation of this chapter is to examine the representation of symbolic archetype and family conflict in *Symbol of a Goddess* and *Cry of a Maiden* and to explore how they have contributed in defining the social, political and cultural embellishments of the plays.

Chapter eleven | *Chidiebere S. Ekweariri, in*
Charles Nwadigwe, Molinta Enendu & Canice Nwosu (Eds.)
Metaphors and Climax, Reminiscences on the Drama and
Theatre of Ogonna Agu
London, Adonis & Abbey Publishers

Clarification of Concepts

Symbolism and archetype share basic similarities and when they are used together, they tend to further accentuate their collaborative functions. However, for the purposes of this study, they shall be independently defined and later fused together in order to create a suitable analytical balance. A symbol therefore is a sign "which acts as substitute for some other sign with which it is synonymous ... all signs and symbols are signal" (Lyons 344). However, it is not necessary that the sign must be synonymous with the symbol represented as implied above. This is because a sign may mean a different thing or different things other than that which it is associated with depending on the perception of the person involved and the context in which the object appeared. In a similar vein, Ohiri affirms the veracity of the above statement when he writes that "a symbol is a token of meaning; that is, it is one thing that stands for something else" (382).

On the other hand, an archetype is equally a symbol but with deeper meaning. It is a universally understood symbol, term or pattern of behaviour, a prototype upon which others are copied, patterned, or emulated. Archetypes are often used in myths and storytelling across different cultures. Archetypes can be found in nearly all forms of literature, with their motifs being predominantly rooted in folklore. According to the Wikipedia (online dictionary), "even in the Noh plays of Japan, the characters are skillfully depicted with exaggerated expressions and elaborate costumes to clearly portray a system of archetypes." Certain common methods of character depiction employed in dramatic performance rely on the pre-existence of literary archetypes. Stock characters used in theatre or film are based on highly generic literary archetypes. In this context therefore, symbolic archetype can be defined as a system of representation that not only captures

Chapter eleven | *Chidiebere S. Ekweariri, in*
Charles Nwadigwe, Molinta Enendu & Canice Nwosu (Eds.)
Metaphors and Climax, Reminiscences on the Drama and
Theatre cf Ogonna Agu
London, Adonis & Abbey Publishers

the underlying discernible and common meanings embedded in dramatic and literary works but also studies the patterns and behavioural traits of individual characters, either as a hero, comic character or villain with the view to having a deeper understanding and appreciation of the dramatic piece. Furthermore, conflict is a term associated with a state of disharmony between incompatible or antithetical persons, ideas or interest. In a dramatic piece, especially, in the context of the discussion, it could be seen as an opposition between characters or forces in a work of drama or fiction, especially opposition that motivates or shapes the action of the plot.

Symbolic Archetypes in the Plays

Symbolism is, unequivocally, a matter of representation. Its meaning is imbued in that which is represented. All through these selected plays of Agu, the use of symbols is quite discernible. As a matter of fact, the plays are enmeshed in symbolic archetypes which are masterfully created to arouse interest and communicate meaning. In the play, *Cry of a Maiden*, the pot has a lot of symbolic undertones which the playwright acknowledges. He expresses the view that all the actions in the play "centres on the image of the pot as symbol" (iii). The significance of this pot, in essence, lies in its symbolic undertones that not only captures the thematic preoccupation of the play but that which is also open to different interpretations. In the context of the play, the pot represents the precarious object which Chidum plays with to the chagrin of Okolo. Pots generally are fragile objects that need to be handled with care. As a delicate object, it has a belly-like structure, designed to house something that should be treasured. A woman's virginity could be likened to a pot in this context which Ada broke. To her, the pot ought to have belonged to Chidum, her preferred love; and even if it was to be broken by Okolo, it should not have

Chapter eleven | *Chidiebere S. Ekweariri, in*
Charles Nwadigwe, Molinta Enendu & Canice Nwosu (Eds.)
Metaphors and Climax, Reminiscences on the Drama and
Theatre of Ogonna Agu
London, Adonis & Abbey Publishers

been in the illicit manner in which it was done. This prompted her to cry because she has shamefully broken that which makes her a woman and the pride of her maidenhood. To buttress the symbolic relationship between the pot and a woman's womb or virginity in the play, Okolo has this to say to Ada:

> OKOLO: . . . you don't know how elated I feel sitting beside you like an important cockerel. Let me have your pot. (*He carries the pot from her and begins to cuddle it*). It is the fertile womb of earth where I raise my nursery. Together we shall cultivate the farm, shall try supply meaning unto our earth. (23)

In the following dialogue, Okolo further alludes to the fact that the pot is a symbolic representation of virginity while responding to the inciting remarks of Ebere the rhapsodist; thus:

> EBERE: This time I'm going home to my mother. Today and tomorrow I'll no more return to your country. No more return to your town. Not till the   damned lot of your crooks are dead and gone beneath my feet. Then I shall have all the women to myself alone.
>
> OKOLO: Pardon him, my people. He's a rhapsodist. Wouldn't mind breaking the pots of those virgins in the presence of their fathers.

(There is a general uproar from within and outside. Okolo looks around. Only a few hang about watch him intently, smiling)

> OKOLO: Lord! What's all this about? Where ... where is my calabash of wine ... my beloved calabash of wine. (43)

In this context, calabash of wine represents his jewel of inestimable value, Ada.

Generally, the symbol of a maiden is her virginity. It is her pride and becomes the centre of attraction whenever a maiden wants to get married. This explains why parents and maidens themselves lose their pride and respect whenever it is revealed

---

Chapter eleven | *Chidiebere S. Ekweariri, in*
Charles Nwadigwe, Molinta Enendu & Canice Nwosu (Eds.)
Metaphors and Climax, Reminiscences on the Drama and Theatre cf Ogonna Agu
London, Adonis & Abbey Publishers

that a maiden has broken her virginity before a calabash of wine is placed for her head. All these are manifest in the play.

Another symbolic archetype used in the play is the cottage or *Obi* in local parlance. In traditional Igbo society, it plays significant role, especially, as it pertains to the welcoming of visitors and the breaking and pouring of libation. According to the playwright:

> Firstly, [i.e. *Obi*] it is like a temple in every sense. There, the ancestral symbols of religious observances are kept. The altar of the ancestors is also arranged here. It is a cultural centre, a museum of antiquities, and a social meeting place all lumped into one. The point therefore is that a homestead without an *Obi* is a dead place, since it is the hub of activities of the household. The early morning kolanut invocation takes place here. The *Chi* shrine is located just outside the obi. The collapse of one's *Obi* under whatever circumstances portends danger for the family. It literally spells death for the head of the household. (iv)

From the foregoing, the place of *Obi* in the cultural and spiritual wellbeing of an average Igbo man in traditional African society cannot be underestimated given its place in every homestead. This became the centre of disagreement between Okolo and his younger brother, Chidum, when the latter hinted the idea to get married and sought the permission of his elder brother. This is captured in the following conversation:

CHIDUM: All I'm asking my brother in your presence is to let me get married now that I'm ready. For three years we fought in the jungle of Burma and Palestine war zones. Now I want to live a settled life with a wife to complete it.

OKPALA: At this point we'll seek his opinion again. Now Okolo, you are directly involved.

OKOLO: ... maybe ... Chidum can do as he pleases. But I must warn that a major task stares us in the face; the task of reconstructing this cottage. As you can see, the Obi building has gone into ruins. And the shrine house has collapsed, thereby exposing the sacred goddess to [bad] weather and inhospitable rains.

Chapter eleven | *Chidiebere S. Ekweariri, in*
Charles Nwadigwe, Molinta Enendu & Canice Nwosu (Eds.)
Metaphors and Climax, Reminiscences on the Drama and
Theatre of Ogonna Agu
London, Adonis & Abbey Publishers

OKPALA: But Chidum, your brother's decision is wise. It's shameful that till now, nothing has been done to secure those crumbling mud walls. This Obi is no longer the usual spot; an Obi in which numerous animal skulls hung to remind us of the valour of our ancestors. Now you want to expose those antiquities to be spoilt ... it makes me feel ashamed!

CHIDUM: Don't you worry, uncle. We'll rebuild our cottage first. (10)

This cottage or *Obi* is a symbolic means of communication between man and the gods, hence its venerated place in the homestead. This is usually inherited by the Diokpara (the first son), hence the desire by Okolo to have it repaired before anything else. Whether the request was born out of real desire or beclouded with ulterior motive and sentimentality in view of the drama that took place thereof is left for critics to decipher. However, the point remains that it was because of the symbolic meanings embedded in the *Obi* that necessitated Chidum's resolve to have it repaired before getting married.

Another symbolic archetype in the play is the use of the flute. A flute, to some Africans is an instrument of music. To others, it is imbued with respect and has other meanings embedded in it. Similar to the *Ikoro* (giant wooden drum), it sounds sparingly and when it does, it calls for attention. In that circumstance, an attention of the community is drawn to an unusual occurrence or calamity. Most times, it is either in celebration of an event or the death of a great warrior. This is exactly the case in the *Cry of a Maiden*. Here, the flute symbolizes death. This is captured in the following conversations between Okpala, and Awili:

(A distant flute is heard. Beneath its occasional soar the slow rhythm of a dirge-grave and slow. It increases in tempo as the players approach. Now and then cries of Huo! Huo! Huo! shoot out above the general noise)

OKPALA: Wait! A great man has died.

Chapter eleven | *Chidiebere S. Ekweariri, in*
Charles Nwadigwe, Molinta Enendu & Canice Nwosu (Eds.)
Metaphors and Climax, Reminiscences on the Drama and Theatre cf Ogonna Agu
London, Adonis & Abbey Publishers

AWILI: The wise men of Akilo are finishing.
OKPALA: Chidum, go and find out at once. (12)

Again, the use of marriage in the play has a symbolic relationship with responsibility, maturity and commitment. Chidum, an ex-serviceman is anxious to settle down after wasting three years fighting in the jungle and desert of Burma and Palestine. He feels his desired lifestyle will not be accomplished without a woman by his side. On the other hand, Okolo's refusal to marry makes him a laughing stock before his uncle, Okpala. He chastises him whenever the opportunity arises. For instance, Okpala had the following to say to Okolo on the subject:

OKOLO: Anene does fine job indeed.
OKPALA: He works hard. At thirty he has tethered another sheep.
OKOLO: You've often said it.
OKPALA: Not without a purpose. At your age you should have done more.
OKOLO: You once suggested it to me.
OKPALA: In private-yes, I did. And which is the point of this meeting. (9)

Okolo's only preoccupation is to drink and fool around with village rascals like Awili. On the other hand, Anene is respected not only because he works hard, but the fact that at his age, he has already married another wife, which makes him responsible and committed. Therefore, one hardly finds him fooling around in the community. He is always focused and committed towards fulfilling his responsibilities and providing for his family. When eventually Okolo decided to be responsible and committed (albeit in a very surreptitious manner) and Chidum tries to scuttle it, Okpala admonishes him thus:

OKPALA: Where is he! I saw him at the door post. When I suspected he was about to dodge, I left him. Can't understand what's come over him. Thinks he can scorn his brother's union-

Chapter eleven | *Chidiebere S. Ekweariri, in*
Charles Nwadigwe, Molinta Enendu & Canice Nwosu (Eds.)
Metaphors and Climax, Reminiscences on the Drama and
Theatre of Ogonna Agu
London, Adonis & Abbey Publishers

> scot free-and defying all authorities. Doesn't know that it is
> the strongest organization in the whole world. (32)

Furthermore, some of the characters in the play portray symbolic archetypes in their roles. Chidum for instance, is created to serve as a catalyst to the expected mental maturity and commitment of his elder brother, Okolo. His destiny had already been defined by the playwright who makes sure that he never fulfils his desire to marry Ada. Furthermore, his friend Awili, who does nothing else other than drinking and making troubles is symbolically the archetypal loafer. Similarly, Anene's role has symbolic archetypes embedded in it. He is portrayed as a hardworking man and an ideal son-in-law. Thus, he works assiduously towards fulfilling his masculine obligations. Anene is the archetypal parameter and reference point for evaluating other young men like Okolo and Awili.

In *Symbol of a Goddess*, the case is not different. As the name implies, everything about the play is a symbolic representation of the dream of Emenike to further propagate the dying image of Biafra. The water goddess, his ankle string and the bird, all symbolize his dreams and aspirations. This is reflected in the following dialogue:

EMENIKE:	You only know my mission.
OKOBE:	Right.
EMENIKE:	To keep our goddess alive
OKOBE:	So? What are you saying?
EMENIKE:	My ankle string – that's what am saying
OKOBE:	But you are not an Ozo.
EMENIKE:	It is only a symbol . . . (17)

Here, the ankle string is a symbolic link between his Biafran dream and the *Agbogho Oke Ego* (Water Goddess) as he calls her. To the villagers, the ankle string is worn only by *Ozo* title holders with

Chapter eleven	*Chidiebere S. Ekweariri, in*
	Charles Nwadigwe, Molinta Enendu & Canice Nwosu (Eds.)
	Metaphors and Climax, Reminiscences on the Drama and
	Theatre cf Ogonna Agu
	London, Adonis & Abbey Publishers

a wife to complement it. But to Emenike, the meaning is different. It symbolizes a psychological connection with an ideal force and condition. With the string, the spirit of Biafra lives not only physically but also in the mind. This dream is also replicated in the use of the bird in the play. This is explained in the following lines:

IGBONEKWU: At present, he is keeping a big bird
COMMANDER: I have heard that. What kind of bird?
IGBONEKWU: Is eagle, yes, eagle ... dat is de bird. The king of bird.
              He calls him Biafra.
COMMANDER: Biafra? Biafra is dead!
IGBONEKWU: Is his problem. He does not believe so. (14)

This is also substantiated by Emenike himself when he affirms that "he is looking for his lost queen in a distant country and strong like the eagle" (19). He therefore admonishes his mother when he learnt that his eagle had flown away saying:

EMENIKE: I was away-fighting for mother land. I begged you to take
            care of the bird. That bird was the nation we were fighting
            for. (45)

In this context, the bird becomes a symbolic archetype used to keep the dream alive. To him, even though Biafra is lost, it should not be forgotten. This is captured thus:

EMENIKE: I will invoke her again, I will sing to her always, chant
            poetry to her, my song will give her body . . . she will come
            back to me, divine goddess incarnate.
OKOBE: Aha! I get you now. You don't want Biafra to die? That is
            dangerous you know?
EMENIKE: I live for her and she for me. (18)

This has always been the nucleus around which his actions revolve; to perpetually keep the dream alive. Towards the end of the play, the people started deciphering the import of Emenike's actions and felt disheartened that they could not support him all

Chapter eleven | Chidiebere S. Ekweariri, in
Charles Nwadigwe, Molinta Enendu & Canice Nwosu (Eds.)
Metaphors and Climax, Reminiscences on the Drama and
Theatre of Ogonna Agu
London, Adonis & Abbey Publishers

along. This is echoed by Igbonekwu when he asserts that "he is asking other converts to come and join in relieving the experience . . . the experience of a nation in turmoil . . ." (64).

Biafra lives in Emenike. It is both his wife and existence. Hence, he refuses to marry in the real sense of the world or allow anybody marry for him. He is indeed married to Biafra and eventually dies for her. He didn't know he was fighting a lost battle and when his goddess did not fully emanate but rather remained elusive, he became, as Ngumoha says, "tormented by a frustrating feeling of abandonment and despondent lethargy" (91). Biafra, which was the basis for the symbols in the first place, finally becomes a lost dream for Emenike but he nevertheless chases that dream on different level of existence.

The representation of symbolic archetypes is quite clear in Agu's dramatic characters. Prominent amongst them is the role of Emenike, an unsung hero who died without realizing his Biafran dreams. His desire was to keep the dream alive through the use of masquerades and other representational objects. This symbolic archetype can also be found in the character of Akudiri, the betrothed wife to Emenike. She was the archetypal sacrificial lamb meant to entrap and tame Emenike and thus bring him to accept reality as perceived by his kinsmen. Akudiri was a symbol of patience and perseverance and meant to endure till the end otherwise she could not have married Emenike in the first instance. Emenike was not around when she came into the house and she spent one year of futile wait, without setting eyes on him. Even when Emenike came back, put Akudiri in a family way and abandoned her, she still claims that she loves him and is ready to stay on. These in essence show that all her actions and how she is to execute them have been planned and predetermined by the playwright.

Chapter eleven | *Chidiebere S. Ekweariri, in*
Charles Nwadigwe, Molinta Enendu & Canice Nwosu (Eds.)
Metaphors and Climax, Reminiscences on the Drama and
Theatre cf Ogonna Agu
London, Adonis & Abbey Publishers

Another striking thing about the two plays is the issue of family conflict. Conflict itself is necessary in every dramatic piece and according to Iji, "it is the main ingredients of dramas or plays, the main raw materials of theatre practice" (117). Theatre in this context connotes both the processes of writing a play and its enactment before a given audience. However, it has to be stated that conflict has different dimensions and types but the nature of conflict under investigation in this context is family conflict. It is true that siblings could be born of the same parents but individually have different perception about things. Okolo and Chidum's relationship in *Cry of a Maiden* is a typical case in point. They are brothers born of the same parents and although they have similar orientation, but their attitude towards life and societal responsibility are different. Similarly, they both share the urge and necessity to get married and repair their father's broken cottage (*Obi*). They also recognize the overriding authority of Okpala over them hence the need to invite him to mediate in their problem. However, the family conflict here comes as a result of betrayal, misplaced priority and personality disagreement. Chidum wanted a wife but was convinced into accepting to repair the broken cottage first. This he heeded but was later betrayed by his brother Okolo, who surreptitiously seduced his intended wife, Ada and put her in a family way. This is gleaned in the play thus:

> UDOKA: Here we are at last, Okpala. This boy ran to me with eyes full of tears. Okolo, where is Okolo? You had an understanding with this child. You did not keep it. You fought and forced him out of his father's compound . . . (40)

This broken promise added to the fact that Okolo also broke Chidum's calabash metamorphosed into a bitter quarrel which leads to fighting between them. Here, the concept of family conflict is predicated on the fact that the wish of Chidum was not granted,

Chapter eleven | Chidiebere S. Ekweariri, in
Charles Nwadigwe, Molinta Enendu & Canice Nwosu (Eds.)
Metaphors and Climax, Reminiscences on the Drama and Theatre of Ogonna Agu
London, Adonis & Abbey Publishers

and to aggravate issues, his intended wife was stolen from him by his own brother. This conflict is also heightened by the nefarious activities of Awili, who claims that he did what he did in order to protect Okolo and his love.

Throughout the play, the urgent need to resolve this family conflict contributes to the heightening of suspense in the play. Okpala's presence is to ward off any acrimony between the two brothers. Mgbochi's efforts are geared towards creating peace and tranquility in the family, especially, as her husband is no more alive. Udoka's spirited effort is also meant for peace. The following lines in the play substantiate this:

> UDOKA: I have not come to that. Now that he's back, swear to me - both of you-that hence forth, you'll not fight again.
> OKOLO: I swear
> CHIDUM: I swear
> UDOKA: Bear witness. O spirits of our fore fathers! Earth and sky bear witness...! (*He hands a pot of concoction to them and they drink in turns as a communion*) Now bring us kolanut to chew. (40)

In *Symbol of a Goddess*, the conflict arises out of Emenike's desire to pursue his dreams instead of settling down to a family life like his mates that returned from the war. He was frustrated after the war and he became agitated and restless. In such a dejected situation, the character involved seriously needed to "cushion the effect of an otherwise bitter experience . . . to mask truth from its bitter and naked self" (Asigbo and Ebo 62). Due to his abrasive behaviour and troublesome nature especially since he came back from the war, the family members decided to marry for him. The assumption is that it will curtail his excesses. But this action escalated the problem because Emenike refused to have anything to do with the girl, Akudiri. Although he had a brief romantic overtures with her that resulted in pregnancy, Emenike's

Chapter eleven | *Chidiebere S. Ekweariri, in*
Charles Nwadigwe, Molinta Enendu & Canice Nwosu (Eds.)
Metaphors and Climax, Reminiscences on the Drama and Theatre cf Ogonna Agu
London, Adonis & Abbey Publishers

vehemence that he has a wife and therefore not in need of Akudiri could not be accepted by his mother. She was overjoyed by the pregnancy believing that the purported spell on her son had been broken. A marriage between Emenike and the girl he impregnated was expected to take place naturally since the culture frowns at anything to the contrary. All efforts were then made to compel Emenike to marry her. This extended the family conflict to a community level. However, unlike Okolo who found himself in a similar situation with Ada in *Cry of a Maiden*, Emenike rejected Akudiri and her unborn baby. The family and community attempts to bend Emenike were futile and all efforts made by Akudiri to draw him to herself proved abortive.

Owing to the family conflict, in *Symbol of a Goddess*, enemies tried to infiltrate, which at a point made Igbonekwu to warn that "Emenike's case is our internal problem, not their problem. Any one of you who will cause Emenike to run away again, the whole town will fight him" (39). He therefore sees the need to resolve the conflict and become one united family again. Although this could not be achieved before Emenike's death, efforts were nonetheless made in that direction. Even when Emenike was brought before the community by Ide, one could say that it was a move designed to foster peace and unity between Emenike and Ide on one hand and Emenike and his betrothed on the other. In all, Emenike's death truncated the move and leaves everybody heartbroken.

Conclusion

The study has attempted an examination of the use of symbolic archetypes and family conflicts in selected works of Ogonna Agu with a view to understanding their overall impact in the appreciation and proper understanding of the play. As plays of African origin with familiar names and settings, their messages, meanings and symbolic undertones have been well delineated and

Chapter eleven | *Chidiebere S. Ekweariri, in*
Charles Nwadigwe, Molinta Enendu & Canice Nwosu (Eds.)
Metaphors and Climax, Reminiscences on the Drama and Theatre of Ogonna Agu
London, Adonis & Abbey Publishers

properly accentuated. The issue of family conflict has also been elaborated upon.

Apart from the use of symbols, the issue of family conflict, as earlier stated, is a factor that cannot easily be ignored. In everyday life, conflict cannot be avoided in its entirety. However, the playwright's attempt in these two plays is not overtly aimed at glamorizing it but essentially designed towards recreating a recurrent phenomenon in most family situations. Furthermore, the essence of this recreation is to further highlight its destructive tendencies with a view to taking a proactive measure in tackling it as soon as it occurs.

The inherent use of symbolic archetypes in the two plays traditionalized them without which most of the messages of the play would have been lost. This is made more obvious by the artistic ingenuity and manipulative prowess of the playwright whose writing inventiveness created the platform for the use and delineation of these symbols. From *Symbol of a Goddess* to *Cry of a Maiden*, the use of symbols heightened the appreciation of the plays and helped in making Agu's drama an interesting theatre experience.

There is therefore the need for budding African playwrights, especially Nigerians, to borrow a leaf from the two plays in order to further advance the use of symbolic archetypes in playwriting instead of the usual writing of plays that lack creativity and offend the sensibility of readers, audience and theatre practitioners. A time has therefore come for playwrights to rethink their writing methods with a view to deftly apply symbolic archetypes that communicate to the senses and arouse interest. Again, family conflict, in all its ramifications, should be given quick attention with visible and practicable solutions offered. This will in the long run help to create an atmosphere of peace and harmony in various homes and the society in general.

Chapter eleven	*Chidiebere S. Ekweariri, in*
	Charles Nwadigwe, Molinta Enendu & Canice Nwosu (Eds.)
	Metaphors and Climax, Reminiscences on the Drama and
	Theatre cf Ogonna Agu
	London, Adonis & Abbey Publishers

Works Cited

Anaguudo-Agu, Ogonna. *Cry of a Maiden*. Calabar: Wusen Press Ltd, 2000.

Anaguudo-Agu, Ogonna. *Symbol of a Goddess*. Calabar: University of Calabar Press, 2005

"Archetype." http://en.wikipedia.org/wiki/archetype. Retrieved 10th October, 2012.

Asigbo, Alex and Emma, Ebo. "Dramatizing Death: Theatrical Dimensions of a Titled Man's Burial in Onitsha: Lessons for National Development." *Theatre Experience: A Journal of Contemporary Theatre Practice*. 2:1 (2003): 62-67.

Edde, Iji M. *Towards Greater Dividends: Developmental Imperatives*. Calabar: BAAJ, 2001.

Euba, Femi. "The Nigerian Theatre and the Playwright." *Drama and Theatre in Nigeria: A Critical Source Book*. Ed. Yemi Ogunbiyi. Lagos: Nigerian Magazine, 1981. 381-398.

Lyons, John. *Semantics*. Vol. 1. New York: Cambridge University Press, 1977.

Ngumoha, Emma. "Initiation and Symbolism in Okigbo's *Labyrinths*." *WAACLALS*. 2:1 (2005): 86-105.

Ohiri, Innocent. "Designing for the Theatre in the New Millennium." *Design History in Nigeria: Essays in Honour of Demas Nwoko*. Abuja: National Gallery of Art, 2002. 380-392.

Chapter eleven | *Chidiebere S. Ekweariri, in*
Charles Nwadigwe, Molinta Enendu & Canice Nwosu (Eds.)
Metaphors and Climax, Reminiscences on the Drama and Theatre of Ogonna Agu
London, Adonis & Abbey Publishers

Chapter Twelve

Biafran Ideology and the Question of Commitment:
A Study of Ogonna Agu's *Symbol of a Goddess*

Charles Okwuowulu

Introduction

Every society has collective interests. These interests are diverse and could range from liberation, oppression, and intimidation to economic equality. The struggle for economic equality either creates a conflict between the ruling class and the masses or between one community and the other. Most times these conflicts degenerate to strong oppositions which lead to war. This was the case with the Nigeria/Biafra War. The year 2014 marks a century of the Amalgamation of the Northern and Southern Protectorates of Nigeria by Lord Lugard in 1914. The amalgamation was done without due consideration to the cultural and religious differences of the many tribes inhabiting the vast geographical region that came to be known as Nigeria. This diversity in thought patterns and worldview has generated series of conflicts in Nigeria.

The year 1960 marked Nigeria's independence from colonialism. Thereafter the challenge of coexistence in diverse cultural and value systems engineered leadership tussles which culminated in different religious crisis and several coup d'état. The Eastern region of the country felt marginalized and intimidated by the Northern region. Achebe states that the Nigerian Civil War arose from an attempt by the Eastern region of Nigeria, led by Emeka Odumegwu Ojukwu to secede in 1967. This was as a result of a massacre of the Igbo in the North and destruction of their property and livelihood. The war which lasted for thirty months

Chapter twelve | *Charles Okwuowulu, in*
Charles Nwadigwe, Molinta Enendu & Canice Nwosu (Eds.)
Metaphors and Climax, Reminiscences on the Drama and
Theatre of Ogonna Agu
London, Adonis & Abbey Publishers

resulted in loss of millions of lives and property worth billions of Naira (qtd. in Ndubisi 145).

The issue of commitment by creative writers has generated a lot of academic debates. Esedebe affirms that one significant service of history for the committed dramatist is the presentation of collective memory as a veritable means for comprehension of the present (qtd. in Ndubisi 144). This study takes a critical look at Ogonna Agu's play, *Symbol of a Goddess,* with the aim of foregrounding Ogonna Agu as a writer who is committed to the cause of Biafra. Ogonna Agu's place of birth, Nnobi in Anambra State, like most communities in Eastern Nigeria, had a collective burning desire which is hinged on actualizing a sovereign state of Biafra. This desire burns like wild fire in the spirit of Ndigbo. This was a course many fought and died for: a course many are still willing to die for.

Having read English and drama at the University of Nigeria, Nsukka, Ogonna Agu proceeded to Leeds and London for his postgraduate studies. Upon his return to Nigeria, he became a lecturer at the University of Calabar and there he yielded to the Biafran course. Until his death in 2011, he was a playwright, novelist and poet who saw literature as effective medium to project the course of his people. His works include *The Strong Boy of the Forest* (novel), *Adiaha the Beauty Queen* (novel), *Odu Okike* (poetry), *Cry of a Maiden* (play), *Symbol of a Goddess* (play) and many other creative works. One outstanding thing about his works is the concept of his commitment on the side of the masses. His commitment is seen in the promotion of African cultural values which *Cry of a Maiden* and *Odu Okike* epitomize. His commitment to the Biafran cause is seen as a subtheme in *Cry of a Maiden* and a major theme in *Symbol of a Goddess.*

Chapter twelve | *Charles Okwuowulu, in*
Charles Nwadigwe, Molinta Enendu & Canice Nwosu (Eds.)
Metaphors and Climax, Reminiscences on the Drama and Theatre of Ogonna Agu
London, Adonis & Abbey Publishers

The Biafra Ideology: Historical Foundations

The ideology of Biafra is enshrined in the captivity of the Easterners. The post-independence period foreshadowed its challenges on the question of coexistence. This is because the 1914 amalgamation by Lord Lugard forced people with diverse cultures to become one country (one people). Nigeria became a jungle plagued by injustice and ethnic distrust. The Nigerian polity became heated up as these policies entrenched poverty and insecurity on citizenry. The military seized power through coup that produced Ironsi as Head of State but their intervention was equally given ethnic interpretation and rejected by some sections of the country especially in the north. This brought tension, insecurity and finally led to a counter coup, murder of Ironsi and further attacks and mass killing of the Igbo and other people from the eastern region that lived in the north. The formation and rise of ethnic-based agitation and vigilante groups was a predicted consequence, especially as successive military and civilian regimes continued the policy of marginalization and discrimination. Prominent amongst these radical groups in the eastern part of Nigeria was Biafra. Lending credence to this, Uwalaka asserts that:

> The reason adduced for the creation of Biafra included: the humiliation, extermination, bloodletting and spilling of innocent blood of the Igbo and those of the people of the eastern region. This made their security and survival impossible. Some months later, Ojukwu said, '. . . worst of all came the genocide in which over 30,000 of our kiths and kin were slaughtered in cold blood all over Nigeria and nobody asked questions, nobody showed regret, nobody showed remorse. Thus, Nigeria has become a jungle with no safety, no justice, and no hope for our people. We decided there to found a new place, a human habitation away from the Nigerian jungle. That was the origin of our Biafra. (13)

Consequently, a genocidal war broke out. The Igbo fought for freedom and for a right to life. But the concept of Biafra has been

Chapter twelve | *Charles Okwuowulu, in*
Charles Nwadigwe, Molinta Enendu & Canice Nwosu (Eds.)
Metaphors and Climax, Reminiscences on the Drama and
Theatre of Ogonna Agu
London, Adonis & Abbey Publishers

misrepresented by some scholars as a mere pressure group. This is because many pressure groups have emerged in Nigeria fighting for one cause or the other. Many of these causes can be considered just while some are mere frivolities. According to Oyeniyi, some of these ethnic-based groups include the Niger Delta Peoples Volunteer Force, Ogoni Youth, Ijaw Youth, Bakassi Boys, Egbesu Boys, Onitsha Traders Organization and so on (qtd. in Okwuowulu 11). Similarly, groups such as the O'Odua People's Congress (OPC) emerged in the southwest while the Arewa Youth Consultative Form (AYCF) and Boko Haram emerged in the North.

Most scholars have condemned Boko Haram's agitation against Western education as a fruitless fight. Thus, some scholars likened the course of Biafra to that of Boko Haram. Besides, the formation philosophies of the other groups which were aimed at achieving a common goal were thwarted along the line. The philosophy of OPC founded in 1995 by Frederick Fasheun as a movement for promotion of Yoruba cultural values was derailed with the continual incarceration of Chief MKO Abiola. The members who saw Frederick as an educated weakling, who could do less for Abiola's release, broke out and engaged in guerrilla fighting. The break-away fraction soon indulged in intra-group fighting, arson, inhuman treatment and extrajudicial killings (Okwuowulu 12). This thwarted philosophy and the failure of Biafra to achieve its aim through the Civil War has equally made scholars to liken the course of Biafra to these other groups. These two reasons account for the misrepresentation of the Biafran ideology by some scholars. To understand the ideology of Biafra, it is necessary to get a historical account of the Nigeria – Biafra War.

Barely five years after independence from colonial rule, Nigeria witnessed the first military coup on 15th January, 1966. The coup plotters, led by Major Chukwuma Nzeogwu, pointed to

Chapter twelve	*Charles Okwuowulu, in*
	Charles Nwadigwe, Molinta Enendu & Canice Nwosu (Eds.)
	Metaphors and Climax, Reminiscences on the Drama and
	Theatre of Ogonna Agu
	London, Adonis & Abbey Publishers

maladministration, nepotism, economic mismanagement, blatant rigging of elections, political intolerance and ethnic competition as reasons for ousting the civilian government. This coup aimed at overthrowing the federal and regional governments (Uwalaka 9-10). Nigeria then was divided into regions. However, majority of these coup plotters were from the Eastern region. The coup succeeded in the North and the West but failed in the East. In the North, Alhaji Sir Ahmadu Bello, the Northern premier was killed, and in the West, Chief Akintola the Western Premier was killed. In Lagos, the Federal Prime Minister, Alhaji Sir Abubakar Tafawa Balewa and his Finance Minister Chief Festus Okotie-Eboh were killed. In the East, the coup was not successful.

The failure of the coup in the East was misinterpreted to be sectional as majority of the coup plotters were of Eastern origin. This sparked off riots and subsequent killings of the Igbo and people of Eastern origin in the north in retaliation for the death of the northern leaders in the perceived sectional coup. People numbering about 30,000 and properties worth millions of Naira were destroyed (Uwalaka 10). On 27 July 1966, Lt. Col. Yakubu Gowon led a counter-coup which led to the death of Major General Aguiyi Ironsi, Lt. Col. Fajuyi, the Military Governor of the Western Province and about 200 officers from Eastern Nigeria. Gowon's counter coup was perceived as a revenge mission against the Igbo. As a result, there was a complete breakdown in the Nigerian Government system.

The imposition of Lt. Col. Gowon as the Head of State raised opposition from Lt. Col. Odumegwu Ojukwu, the Military Governor of the Eastern region. Ojukwu refused to take orders from Gowon who was a junior officer in the army and alleged that there were other senior military officers who could take up the role as Head of State like Brig. Ogundipe (Uwalaka 11). This heightened the political and civil unrest. Consequently General

Chapter twelve | *Charles Okwuowulu, in*
Charles Nwadigwe, Molinta Enendu & Canice Nwosu (Eds.)
Metaphors and Climax, Reminiscences on the Drama and
Theatre of Ogonna Agu
London, Adonis & Abbey Publishers

Ankrah (The Ghanaian Head of State), in January 1967 invited Nigerian leaders to find lasting solution to the Nigerian problem. An agreement known as the Aburi Accord was reached in Ghana. Returning to Nigeria both parties gave conflicting interpretations to the accord. Citing *Africa Today*, Uwalaka states that:

> The printed verbatim report and the tape-recorded account of the proceedings of the conference showed that there was agreement to introduce a greater measure of decentralization by increasing the powers of the regions vis-à-vis those of the federal government. (12)

This lends credence to Ojukwu's interpretations of the Accord as confederation. Gowon on the other hand claimed ignorance of confederacy decision, while his top bureaucrats asserted that he was duped to accept the term he did not understand. On 26th May 1967, Ojukwu summoned an emergency meeting of the Eastern Nigerian Consultative Assembly to discuss the Nigerian issues as it affected the security of life and property of the Eastern region. In reaction to this, Gowon on 27th May 1967 created more states in Nigeria, dividing the Eastern region into three; (East Central, South Eastern and Rivers). This was a stroke aimed at weakening and destabilizing the Eastern region from forging a common front and solidarity. Reacting to Gowon's State creation and destabilizing technique, the Assembly empowered Lt. Col. Ojukwu to declare the Eastern region, the Independent Republic of Biafra. This Ojukwu did on 30th May, 1967.

Consequently, a "Clinical Police Action" was ordered by the Gowon led administration to stop the rebellion in the East. Biafra's resistance made the Nigerian Supreme Military Council on 26th August 1967 to declare total war against Biafra, resulting in a genocide which lasted for thirty months, during which millions of Biafra lives and property were lost. On Jan 15, 1970, the Eastern region, after about three years of resistance, untold hardship and

---

Chapter twelve | *Charles Okwuowulu, in*
Charles Nwadigwe, Molinta Enendu & Canice Nwosu (Eds.)
Metaphors and Climax, Reminiscences on the Drama and Theatre of Ogonna Agu
London, Adonis & Abbey Publishers

induced hunger meted by foreign support, empowered Major General Effiong on behalf of Biafra to surrender. General Ojukwu was granted asylum in Ivory Coast (Uwalaka, 13-15).

The ideology of Biafra is hinged on the captivity of her people in the land of Nigeria. This oppression did not stop even after the Civil War. Hence, the Biafra cause will continue to live in every Igbo man unless the reason which was adduced for the creation of Biafra is addressed. It was hoped that the postwar period and civilian rule would address these grievances and injustice but rather it deepened the marginalization of the Igbo through political scheming and obnoxious policies. This equally rekindled the Biafran agitation as groups such as the Movement for the Actualization of Sovereign State of Biafra (MASSOB) emerged.

The Concept of Commitment

The concept of commitment in creative writing has received an avalanche of academic discourse. Ngugi wa Thiong'o's *Writers in Politics* is a lucid conceptualization of writers' commitment towards particular goals. He argues that a writer born in a particular society is confronted with the values and problems of that society. Faced with these, the collective unconscious state of the writer's mind will at best take ideological stand, either on the side of the masses or those in power. Foregrounding Kenya's experience, he recounted the African struggle against foreign domination in economics, politics and cultural values (5-6). Literature mirroring the society therefore reflects the political, economic and cultural struggles of Africans which have consisted of slavery, colonialism, neo-colonialism, war and the siege of negative social forces. Ngugi wa Thiong'o's further states that:

> . . . a writer has no choice, whether or not he is aware of it, his works reflect one or more aspects of the intense economic, political, cultural

Chapter twelve | *Charles Okwuowulu, in*
Charles Nwadigwe, Molinta Enendu & Canice Nwosu (Eds.)
Metaphors and Climax, Reminiscences on the Drama and Theatre of Ogonna Agu
London, Adonis & Abbey Publishers

and ideological struggles in a society. What he can choose is one or the other side in the battle field: the side of the people, or the side of those social forces and classes that try to keep the people down. What he or she cannot do is to remain neutral. Every writer is a writer in politics. The only question is what and whose politics. (preface)

He reiterates that a writer having come from a particular class, race and nation; being a product of a particular culture and social process always makes us view life, perhaps unconsciously, from his socio-cultural perspective. This he achieves with his pen through different techniques such as persuasion or direct appeal towards his doctrine, goals and set values consciously or unconsciously held by him (6). He posits that commitment of a creative writer should also reflect in the use of his local language for creative works. This language question has generated a lot of academic controversies. Thus two schools of thought emerged. The school of Ngugi wa Thiong'o and Obi Wali believes that African literature written in English language is a form of imperialism. The school asserts that African literature can be authentic if written in an African language. Consequently, African literature in European language should be classified as Afro-European literature (Nwabueze 13). The second school of thought propounded by China Achebe and Wole Soyinka believes that literature written in European language is legitimate; European language being more universal, thus serves as a vehicle for transmission of African Experiences (Nwabueze 13). The criticism that greeted Ngugi wa Thiong'o and Obi Wali's school is anchored on the plethora of indigenous African languages. However, the concept of transliteration which posits that a writer should think in mother tongue and write in European language justifies Chinua Achebe and Wole Soyinka's school of thought.

Ogbolosingha observes that the motivational factor for literary commitment is the anomalies in the socio-political structures put

Chapter twelve | *Charles Okwuowulu, in*
Charles Nwadigwe, Molinta Enendu & Canice Nwosu (Eds.)
Metaphors and Climax, Reminiscences on the Drama and
Theatre of Ogonna Agu
London, Adonis & Abbey Publishers

in place by the ruling class to drive their dominant ideology to the masses. The position of the writer in such cases which is on the side of the greater percentage of the citizenry, rejecting situations, experiences and actions that run contrary to the aspiration of the people is equated with commitment on the side of the masses (12). Furthermore, Ogbolosingha identifies the ultimate form of commitment which is known as protest literature, asserting that every protest writer is a committed writer. A protest writer is thus committed to the well being of the generality of the people, putting the interest of the masses before his personal interest. Therefore, the "protest writer is both persuasive and coercive and does not hesitate to recommend the use of force, if necessary" (15). Emmanuel Obiechina explains that the question of commitment which is as old as creativity itself makes the writer think of himself as spokesman, prophet, teacher, moral legislator and an entertainer (qtd. in Ogbolosingha 15).

Having established the theoretical formula for studying commitment in writing, the question of the side now arises. How committed are Nigerian writers to the several problems of the state? Ndubisi affirms that the subject of Nigerian Civil War and the quest for the Biafra nation has been a burning issue in Eastern part of Nigeria. He argues that the Biafran cause is too big to be ignored or neglected by writers in their creative works. He makes no excuses for such literary neglect since war as a topical issue has been given adequate academic attention (144). Citing the view of Biodun Jeyifo, he affirms the dearth of literature on the Biafran experience and listed the few Nigerian creative works in English that centred on the Nigeria-Biafra War to include *The Last Battle and Other Stories* by Ossie Enekwe, novels like Kalu Uka's *Colonel Ben Brim* and War Diaries in the manner of Elechi Amadi's *Sunset in Biafra* and in poetry there are Achebe's *Beware Soul-Brother*, Enekwe's *Broken Pots, Don't Let Him Die*, co-edited by Achebe and

Chapter twelve | *Charles Okwuowulu, in*
Charles Nwadigwe, Molinta Enendu & Canice Nwosu (Eds.)
Metaphors and Climax, Reminiscences on the Drama and Theatre of Ogonna Agu
London, Adonis & Abbey Publishers

Dubem Okafor, Nnamdi Azikiwe's *Civil War Soliloquies, Causalities* by J.P Clark-Bekederemo and Maman Vatsa's *Voices from the Trench* (146).

Furthermore, Ndubisi asserts that there has not been a play in English that deals specifically or comprehensively with the Nigerian Civil War. According to him, there may be subtle references of Civil War in some modern Nigerian plays in English which are usually infinitesimal to be regarded as a minor theme. Wondering if Nigerian dramatists are not interested in history, he concludes that for theatre to survive, theatre must proffer solution to the National problems and serve as a directional compass for social change (146).

Similarly, Ogbolosingha equally expresses the view that there is lack of literary commitment on the side of the masses among the first generation Nigerian writers. He asserts that a crop of new writers known as second generation writers believe that the Nigerian solution in the 1960s demanded and deserved more literary, artistic and dramatic radicalism. He listed such second generation writers and scholars as Biodun Jeyifo, Femi Osofisan, Olu Obafemi, Chidi Amuta, Kole Omotoso, Tanure Ojaide, Niyi Osundare, Odia Ofeimun, Harry Garuba, and Festus Iyayi. These writers debunk what they consider the escapist attitude of their predecessors and are poised to enforce change on their society through literature (16).

However, this study foregrounds Ogonna Agu's *Symbol of a Goddess* as a quintessence of commitment in the Biafran cause. Currently, there is lack of critical attention on the work in the light of its significance to the society. The study further argues that a high sense of commitment to the masses, which scholars believe is lacking in the present day literature, is epitomized in Ogonna Agu's *Symbol of a Goddess*. The exclusion of Ogonna Agu's name as a second generation committed Nigerian writer by Ogbolosingha,

Chapter twelve | *Charles Okwuowulu, in*
Charles Nwadigwe, Molinta Enendu & Canice Nwosu (Eds.)
Metaphors and Climax, Reminiscences on the Drama and Theatre of Ogonna Agu
London, Adonis & Abbey Publishers

and the assertion by Ndubisi that modern Nigerian plays do not treat the theme of war adequately cannot be adjudged correct based on the findings of this study. Ndubisi made his assertion after citing the lacuna which Musa Abiodun had pointed out in an earlier study; and hence submits that "the Nigerian-Biafran civil war and the numerous coup d'états are long overdue to be subject matters of play texts" (Ndubisi 147). Musa's study carried out in 2002 (the same year Chukwuma Okoye's *We the Beast* was published), predated the publication year of *Symbol of a Goddess* which is 2005. However, Ndubisi's study in 2008 was done after the publication year of *Symbol of a Goddess*. Thus, the purported lacuna Musa discovered had been filled by Okoye's *We the Beast* and Agu's *Symbol of a Goddess* even before Ndubisi's study. A critical analysis of Ogonna Agu's *Symbol of a Goddess* justifies this claim.

Ogonna Agu's *Symbol of a Goddess*

Agu's *Symbol of a Goddess* is one of the Nigerian plays with overriding theme in the struggle for the actualization of sovereign state of Biafra. The Biafran spirit which resides in every Igbo man is highly expressed in the dramatic text. The refusal of Emenike to drop arms at the end of war against the wishes of his community sparks off the conflict of the play. Emenike terrorizing the villagers with his gun and his Biafra ideologies is chased out of the village by the commandant, a military officer to whom the villagers report. During the attempts to capture Emenike, his bird, his symbol of Biafra flies away. This further heightens the dramatic conflict as Emenike refuses to marry in the belief that the bird being his wife lives in the rivers. However, Emenike's mother, Iluka marries a wife, Akudiri for Emenike whom he (Emenike) gets pregnant but refuses to marry. Emenike's refusal to accept Akudiri takes the dramaturgy to a resolution at the king's palace.

Chapter twelve | *Charles Okwuowulu, in*
Charles Nwadigwe, Molinta Enendu & Canice Nwosu (Eds.)
Metaphors and Climax, Reminiscences on the Drama and
Theatre of Ogonna Agu
London, Adonis & Abbey Publishers

Ide's accusation that Emenike abandoned his wife for a water goddess makes no impetus as Emenike's heed to the call of the *agboghommuo* (his goddess) justifies his mission and commitment to the Biafran spirit.

The playwright uses a lot of narrative techniques and motifs to propel the theme of the text which epitomizes Biafran ideology in Emenike's captivity. Emenike is faced with different levels of captivity. First by the soldiers who try to arrest and take him captive and then by his kinsmen who marry a wife for him to take him into family captivity. The failure of these captive intents asserts the survival of Biafra. The play gives a historic insight into Biafra which is realized through a flashback technique using the narrator as authorial voice to recount war sorrows through war songs. During the war memoirs, the playwright informs that Emenike fought in Abagana, Gekem, Ore, and Otuocha which are significant battlefields in Biafran war experiences. The diction of the play combines pidgin English with Igbo language; thus creating the locale and giving a historic perspective to the playtext. The commandant and soldiers speak Pidgin English while Illuka speaks Igbo. This concept of transliteration in diction is apt in the area of music which, created in local dialect, depicts the sorrows and anguish of war thereby generating palpable empathy. The concept of dance which the playwright equally introduces in the text embodies African cultural spirit. The masquerade and romantic dances of Emenike and Akudiri capture the core African values.

The play is filled with symbolism. The creation of eagle as a symbol of Biafra sustains the tempo of the text. The eagle symbolizes strength and freedom from captivity. Upon attack by the soldiers, the eagle flies away and this metaphorically portends that the Biafran struggle can no longer be held captive. This is

Chapter twelve | *Charles Okwuowulu, in*
Charles Nwadigwe, Molinta Enendu & Canice Nwosu (Eds.)
Metaphors and Climax, Reminiscences on the Drama and
Theatre of Ogonna Agu
London, Adonis & Abbey Publishers

buttressed in the final scene where the bird flies back. Emenike ululates her symbolic return:

> EMENIKE: There she comes... my egret!
> O! what a presence! Gold crop sinking...
> O! how can I gather you in my palms.
> Lady of the Red Eyes... mother of the nation...
> Agboghommuo...God! Humbled am I, by your majesty.
> (65)

Symbolism in the play is further buttressed by the fact that the egret never existed physically but in Emenike's imagination, though represented by the spirit mask as the textual direction suggests. The author presents two symbols of authority which Emenike uses to enforce his Biafran ideology. The European form symbolized in the gun which Emenike uses to terrorize the whole village whom he perceives are opposed to continuing the Biafran struggle; and the African form symbolized in the masquerade which Emenike eventually uses to enforce his mission. The superseding of the African symbol of authority over the European symbol reiterates the playwright's commitment to African cultural values. Furthermore, the playwright presents Emenike as a down-to-earth man committed to the Biafran cause.

The challenge of the Biafran struggle is depicted in the character of Emenike who is torn between two different forces. The force of nature symbolized in Akudiri, the lady Emenike's mother, Illuka married to charm him back from exile; and the force of Biafran ideology symbolized in the eagle which the playwright presents as being more important to Emenike than his earthly mother. Nevertheless, the concept of sabotage which Biafrans believe accounted for their loss of the war is characterized in Igbonekwu and Ide. On Igbonekwu's suggestion, the commandant orders the soldier to capture Emenike's eagle in place of his mother, Illuka. This process leads to the escape of the eagle. Ide is

Chapter twelve | *Charles Okwuowulu, in*
Charles Nwadigwe, Molinta Enendu & Canice Nwosu (Eds.)
Metaphors and Climax, Reminiscences on the Drama and
Theatre of Ogonna Agu
London, Adonis & Abbey Publishers

221

known for inviting the military to capture Emenike who is his cousin.

The Biafran struggle culminates to a climax when Emenike is confronted with the question of choice and he opts for the woman of the waters (Biafra) instead of his pregnant wife. This dramatic twist inflames the Biafran spirit as his subsequent death for Biafra does not only make him a tragic hero but culminates in winning more converts to the Biafran cause. Igbonekwu thus turns from a presumed saboteur and opponent an advocate and devotee-the new hope of Biafra. He speaks:

> IGBONEKWU: Emenike is like a ram-headed one with crooked horns... he retreats before he strikes. Biafra is alive, living in him... The other issue to consider is how he has put his intellectual and emotional strength into great use. At first he came with guns. Now the guns are gone, and he is stirring the whole village with scenes of a magnificent masquerade. What a way to engage his mind, and pull it from its destructive tendencies. I myself have become his convert. He is asking other converts to come and join him in reliving an experience... the experience of a nation in turmoil . . . (64)

Even on the earthly plane of existence, the spirit of Emenike and his ideals live on, symbolized in the unborn child, a metaphor for the future.

Conclusion

This study has drawn a critical attention to Ogonna Agu's *Symbol of a Goddess* as an epitome of Biafran commitment which scholars believe is lacking in the modern Nigerian drama. It has equally presented Ogonna Agu as a committed writer who is given to the plight and the struggles of masses. Beyond drawing attention to the Biafran movement, this study creates spiritual consciousness in

Chapter twelve   *Charles Okwuowulu, in*
Charles Nwadigwe, Molinta Enendu & Canice Nwosu (Eds.)
Metaphors and Climax, Reminiscences on the Drama and
Theatre of Ogonna Agu
London, Adonis & Abbey Publishers

the belief that Biafra will achieve its purpose of liberation one day as the play text suggests. To be a free citizen in his fatherland, Biafra has been the desire of every Igbo man; a cause many fought and died for; a cause many are still willing to die for. Biafra, seen through Agu's play, is more than a sovereign state; it is an index of freedom in all its ramifications.

Works Cited

Anaagudo-Agu, Ogonna. *Symbol of a Goddess*. Calabar: University of Calabar Press, 2005.

Ndubisi, Nnanna. "The Nigerian Civil War in Modern Nigerian Drama: Selective Amnesia or Wisdom of the Ostrich?" *Trends in the Theory and Practice of Theatre in Nigeria*. Eds. Duro Oni and Ahmed Yerima. Lagos: Society of Nigerian Theatre Artistes (SONTA), 2008. 143-152.

Nwabueze, Emeka. *Visions & Revisions, Selected Discourses on Literary Criticism*. Enugu: Abic Publishers, 2005.

Ogbolosingha, Michael. Commitment and Conflict in the Dramaturgy of the Niger Delta: An Examination of Select Works of Six 21st Century Playwrights. A Ph.D. Seminar Paper Presented to the Department of Theatre Arts, University of Port Harcourt, September 2012.

Okwuowulu, Charles. "Waging War Against Domestic Terrorism in Nigeria Through Video Films: A Critical Appraisal of *The Liquid Black Gold*." Paper Presented at the Convention of the Society of Nigerian Theatre Artists. Department of Theatre Arts, University of Calabar, 12-15 Sept. 2012.

Uwalaka, Jude. *The Struggle for an Inclusive Nigeria. Igbos to be or not*

Chapter twelve | *Charles Okwuowulu, in*
Charles Nwadigwe, Molinta Enendu & Canice Nwosu (Eds.)
Metaphors and Climax, Reminiscences on the Drama and
Theatre of Ogonna Agu
London, Adonis & Abbey Publishers

to be? A Treatise on Igbo Political Personality and Survival in Nigeria. Enugu: Snaap Press Ltd, 2003.

Wa Thiong'o, Ngugi. *Writers in Politics.* London: Heinemann Educational Books, 1981.

Chapter twelve	*Charles Okwuowulu, in*
	Charles Nwadigwe, Molinta Enendu & Canice Nwosu (Eds.)
	Metaphors and Climax, Reminiscences on the Drama and
	Theatre of Ogonna Agu
	London, Adonis & Abbey Publishers

Chapter Thirteen

Evaluating Dance and Music in Ogonna Agu's *Cry of a Maiden*

Ikike Ufford

Introduction

Dance and music have over the years been veritable materials that playwrights employ in sending conscious messages to their audience. These art forms have helped to arouse in-depth sensory manifestations capable of redesigning the desire and aspirations of the common man in a vicious society. Dance is a way of thinking and living. It is true that all facets of life find emotional release and expression through body movement. Due to the profound connection with the habits of the periods in which it is created, many dances depict human body in time and space. It employs highly structured patterns of movement units which are used to capture the essence of the object, feeling or thought. The language of dance which could be called "body codes" is constructive and concentrated. The combination of the movement units into a harmonious presentation makes a pleasing perception and admiration.

Similar to dance, music has powers. The power of music comes from its ability to arouse a certain feeling or mood in the listener. Music can relax, soothe, refresh, enliven and stir up every human emotion. Throughout history, men have recognized the powers of music and used it to satisfy people in various ways. Music is a universal human entity applied either for its own sake or as part of other activities paramount of which is dance. Music is abstract because it cannot be seen or touched. In some cases, one may not

Chapter thirteen | *Ikike Ufford, in*
Charles Nwadigwe, Molinta Enendu & Canice Nwosu (Eds.)
Metaphors and Climax, Reminiscences on the Drama and Theatre of Ogonna Agu
London, Adonis & Abbey Publishers

be inclined to dance, but music creates the mood and motivates a listener to dance. The pulsating rhythm of music sets fire to one's imagination and so, without any conscious effort one's spirit is lifted, the feet begins to tap, the head nods to the beats of the sound, a smile comes to the face, little by little, enjoyment of the music sets in and the problem and frustrations of the body are momentarily forgotten as the listener melts into the sound, becoming one with the music and dance. This is the magical potential of music. Music like a human being has a soul, a heart, a mind and a skeleton. The soul of music is melody which is a succession of tones that make up a pleasing composition, the heart of the music is rhythm and tempo, the mind of music is the harmony while the skeleton is the form.

Dance and music have featured in some African plays such as the *Death and the Kings Horse man"* by Wole Soyinka where dance and music create a path or bridge between the living and the dead; they become a vehicle for ritual transmutation and spiritual cleansing in Uwemedimo Atakpo's *Isadok* and celebration of life in Ola Rotimi's *The Gods are not to Blame*, to mention but a few. Ogonna Agu has creatively used dance and music in multidimensional perspectives ranging from native festival experience to stylized and codified symbolic conjectures. Such movement simulations also express philosophical and phenomenal subjections of human frailties. Though Agu's use of dance and music is not elaborate, in its unit of purpose, the symbolic parlance reveals the essential excitement and power in the human march towards exposing the major disputes in man's desire to satisfy his wants in all ramifications.

Chapter thirteen | *Ikike Ufford, in*
Charles Nwadigwe, Molinta Enendu & Canice Nwosu (Eds.)
Metaphors and Climax, Reminiscences on the Drama and
Theatre of Ogonna Agu
London, Adonis & Abbey Publishers

Dance and Music in *Cry of a Maiden*

Cry of a Maiden opens with a sensational use of music as a lubricator of one's working habit and love world. Ada is seen plaiting the hair of Mgbochi in a relaxed atmosphere. The ballad which is masterly rendered by Ada sends Okolo to early sleep, where the joy that filled her heart leads her to a eulogy of the essence of beauty and royalty. In her ballad she sings:

ADA: If the oil carries dignity
Let it dignify me
If the oil carries dignity
Let it dignify
This oil of kings
I asked Nwadike at his home
Nwadike, who will lead
This great nation?
And he stood up fine fine
He is also in the dance
Be quick, Nwadike, be quick
Racing, walking and with
Your staff of office.
I went to Lagos
I went to Lagos . . . but
You have a diver . . .
I wrote to our father Okoye
He replied in this town
The police will charge your soul
Arrear is in the government
Arrear is also in my dance (1-2).

Ada in her ballad freely expresses her innocent feelings about her cultural resilience and fear of unwanted commentary about the government of the day. This ballad is so interesting and intriguing that Chidum wishes to hear more:

CHIDUM: I mean the song you sang a
moment ago. At one time you

Chapter thirteen | *Ikike Ufford, in*
Charles Nwadigwe, Molinta Enendu & Canice Nwosu (Eds.)
Metaphors and Climax, Reminiscences on the Drama and
Theatre of Ogonna Agu
London, Adonis & Abbey Publishers

were talking on your fortunes, at
other times you were dreaming of
Lagos. You stopped. Wiped your
eyes and shook your head as if
gripped by the pathos of music . . . (2)

Ada goes on to inform him that the maiden dancers of the ballad are making an appearance before the governor in a welcome ceremony. Chidum in his response remembers complementary performances and their seasons in the society:

CHIDUM: A'ah, I love it. Reminds me of long
forgotten jungle drums. The new moon-when the
maidens wriggle a dance of the waist and great
warriors during the festival of the skull. (2)

The above piece highlights the two very important groups in the traditional society. The waist dance is graciously displayed by flexible and alluring maidens, while the warriors in a more vibratory dance form perform with the skull of their prey, suggesting celebration of valour and reassurance of basic security for the society. With these conversations Ogonna Agu successfully uses the festival as an avenue for exhibiting the rich cultural performance contents in the society and the affinity that comes with the spree of music, dance, songs and mimetic displays amongst the people.

Not being enraptured in the symphony of the performing arts, the playwright once again established the essence of the conflict in the play as Ada through a musical rendition asks: who and who will marry me? This rhetorical question begins the riddle that encircles the destiny of the crying maiden and the two brothers (Okolo and Chidum) in the course of the play. We can essentially see that the playwright drops vital points in sublime manner in the process of exhilaration in the maidens' ballad. This whole scenario justifies Akpabot's submission that "music exist only in terms of

Chapter thirteen | *Ikike Ufford, in*
Charles Nwadigwe, Molinta Enendu & Canice Nwosu (Eds.)
Metaphors and Climax, Reminiscences on the Drama and
Theatre of Ogonna Agu
London, Adonis & Abbey Publishers

social interaction and it is a learned behavior... it involves the behavior of an individual and groups of individuals" (1).

Chidum is saddled with the urge to learn what Ada composed and develop more interest in patronizing her creative, innocent and adorable skills:

> CHIDUM   ... and yet it is your voice that is ringing.
> Can't you hear it? How it
> flows like a fresh spring in the rocks;
> spurring the reeds to dance. You hear?
> Mellow to its depths ... it rises and falls
> with the heartthrob of a man poised
> between love and ownership. (4)

The irony of Ada's ballad is that, while she was singing it, Okolo was engrossed in deep sleep while Chidum savoured the grace that came with it. Ada consciously controlled the emotional state of Chidum, making him to raise stakes and desire to marry her by all means. However, when Okolo began to intoxicate Ada with his music of love, Chidum was away while Ada got submerged in the ineluctable power of his love promise and passionate diction. One will see Chidum as a person who only listened and cherished Ada's ballad without engaging her in a dance which would have finalized their urge and desire to be one. Okolo succeeded based on his demanding power and the maiden was seduced. The ensuing interaction between Okolo and Ada on their match to breaking the "pot" is worthy of analysis:

> OKOLO: You are a treasure to me Ada. Our love is at stake this way you do. Can't you see it? How long must you keep tottering on the scale? But this is the plight of one who must love! Now look, Ada – PEAR the blackest of them all.

He tantalizes Ada with a prized pear. Ada attracted stretches her hand to see but he drags her to himself in a firm embrace. At

Chapter thirteen | *Ikike Ufford, in*
Charles Nwadigwe, Molinta Enendu & Canice Nwosu (Eds.)
Metaphors and Climax, Reminiscences on the Drama and
Theatre of Ogonna Agu
London, Adonis & Abbey Publishers

this point the ballad singers begin to chant a favorite song supplying background music to the dance that follows. Throughout the dance, the lovers remain in the same firm embrace on a spot. Okolo determines the motion which he maintains strictly to rhythm. Ada having to make herself malleable to any course he steers. The essence of the art of this dance is to evoke an emotion of love. Hence, the lovers are dancing dreamily, oblivious of the world around them and rapt in the joy of it as the song continues. This scenario shows how intensive the power of music and dance could be. The music is used as bedrock on which the dance is constructed. The rhythm directs the choice of movement and together launches the performance into a realm where the characters can no longer identify themselves with the world around them. This performance by Okolo and Ada is a demonstration of an "attempt to control and communicate with the forces around their developed symbolic gestures and movements that expressed the way they felt . . . " (Lange 5). Ideally, this dance is seductive and in all gestures simulates the art of lovemaking presented in a symbolic form. In this realm of performance the playwright reveals the sacred sensations influenced by the deep passion in their surreal state. Their discussion while in the state of trance in the "dance of love" can be imagined.

OKOLO:	Adakego in town
ADA:	Yes
OKOLO:	Adakego in town!
ADA:	Yes
OKOLO:	You and I shall be friends by God's grace
ADA:	It's alright
OKOLO:	If not in this world in the next
ADA:	It's alright
OKOLO:	If you are eating do not boast
ADA:	It's alright

Chapter thirteen | *Ikike Ufford, in*
Charles Nwadigwe, Molinta Enendu & Canice Nwosu (Eds.)
Metaphors and Climax, Reminiscences on the Drama and Theatre of Ogonna Agu
London, Adonis & Abbey Publishers

All that Okolo chanted in the process are affirmed by Ada in a relaxed and submissive atmosphere. Even when Ebere comes in they were still locked in their warm embrace in total submergence to the power of love orchestrated in the spirit of dance and music.

It should be understood that in this context the playwright uses dance in two basic perspectives. The first shows dance from the perspective of what Sonny Sampson-Akpan described as "man's mimetic or dramatic way of representing emotion or producing entertainment" (Oko-Offoboche 2). This is supported by Meki Nzewi when he explained that "dance movement motif are use for character delineation . . . and employed as symbolic element to sketch the theme of drama" (477). The dance between Okolo and Ada strongly shows the delineation of the protagonist (Ada) and antagonist (Okolo). The action they are engulfed in is central to the theme of the play because the pot got broken in the performance process. Dance in this case is seen as movement designed to fashion out and heighten the topical issues in a dramatic form.

The second approach by the playwright is phenomenological because the dance between Okolo and Ada is phenomenal in the play. It is central to the conflict and resolution of the play. The dance is phenomenological because it has not existed prior to its creation and exhibition. This leads us to the theory of "kinestruct", "kinecept" and "kinesymbol" as propounded by Eleanor Metheny as concepts of dance. She focuses on the philosophical angles of the theory of symbolic transformation of movements and examines the ideas inherent in human movement (qtd. in Forry 93). Metheny thus presents three ways of appraising movement to include visually perceivable patterns (as seen in the constant maneuvering of body movement by Okolo and Ada at a fixed spot), nonverbal symbolic form (as seen in the movement of the transfixed bodies in a witty exposition of sexual activity displayed in an imaginary form), and the perceptual form which incorporates all the sensory

Chapter thirteen | *Ikike Ufford, in*
Charles Nwadigwe, Molinta Enendu & Canice Nwosu (Eds.)
Metaphors and Climax, Reminiscences on the Drama and Theatre of Ogonna Agu
London, Adonis & Abbey Publishers

perceptions (that evoked total loss and surrender of will between the "love birds").

The consequence of the "love dance" leads to regrets of some sort by the maiden who thought she had finally broken her pot through the intrigues of a man she never really loved. Caught at this emotional crossroads, she apologizes to Chidum with another folk ballad:

> ADA: (*singing off stage*)
>   Mother o mother!
>   My pot has betrayed me
>   My clay pot
>   Mother o mother!
>   My pot has betrayed me
>   My clay pot
>   My pot for drawing water
>   Suddenly broken from my hands
>   My clay pot
>   Shall I follow
>   Or shall I leave the pot and return?
>   My pot!

Ada enters crying and expressing her sorrow as she presents Okolo with the piece of a broken pot which openly shows that Okolo was instrumental to the pot being broken. Okolo on his part takes up the challenge to comfort her and fight against all odds. His desire to get on with Ada in order to wipe away shame continues as the community eventually settles for their union.

Conclusion

The playwright made creative use of dance and music in weaving the dramatic plot. He theatrically used music to establish the riddle and equally used dance to resolve those riddle in the play. Chidum loved the ballad sung by Ada and even recorded her voice offering to teach her how to use the buttons of the recorder for more

Chapter thirteen | *Ikike Ufford, in*
Charles Nwadigwe, Molinta Enendu & Canice Nwosu (Eds.)
Metaphors and Climax, Reminiscences on the Drama and
Theatre of Ogonna Agu
London, Adonis & Abbey Publishers

exciting moments. She obliged but there was no follow up. Okolo tricked Ada into a dance with sweet words sang into her ears in an irresistible manner. His persistence saw Ada join him in the dance and consequently got engulfed and ultimately lost her virginity to the man she never really loved. Music is pleasurable but dance attracts bodies that come together for a given purpose. The playwright is suggesting that there is an intimate marriage between music and dance which potentially produces ecstasy beyond human comprehension.

However the playwright fails to elaborate on the form of music thereby making it subject to various rhythm, tone and composition. There was no cogent interpretation of instrumentation in the ballad as well as the maiden dances. The masquerade dance was fleeting without in-depth interpretation; the maiden dances or performance was mostly not defined. Generally Agu used dance and music to bridge the scenes and any gaps in the narration. They were also deployed as imaginary, stylized weapons to dramatize what would have been vulgar if it were enacted ordinarily in the real sense of it. Hence, beyond spectacle and entertainment, the love dance between Ada and Okolo which was highly symbolic and intriguing helped to advance the dramatic action towards the climax.

Works Cited

Anaagudo-Agu, Ogonna. *Cry of a Maiden*. Calabar: Wusen Publishers, 2000.

Akpabot, Samuel Ekpe. *Foundation of Nigerian Traditional Music.* Ibadan: Spectrum Books, 1976.

Forry, Joan G. *The Gender Politics of Contemporary Sport: Ethics, Power and the Body*. Michigan: BiblioBazaar and ProQuest, 2011.

Chapter thirteen | *Ikike Ufford, in*
Charles Nwadigwe, Molinta Enendu & Canice Nwosu (Eds.)
Metaphors and Climax, Reminiscences on the Drama and
Theatre of Ogonna Agu
London, Adonis & Abbey Publishers

Lange, Roderyk. *The Nature of Dance and Anthropological Perspective.* London: Macdonald and Evans, 1975.

Nzewi, Meki. "Music, Dance, Drama and The Stage in Nigeria." *Drama and Theatre in Nigeria: A Critical Sourcebook.* Ed. Yemi Ogunbiyi. Lagos: Nigeria Magazine, 1981. 433-456.

Oko-offoboche, Edisua. *The ABC of Dance Arts.* Calabar: Uptriko Press, 1996.

Chapter thirteen | *Ikike Ufford, in*
Charles Nwadigwe, Molinta Enendu & Canice Nwosu (Eds.)
Metaphors and Climax, Reminiscences on the Drama and Theatre of Ogonna Agu
London, Adonis & Abbey Publishers

Chapter Fourteen

The Musical Idiom in Modern African Drama: A Study of Ogonna Agu's *Symbol of a Goddess*.

Nicholas C. Akas

Introduction

In traditional Africa, music is an integral part of life and linked with the worldview of the society in which it is produced. It has social, cultural and political functions as well as deployed for recreational purposes. Harvey states that:

> Traditional art forms including music are rooted in mythology, legends and folklore and are associated with gods, ancestors and heroes. Musical activities are ritualized and intended to link the visible world with the invisible (1)

Music as one of the arts of theatre serves an important role by using the didactic essence in indigenous songs as a means of sustaining a people's cultural heritage. It has in many ways helped to preserve, nurture and promote a community's norms and values. Music is equally used to conscientize the society and guide the people towards the right path of life. Oshionebo is of the opinion that "music features so much in our daily lives. It is everywhere among us and the most accessible of all the performing arts because in all other activities music is played" (70). Music occupies a vital place in the cultural life of any society. It carries the culture of the people through which it portrays their habits, and life activities. Therefore, music has traditionally played diverse and essential roles in the African society. Hence, Onwuekwe affirms that:

Chapter fourteen | *Nicholas C. Akas, in*
Charles Nwadigwe, Molinta Enendu & Canice Nwosu (Eds.)
Metaphors and Climax, Reminiscences on the Drama and Theatre of Ogonna Agu
London, Adonis & Abbey Publishers

> Music is an integral part of the African cultures with various ceremonies being preceded by some sort of music. It is used to communicate, pass literature, welcoming heroes among other ritual functions. (121)

Indeed, "the mythology of some traditional festival is hidden or portrayed in their indigenous music" (Akas 75). Traditional African music does not have a written tradition. It is difficult to notate the music using Western staff nevertheless it transmits its idioms through various dimensions such as the musical text, melody, tempo, rhythm and orchestration.

Musical Genre and Functionality

Folk Music: Folk music is kind of traditional music that is handed down from generations in every culture. This type of music reflects the emotions of communality and captures the social bond that lies among various classes of people.

Opera music: Opera music first emerged in Italy in the 1600s. This genre had a remarkable combination of dramatic and musical arts, hence, it is specifically played in the theatres. This composition has greater appeal due to its delightful orchestral accompaniment. The preludes and interludes of this music set the tone for the action on-stage.

Metal Music: Metal music emerged after the Second World War. In this genre, the central melody of the composition is heavily influenced by and decides the structure of the songs. It is also known as "Information music".

Techno Music: Techno music is also known as fusion music. This became popular towards the middle of the 1980s. It is a form of electronic dance-music often based on African-American music styles. It features electronically induced fast beats as its musical style and is basically influenced by music technology.

Chapter fourteen | *Nicholas C. Akas, in*
Charles Nwadigwe, Molinta Enendu & Canice Nwosu (Eds.)
Metaphors and Climax, Reminiscences on the Drama and Theatre of Ogonna Agu
London, Adonis & Abbey Publishers

There are many other types of music but whatever the genre, music remains one of the most beloved human experiences. Everyone enjoys some sort of music as an accompaniment in almost every situation or human event. Paul states that:

> Man enters into this universe and exits with music. Music is the only common thing to everyone in the world. Though there are many different kinds of music, it is only one and the same. Music is one even though we call them by different names. It is just a part of whole music. (48)

Music is one of the greatest creations of humankind in the course of history. It plays a complementary role in man's emotional states. Prabhjit Singh explains that:

> Music is a way to escape life which gives us relief in pains and helps us to reduce the stress of daily routine. It helps us to calm down, and even excites us in the moment of joy. Moreover it enriches the mind and gives us self confidence. (45)

Music surrounds our lives at different moments whether we hear it over the radio, on television, from our car, in church and or at home. It is simply geared towards developing human beings mentally, socially, economically, and culturally in their daily existence. Sociologically, music serves as entertainment tool, corrective resource, arbitration support, means of livelihood, and a mark of identity. Modern African dramatists apply the vehicle of music in varying degrees and dimensions to achieve their artistic objectives. It is therefore necessary to investigate the application of music in Agu's drama.

Brief Insight into the Play

The play *Symbol of a Goddess* centres on the multiple impacts of the Biafran war especially how it affected the people sociologically, psychologically and politically, culturally and even sociologically,

Chapter fourteen | *Nicholas C. Akas, in*
Charles Nwadigwe, Molinta Enendu & Canice Nwosu (Eds.)
Metaphors and Climax, Reminiscences on the Drama and Theatre of Ogonna Agu
London, Adonis & Abbey Publishers

psychologically, morally. The Civil War ended but its long-term aftermath in the lives of the soldiers who fought at the battlefields remained to haunt their families and communities. To some of these people, such as Emenike, the war has not ended. Agu's *Symbol of a Goddess* therefore raises a number of questions that need to be answered urgently.

The music used in the play *Symbol of a Goddess* is of didactic essence. The playwright's good choice of music at any given time in the play semiotically gave an in-depth depiction and painted the colour of the action or situations portrayed in the play. Music was used as mental boost, a tool for tactical preparation, spiritual motivation and body fitness in the minds of Biafran soldiers. While getting ready for the big task of defending their country, music becomes a vehicle for raising the morale of the combatants, to shun any attempt to retreat, no matter the pressure mounted on them. Their watch word is forward ever and backwards never. This was abundantly shown in the song below:

> SOLDIERS: Agawalam Ikwa mgbo n'Otu Onitsha-Aye! Agawalam Ikwa mgbo Bebim ana-ebe si mgbo atukwala m n'amu. Bebi I si m'gbalaga, onye ga-akwanu mgbo ma m'gbalaga. Bebi I si m'gbalaga, onye ga-akwanu mgbo ma m'gbalaga. (6)

This song portrays Biafran soldiers as determined, strong-willed men that never believed in defeat or considered danger and other associated challenges as a stumbling block.

Furthermore, in *Symbol of a Goddess*, music still maintains its communicative potency by serving as a consoling tool in the minds of the refugees. The refugees were held hostage by their enemies, but with the aid of the consolatory message in their music, they are encouraged to be strong at all times no matter the pains they might be experiencing. For the stronger they remained in the pains without losing hope, the more they show themselves as worthy

Chapter fourteen | *Nicholas C. Akas, in*
Charles Nwadigwe, Molinta Enendu & Canice Nwosu (Eds.)
Metaphors and Climax, Reminiscences on the Drama and Theatre of Ogonna Agu
London, Adonis & Abbey Publishers

and true sons and daughters of Biafra. So the key word inside the refugees camp is endurance, for it is endurance that sustains the Biafra soldiers in the battle field to win the war, but lamentations bring discouragement and failure in the warfront where the Biafra soldiers are fighting the enemy. Good endurance with hope motivates the soldiers to win the war. This ideology was captured in song and music as shown in the narrator's comment:

> NARRATOR: (The refugees begin to enter still singing)
> Dibe Dibe Dibe Ndidi K'mma
> Dibe Dibe Dibe ndidi K'mma
> Onye omere ya dibe n'uwa Na Biafra nwe mmeri. (8)

Emenike who is an ex-Biafran solider adjusted the perception of the music by using it as a tool for self lamentation to depict his confusion and hopelessness in the hands of love. Emenike's dejection was shown in his adoring and constant sacrifices to the Queen Goddess without knowing when he will see her again. He bitterly laments by singing:

> EMENIKE: Lady of the red eyes where are you? You said you will tell me where you will be, I am waiting by the riverside, waiting by the bush paths, waiting by the forest, waiting by the mountain. Lady of the red eyes. When are we meeting again? I have not told you jeje, since you left me jeje. The ground is hot and the sky is red, since you left me. (19)

The above cry of lamentation by Emenike using music clearly placed him as a sacrificial lamb on the altar of compassion. He also goes further to show his love for birds through music. Emenike's love for the bird in this play goes far beyond the love for mere pets as erroneously conceived by his two relatives, Ide and Igbonekwu. To Emenike, the eagle is sacred and must be accorded the necessary respect. He sees the bird as his source of inspiration before and after war, therefore he named the bird Biafra. So, he felt

---

Chapter fourteen | *Nicholas C. Akas, in*
Charles Nwadigwe, Molinta Enendu & Canice Nwosu (Eds.)
Metaphors and Climax, Reminiscences on the Drama and
Theatre of Ogonna Agu
London, Adonis & Abbey Publishers

depressed when no one could give account of the bird's whereabouts. He portrays this in his song of lamentation:

EMENIKE: Kwolu m, Kwolu mmilo, Kpalanuma. Kwolu m, Kwolu mmuo Kpalanuma. Kwolughu m n'obu taa Kpalanuma Ukwolighi m n'obu taa Kpalanuma. Ogilisi nwa Eze Elo na ekwu okwu Kpalanuma. Kwolum m do-oo Kpalanuma. (22)

But his uncle Igbonekwu does not see any reason why Emenike should be angry or lament over the disappearance of a mere birds. He questions Emenike:

IGBONEKWU: Emenike, are you a bird? Do you live on a tree? Why must you go mad because a bird, a common bird flew out of the cage and found freedom in the forests? Why? (23)

The above utterance really provokes more anger in Emenike, therefore he warns against serious danger that will befall them if the birds were not found. The playwright also used folk musical heritage of the Igbo to address different situations as shown below:

EMENIKE: Okereke Okereke
Dududu gem-gem
Okereafo Okereafo
Dududu gem-gem
Kwe n'o gana-aga
O gana aga njem . . . (23)

Hence, Ogonna Agu used well-known indigenous music idioms in painting the true picture of the Biafra War and its side effects on ex-Biafra soldiers. The music reminds the audience that even though the Biafra War has come and gone, its aftermaths still remain evergreen in the minds of those who agitated and fought for Biafra.

Chapter fourteen | *Nicholas C. Akas, in*
Charles Nwadigwe, Molinta Enendu & Canice Nwosu (Eds.)
Metaphors and Climax, Reminiscences on the Drama and Theatre of Ogonna Agu
London, Adonis & Abbey Publishers

Conclusion

In many African plays, playwrights constructively infuse didactic elements using music as a vehicle for communicating the theme of the play. Music in Agu's *Symbol of a Goddess* sets the cultural environment, reinforces moods and aids in the understanding of the characters' state of mind. The environmental, sociological and cultural factors surrounding various dramatic scenes were obviously spelt out using the musical idiom of expression. Having critically analyzed Ogonna Agu's *Symbol of a Goddess* and established the communicative potency of the songs used in the play, the study concludes that the use of relevant indigenous musical idiom in the play significantly reveals the playwright's passionate intention to keep the Igbo and African heritage alive.

The dramatist applied the music idiom to arouse strong feelings towards visualizing and appreciating the philosophy, enthusiasm and pain of Biafra among its advocates. The songs are semiotic in the sense that they portray deeper meanings beyond the surface. The hopes and excitement of the soldiers, their anger and disappointment, their fear of the unknown, the lack of trust and eventual frustration and hostility experienced by the soldiers during and after the war were reflected by the songs and music which raised their emotional impact. Based on the communicative use of music in *Symbol of a Goddess*, music to Ogonna Agu seizes to be a mere medium for entertainment and becomes a positive tool for propagation and cultural nationalism. Conclusively, the potency of the music idiom in *Symbol of a Goddess* is not in doubt, it goes beyond conventional aesthetic melodic rendition for entertainment. Music, as an expressive idiom, in the hands of Ogonna Agu metamorphoses into a strong reflective device.

Chapter fourteen | *Nicholas C. Akas, in*
Charles Nwadigwe, Molinta Enendu & Canice Nwosu (Eds.)
Metaphors and Climax, Reminiscences on the Drama and Theatre of Ogonna Agu
London, Adonis & Abbey Publishers

Works Citied

Akas, Nicholas. "Expressing Indigenous Knowledge Through Dance." *African Journal of History and Culture.* 4:5 (2012): 69-73.

Anaagudo-Agu, Ogonna. *Symbol of a Goddess.* Calabar: Wusen Publishers, 2005.

Harvey, Alan. *A History of Western Music.* New York: Lawrence Hill Press, 2000.

Oshionebo, Barth and Akazue, Emem. "Music and Cultural Development in Nigeria." *Theatre Experience*: *Journal of Contemporary Theatre Practice.* 1:1 (2002): 70-79.

Onwuekwe Agatha. "The Socio-Cultural Implications of African Music and Dance." *The Creative Artist: A Journal of Theatre and Media Studies* 3:1 (2009): 171-185.

Paul, Ken. *African Music: A People's Art.* New York: Harcourt Brace Publishers, 2001.

Prabhjit, Singh. *Slave Songs of the United States.* New York: Peter Smith Publishers, 1999.

Chapter fourteen | *Nicholas C. Akas, in*
Charles Nwadigwe, Molinta Enendu & Canice Nwosu (Eds.)
Metaphors and Climax, Reminiscences on the Drama and Theatre of Ogonna Agu
London, Adonis & Abbey Publishers

Chapter Fifteen

Love and Responsibility: The Image of Women in Ogonna Agu's *Cry of a Maiden* and *Symbol of a Goddess*

Chidiebere Ekweariri & Ifeyinwa Uzondu

Introduction

Ogonna Anaagudo-Agu, a dramatist of humorous and friendly disposition, is a creative artiste who uses women as a centre-piece in most of his writings and treats love with utmost sense of seriousness. From *Adiaha the Beauty Queen* (a novel) to *Cry of a Maiden* and *Symbol of a Goddess* (plays), the story is the same. In these works, the issues of romance and relationship, apart from other noticeable themes, highlighted the images of love and responsibility on one part and the treatment of women, both positively and negatively on the other part. These relationships between the opposite sex are skillfully portrayed and used to advance the plot in the plays, sometimes with comic undertones.

Generally, the concept of love has been given different interpretations by people seeking to clarify its ubiquitous nature. It is an attribute of humans and as such exists in various dimensions and orientation between man and woman, man and man, as well as woman and woman. This also extends to brothers and sisters and extended family members. Thus, love according to Iferi manifests in the "individual's care for one another; to share emotions and to identify with the other beings" (230). Love and responsibility are not usually expected to be opposed but emanate out of sharing things in common and aim towards affection, care and attendant obligations. This is because responsible conduct may be an initial expression of love; similarly love could evolve or

Chapter fifteen | *Chidiebere Ekweariri & Ifeyinwa Uzondu, in*
Charles Nwadigwe, Molinta Enendu & Canice Nwosu (Eds.)
Metaphors and Climax, Reminiscences on the Drama And Theatre of Ogonna Agu
London, Adonis & Abbey Publishers

be reinforced through responsible behaviour. In other words, there is a symbiotic relationship between the two and quite often, women are usually at the forefront in most conventional love relationships whereas responsibility is often considered (rightly or wrongly) to be a man's problem especially in traditional environments.

Due to the universality of love and its primordial importance in the existence of man, it has become the focal point of most writers. In the long history of drama, the question of love and the issues connected with it have been recurrent. However, depending on their individual experience and perspectives, "playwrights tend to treat it from various viewpoints and in varying contexts" (Effa-Attoe 234). Love, to a large extent, revolves around women and tends to make them the cynosure of all eyes, the focal point and one essence of man's existence. Historically, man's existence has been influenced by the power of love-love for his God, love for his mother, love for his wife, love for his children and love for material things.

In the Nigerian context, many dramatic plots have been built on the themes of love and the responsibility that accompanies it. This study therefore aims at analyzing the dynamic relationships of love and responsibility and how the women are portrayed in the two plays. However, it has to be stated that the kind of love under discussion in this study does not include agape or Christian love but that which concerns deep-rooted emotions and passion that often result in a sexual relationship, intercourse and consequently, marriage.

Love, Lust and Responsibility: The Two Plays Juxtaposed

As earlier stated, attraction precedes love. Sometimes, the attraction begins as mere lust but invariably, it means that for love to exist there has to be an element of appeal, a kind of magnetism

Chapter fifteen | *Chidiebere Ekweariri & Ifeyinwa Uzondu, in*
Charles Nwadigwe, Molinta Enendu & Canice Nwosu (Eds.)
Metaphors and Climax, Reminiscences on the Drama and
Theatre of Ogonna Agu
London, Adonis & Abbey Publishers

between the persons intending to love and be loved. This is clearly the case in the two plays. In *Cry of a Maiden*, Chidum comes back from the Burma and Palestine war zones, and was magnetized by the transformation in Ada. He develops interest in her and wants to marry Ada. But, Okolo on the other hand, had all along liked Ada but could not make his intentions known until it dawned on him to make haste because of Chidum's declaration to get married. On the part of Ada, even though she finally married Okolo, her heart was with Chidum and would have married him if not for Okolo's antics. In all these, the love for a woman becomes glaring.

The fight that ensued between Okolo and Chidum was not necessarily caused by the sudden realization of the fact that Chidum had broken Okolo's calabash, but rather their different love aspirations and desire to own Ada. All other actions in the play are used to expatiate this. When Okolo's attraction began as lust, hence he sought to "break her calabash of wine", encouraged by Awili. When the romance develops to the point of impregnating Ada, his lust metamorphosed into love which blossomed. He became ready to take full responsibility in order to be with her forever. This can be seen in his lines when he declares; "in your name shall I challenge the demons, whoever dares to touch the maiden calabash of wine" (36).

In *Symbol of a Goddess*, love is represented as having complex dimensions-love for one's country, love for one's child and the love for the water goddess-a woman. Below these love relationships are the shadows of infatuation, lust and responsibility. Emenike's behaviour is ruled by love for the only thing that is close to his heart-Biafra. There is no doubt that he is attracted to Akudiri and would have accepted her if not for the ego in him and his dream. At some occasions, his lust provokes intermittent romance with her and this resulted in pregnancy. But Emenike would not assume responsibility by accepting Akudiri

Chapter fifteen | *Chidiebere Ekweariri & Ifeyinwa Uzondu, in*
Charles Nwadigwe, Molinta Enendu & Canice Nwosu (Eds.)
Metaphors and Climax, Reminiscences on the Drama and
Theatre Of Ogonna Agu
London, Adonis & Abbey Publishers

and her baby. He felt it would be a distraction to the one and only dream he was pursuing. The river goddess symbolizes his desire for Biafra. In the play, Emenike becomes sober and somewhat elated each time he remembers his first encounter with her. The urge to see her again intoxicates him and beclouds his sense of reasoning and all effort made by his mother and brothers to bring him back to his right senses were fruitless.

Iluka, driven by motherly love, was more concerned with Emenike consummating his proxy marriage to Akudiri (through sexual intercourse), hoping that out of such infatuation and lust, an enduring love would be kindled. But Emenike's affection was directed elsewhere; he was more willing to die for his true love, the woman of the deep waters and that was exactly what happened at the end of the play. On the part of Akudiri, she liked Emenike and accepted to marry him even when he was not physically present on the day she arrived his home. She was docile, obedient and patient enough to allow love to incubate, hatch and grow between him and Emenike. She also accepted the responsibility traditionally expected of a good wife. For one year, she lived without seeing her husband; but she continued to stay even against her mother's wish; believing that all would be well. The more she longed to see him, the more her love grows. When eventually Emenike resurfaced, her joy knew no bounds. She loved him the more and made concerted efforts to woo him to herself. When she cries, she does so because her love has not been reciprocated. When Emenike's attention is momentarily drawn away from her goddess back to his environment, he gets attracted to Akudiri. But his infatuation was not accompanied by commitment and responsibility. They remained strange bed fellows and often Emenike bluntly rejects and dismisses her without any feeling. Judging from these, it will be right to say that in the two plays, love and lust play both symbiotic and alternate

Chapter fifteen | *Chidiebere Ekweariri & Ifeyinwa Uzondu, in*
Charles Nwadigwe, Molinta Enendu & Canice Nwosu (Eds.)
Metaphors and Climax, Reminiscences on the Drama and
Theatre of Ogonna Agu
London, Adonis & Abbey Publishers

relationships and as such complement or confuse each other depending on the circumstance.

The Image of Women in the Plays

In the context of the discussion, this image revolves around how women are portrayed by the author through their actions and inactions. According to Worugji *et.al* "an image is a personification or a picture an individual has of himself or another person. Thus, the pictures or impressions we carry about others are hardly correct descriptions of the people they refer to" (143). Therefore, whether the opinions expressed in this study are in tandem with the perceived nature of women generally or otherwise does not in any way undermine the collaborative functions of women in the society. Although this may be termed a feminist study, the researchers are not in any way advocating for "equal social and political rights for women to those of their men" (Lerner 236). The presentation in most cases, is not rigorous or ideologically framed, but rather depends on the content of the play. Therefore, the analysis can be seen as conventional while operating within a cultural reality. This is captured more by Yerima when he opines that "the situation the woman finds herself in some Nigerian plays reflects on how the playwright had chosen to present her within the cultural reality and practice of the people she emerges from or represents in the play" (61). This argument forms the basis upon which the image of women is interrogated in the two plays of Ogonna selected for this study.

In both plays, the men dominate major roles while women play complementing parts. Nevertheless, the images of the women are portrayed in different lights, both positively and negatively. One of such depictions is that the women are represented as weaklings and incapable of solving knotty problems. For instance, when Chidum wanted to get married, even when the mother was

| Chapter fifteen | *Chidiebere Ekweariri & Ifeyinwa Uzondu, in* Charles Nwadigwe, Molinta Enendu & Canice Nwosu (Eds.) *Metaphors and Climax, Reminiscences on the Drama and Theatre Of Ogonna Agu* London, Adonis & Abbey Publishers |

around, he did not ask for her assistance in convincing Okolo to allow him do so, rather he sought Okpala's intervention. This is based on the custom and belief system that a guardian's opinion is usually weighty during such occasions and that women usually play the second fiddle in that respect.

Another point is that in the two plays, the women are portrayed as always being at the mercy of men. The events and happenings between Okolo and Ada are testimonies to this fact. Ada was wooed and impregnated and thereafter becomes solely dependent on Okolo's conscience either to formally accept the pregnancy and present a wine on her head or not. In the *Symbol of a Goddess*, Emenike's mother could not take decisions on her own to marry for Emenike without the consent of her extended family members. She begged for support in the following lines.

ILUKA: Am saying that he should marry-
IDE: Igbo, have you heard? (*bursts out laughing*) Emenike to marry and bear children. When will it happen in this world!
ILUKA: I am telling you people to support me. I will marry for him!
(20-21)

This affirms the cultural fact that in the issue of marriage, men play major roles and decide who comes in and who goes out. This also places women in a disadvantaged position and makes their place less important. Similarly, Akudiri is made to tolerate the overbearing negligence of her husband, Emenike even when she has not met him before. To further buttress her subordinate nature, each time she is aggrieved and downcast because of Emenike's attitude to her, she merely cries and finds solace in lamentation; thereby proving that women can hardly hold their emotions and do not take commanding positions when it comes to relationships and marriage. Under such emotional burden, "this supposed 'weakness' of the women now becomes a ploy in the hands of her user a male mentor who determines her life and roles in society"

Chapter fifteen | *Chidiebere Ekweariri & Ifeyinwa Uzondu, in*
Charles Nwadigwe, Molinta Enendu & Canice Nwosu (Eds.)
Metaphors and Climax, Reminiscences on the Drama and
Theatre of Ogonna Agu
London, Adonis & Abbey Publishers

(Ekpa 3). They must dance to the whims and caprices of their male counterparts.

However, it has to be pointed out, at this juncture, that it is not all about negativity as far as women are concerned in the two plays. There are positive elements of femininity and power in them, to the extent that their powers are also felt. In this context, the women showed some strength to illustrate their doggedness and determination especially when aggrieved. For instance, the woman whose basket of fish was stolen by Awili shows all these. She was bold enough to confront him when she saw him with her basket of fish and made her promise of making life uncomfortable for him in the village. They argue thus:

WOMAN: The thief you are, do you know what you've done?
AWILI: What is it I've done?
WOMAN: Fox!
AWILI: Enough woman. You're talking to a man
WOMAN: Shut up! The man you are! If you don't know you are a blot on this village
AWILI: Thank you
WOMAN: By the way what do you think you are?
AWILI: Yours sincerely
WOMAN: Ssssssh. Don't talk. You think I'm those women with whom you frolic under the dim lamps at night?
AWILI: My God! How this woman renders me valueless!
WOMAN: Thief! Thief! That's what you are! (*Picking the bone and throwing at him*) You wait. I'll see you executed in public (*exit woman*) (24-25).

This shows courage and implies that even though women are presumed the weaker sex, they still possess some power and whenever they are aggrieved and determined, they can really be difficult to control.

The women are also portrayed as "necessary evil" and stabilizing agents in the lives of men. Emenike's mother felt that

Chapter fifteen | *Chidiebere Ekweariri & Ifeyinwa Uzondu, in*
Charles Nwadigwe, Molinta Enendu & Canice Nwosu (Eds.)
Metaphors and Climax, Reminiscences on the Drama and
Theatre Of Ogonna Agu
London, Adonis & Abbey Publishers

the only way to tame the behaviour of Emenike was to marry a woman for him; a woman who will refocus his attention and interest for good. Chidum and Okolo knew that without a wife by their side, their potential may not be realized, hence the frantic effort to get married. In addition, within their cultural environment, a male can only be regarded a man and considered responsible if he takes a wife. Hence, all the intrigues in the plays are played around this desirable model of masculinity.

Observations

Although men are often assumed to rule and control the world, but in reality, according to Chinweizu "the women rule and control the men that rule the world" (12). This is in line with the old adage that "the hand that rocks the cradle rules the world" (Ajayi 11). These maxims become relevant in the worlds of the characters especially as it concerns the role of women in the two plays. All the actions and inactions of the men in the two plays are clear cut examples. Anene's doggedness and untiring spirit is geared towards satisfying his wives and making them happy. This agrees with Esther's opinion that "man's work is only done with women in view" (qtd. in Chinweizu 12). Okolo and Chidum's resolve to kill themselves in a physical combat is basically to prove their love for Ada and win her in the process. On the other hand, Emenike's recalcitrant behaviour is controlled by the decision to meet his love-the water goddess.

Indeed, nature has placed women in the position they have found themselves and men seem to be merely obeying the laws of nature. There is therefore no basis for "some women trying to take over from the men the work already planned for them by providence" (Anedo 141). For the feminist, it should be understood that the seemingly prejudiced stance of the playwright in terms of the position he gave the women in these plays is not

Chapter fifteen | *Chidiebere Ekweariri & Ifeyinwa Uzondu, in*
Charles Nwadigwe, Molinta Enendu & Canice Nwosu (Eds.)
Metaphors and Climax, Reminiscences on the Drama and
Theatre of Ogonna Agu
London, Adonis & Abbey Publishers

aimed at subjugation and exhibition of man's dominance over women but rather designed to show the inalienable relationship that exist between man and woman. It further goes to represent a cultural reality, a kind of mutual cooperation or oppression in the gender relationships. The plays also highlight the subordinate place of women in the lives of men and also substantiates the fact that men are pawn in the hands of women. The picture is dynamic and depends on the circumstance.

Conclusion

Creative writers and artists draw inspirations from their culture and environment. They draw from such backgrounds and use their literary prowess to create realistic characters and assign responsibilities to them. The nature of this responsibility is defined by the culture and thematic preoccupation of the playwright. The two plays investigated are culturally grounded and deal with aspects of Igbo traditions that are often dominated by men. However, the culture also recognizes the position of women in the society and their pride of place in the heart of men. From the two plays, what nurtures this affection is love and responsibility. When love blossoms, responsibility is expected to take centre-stage to on the parts of both parties to nurture the relationship.

The dramatic situations created in both plays by Agu also suggest that infatuation and lust often come into play in gender relationships and this is sometimes confused as love. It does not usually involve commitments and responsibility. But love sometimes grows out of initial show of infatuation or lust and this brings about attitudinal change and more responsible behaviour from the man thereby mystifying the field of love and affection. Women's role therefore is a reflection of the cultural exigencies established by nature. Playwrights merely recreate (or subvert) that cultural experience. Hence, culturally and biblically, the image

Chapter fifteen | *Chidiebere Ekweariri & Ifeyinwa Uzondu, in*
Charles Nwadigwe, Molinta Enendu & Canice Nwosu (Eds.)
Metaphors and Climax, Reminiscences on the Drama and
Theatre Of Ogonna Agu
London, Adonis & Abbey Publishers

of African women in creative writings, from all ramifications has continued to be misinterpreted especially by the feminist scholars in their bid to bridge the gap between man and woman in society. This is quite unnecessary because naturally man and woman complement each other and whatever role women and men perform as portrayed in creative arts are mere manifestations of their natural roles other than the so-called gender roles imposed by the society.

Works Cited

Anaagudo-Agu, Ogonna. *Cry of a Maiden*. Calabar: Wusen Press, 2000.

Anaagudo-Agu, Ogonna. *Symbol of a Goddess*. Calabar: University of Calabar Press, 2005.

Ajayi, Frank. "The Image and Influence of Women in Traditional Times: The Nigerian Example." *Arts Courier: African Journal of Arts and Idea*. 9 (2011): 11-56.

Anedo, Onukwube, A. "Culture and Women Empowerment in Contemporary Africa: Igbo Women in Perspective." *AMA: Journal of Theatre and Cultural Studies*. 5:1 (2010): 141-159.

Chinweizu. *Anatomy of Female Power: A Masculinist Dissection of Matriarchy*. Lagos: Pero Press, 1990.

Effah-Attoe, Stella. "The Concept of Love in African Theatre." *The Dramaturgy of Liberation and Survival: Festschrift Essays on Chris Nwamuo's Scholarship*. Ed. Andrew Esekong and Babson Ajibade. Calabar: University of Calabar Press, 2009. 234-237.

Ekpa, Anthonia A. "A Demythification of Gender Power: Jacob Hevi's Celebration of Woman's Strength and Invincible Spirit in *Amavi*." *UNICAL Quarterly: A Journal of the Academic Staff Union of University of Calabar*. 1:2 (1996): 1-15.

Chapter fifteen | *Chidiebere Ekweariri & Ifeyinwa Uzondu, in*
Charles Nwadigwe, Molinta Enendu & Canice Nwosu (Eds.)
Metaphors and Climax, Reminiscences on the Drama and Theatre of Ogonna Agu
London, Adonis & Abbey Publishers

Iferi, Patience. "The Theme of Love in African Drama: A Study of *The Substitute* and *Wedlock of the Gods*. *The Dramaturgy of Liberation and Survival: Festschrift Essays on Chris Nwamuo's Scholarship*. Ed. Andrew Esekong and Babson Ajibade. Calabar: University of Calabar Press, 2009. 230-233.

Lerner, Gerda. *The Creation of Patriarchy*. New York: Oxford University Press, 1986.

Worugji, Gloria, Bojor Enamhe and Eton Simon. "Image of Women: Custom and Modernity in Selected Plays of James Ene Henshaw." *Applause: Journal of Theatre and Media Studies*. 1:4 (2008): 141-158.

Yerima, Ahmed. "The Woman as Character in Nigeria Drama: A Discourse of Gender and Culture." *Trends in the Theory and Practice of Theatre in Nigeria*. Eds. Duro Oni and Ahmed Yerima. Ibadan: SONTA. 2008. 59-75.

Chapter fifteen | *Chidiebere Ekweariri & Ifeyinwa Uzondu, in*
Charles Nwadigwe, Molinta Enendu & Canice Nwosu (Eds.)
Metaphors and Climax, Reminiscences on the Drama and
Theatre Of Ogonna Agu
London, Adonis & Abbey Publishers

Chapter Sixteen

Individuality and Reconciliation in Agu's *Symbol of a Goddess*

Edet Essien

Introduction

The arts including drama, remain veritable avenues for human expression. Zulu Sofola underlines the fact that from the perspective of African worldview, art is meant to heal and restore life to a sick and battered humanity. This paves way for growth, renewal, regeneration and edification of man for a fulfilling life and better community. It is equally to harness the collective conscience for a particular desired objective (qtd. in Iji 116). Drama, an arm of the performing arts, has through centuries performed the task of projecting society's ethos using raw materials extracted from the community itself. Thus, drama and society operate from a mutual and symbiotic pedestal. Tse confirms that "theatre and society enjoy a symbiotic relationship. . . because drama and theatre act as mirror through which the society sees itself and takes corrections" (68).

In the course of its endeavour, drama makes prescriptions aimed at solving societies' problems. These are often pungent and the expected corrective actions lie within the threshold of the individual and the environment under the prevailing circumstances. The roles of these sub-sets are critical and hinge on the capacity to harmonize and reconcile towards progressive and developmental gains. The overall aim of drama in this regard is to help create a desirable atmosphere within the society, where the constituent parts can adequately function without encumbrances,

Chapter sixteen | *Edet Essien, in*
Charles Nwadigwe, Molinta Enendu & Canice Nwosu (Eds.)
Metaphors and Climax, Reminiscences on the Drama and Theatre of Ogonna Agu
London, Adonis & Abbey Publishers

towards the growth and development of the entire system. All the component parts are vital in this exercise. A flaw in one affects the others as well.

Consequently, this study examines the play, *Symbol of a Goddess* with particular critical focus on the personality of Emenike as an individual in society, his inability to adequately reconcile to the environment and prevailing circumstances after the Biafran War, and the attendant effects.

The Play

Ogonna Agu's *Symbol of a Goddess* begins with a Narrator who gives a background to the Biafran War and its effect on the citizenry. Emenike is introduced as a courageous soldier. He is said to have fought at Abagana, Gekem, Ore and Otuocha. He is not willing to lay down his arms, even when Ojukwu, hero of the battle left in search of everlasting peace. The war ends but some soldiers, Emenike inclusive return home with their guns. The Narrator wonders what this portends for the people and communities. The message spreads to Emenike's village; the war has ended. People are happy, but Iluka (Emenike's mother) weeps for her child. She is consoled by Igbonekwu and Ide that Emenike will be back. True to their words, Emenike soon enters with his gun but starts unleashing terror on them. Ide narrowly escapes being shot and invites Commander and the Federal forces.

They arrive in the absence of Emenike and destroy his eagle's cage and take his mother away as hostage and bait to make him come out. They do this in spite of entreaties from Igbonekwu. Meanwhile, Emenike is with Okobe the masquerade leader requesting for an anklet even though he is not an *Ozo* title holder. When Emenike returns, he learns of the visit by Commander. His mother advises him to marry and settle down to no avail. The Commander and his group re-visit. Emenike hides but is nearly

Chapter sixteen | *Edet Essien, in*
Charles Nwadigwe, Molinta Enendu & Canice Nwosu (Eds.)
Metaphors and Climax, Reminiscences on the Drama and
Theatre of Ogonna Agu
London, Adonis & Abbey Publishers

caught when a search ensues. They pull down his hut revealing a mask head.

Six months after Emenike's escape, his mother marries Akudiri for him. The Old Man (Village Head) uses spiritual powers to bring Emenike back. Finally, Emenike resurfaces. He does not appreciate what his mother did; marrying for him, when he is already married to the woman of the sea. However, later, he could not continue to resist the girl; to the admiration and satisfaction of Ugonne and Iluka. This does not prevent him from resenting Akudiri and quarrelling with Iluka for bringing her. He equally fights with Ide whom he sees as a collaborator. In anger, he smashes the mirror in his inner room with his bare hand and asks Iluka to return Akudiri, who is now pregnant.

The play ends at the domain of the Obi of Ezeala with the elders and town folks. Here, Ide tries to show what a nuisance Emenike has been. Igbonekwu seems to have changed his mind and believes that Emenike should be left alone to practice his art. Emenike invokes the spirit of *Agboghommuo* and the masked spirit appears briefly and does a fast movement before collapsing into a mass of cloth. Emenike raises a song, collapses midway and dies, leaving Akudiri who is now heavily pregnant. Okobe enters and loosens his ankle string as mourners sing a dirge and take the body off the stage.

Self and Opposition in *Symbol of a Goddess*

Wars are borne out of disagreement. Individuals with varying wishes and aspirations are often compelled to be part of wars in order to realize a particular goal. In the end, the envisaged goal may be achieved fully, in part or not at all. The end of war often comes with reconciliation. Here, the individuals who prosecuted the war are expected to reconcile themselves to the environment and prevailing circumstance and forge on. This was the case with

Chapter sixteen | *Edet Essien, in*
Charles Nwadigwe, Molinta Enendu & Canice Nwosu (Eds.)
Metaphors and Climax, Reminiscences on the Drama and
Theatre of Ogonna Agu
London, Adonis & Abbey Publishers

the Biafran War. It ended with the slogan "No Victor, No Vanquished". Emenike as a veteran of the war needed to face reality and embrace the new order. He did not. He seemed to believe so much in the cause:

IGBONEKWU: I am a true born of the land... nwodinana ka m bu. True born original...

EMENIKE: Shut up! (*He points the gun at Ide still lying prostate on the ground*).

IGBONEKWU: (*moves closer*). No no no. Emenike keep that gun... don't shoot please don't shoot. The war has ended.

EMENIKE: (*shouts*) It has not ended!

IGBONEKWU: You have not come here to continue the war?

EMENIKE: I say it has not ended! We'll continue the fight! (*Emenike brings down his gun, looks at the body on the ground and turns to go*). (Agu 12)

Emenike should have reconciled his belief in Biafra with the prevailing circumstance and realize that the war has ended; he needs to get on with normal life. Every individual is free to hold an opinion and ideology but these should be in consonance with the environment and the prevailing circumstances. Where such ideologies appear detrimental to the individual and the environment (society), it is expedient to resolve it in the interest of the individual and society. These (individual and environment) are the backdrops and canvas upon which ideologies and opinions are painted. Without them, what exists is a vacuum. Emenike, for holding tenaciously to a moribund cause, became a nuisance to himself, his family and the society.

ILUKA: Emenike are you well at all?

EMENIKE: I don't want to set eyes on them again

ILUKA: Your relatives? Now you have asked them to go, are you satisfied?

EMENIKE: Yes! I am satisfied!

ILUKA: Now you are divided

Chapter sixteen | *Edet Essien, in*
Charles Nwadigwe, Molinta Enendu & Canice Nwosu (Eds.)
Metaphors and Climax, Reminiscences on the Drama and Theatre of Ogonna Agu
London, Adonis & Abbey Publishers

EMENIKE:	Who divided us?
ILUKA:	The Commander. Now people will laugh at you.
EMENIKE:	Why? Is my head like the head of their children?
ILUKA:	They have the Commander on their side.
EMENIKE:	The enemy!
ILUKA:	All the men in your age grade have gone to thank him for chasing you out of the village. (Agu 25-26)

The eagle symbolizes strength and power. On the other hand, it represents ruthlessness. The disappearance of the eagle and the destruction of the nest by Commander and his lieutenants seems to show the evaporation of Biafra's power and the removal of its pedestal. Emenike himself names the bird, Biafra.

It is the dream of every good mother to see her children grow and build up their own families. Where there seems to be a problem, the mother and other concerned relatives are expected to take remedial measures towards the path of rectitude. So, Iluka did exactly what every caring mother should do for a son who has refused to settle down. By marrying Akudiri for him, she was trying to bring her son to the path of rectitude. But Emenike was busy celebrating his love for the woman of the sea. However, he could not help singing love songs to Akudiri and making love to her. This is because, no matter what one does or professes, the real and natural self comes to the fore, from time to time. Emenike's tenacious belief in Biafra and the woman of the sea, seriously affected his interpersonal relationships.

Every African community necessarily has a Village Head; the chief security officer saddled with the maintenance of law and order and the protection of life and properties within the parameters of the community. Emenike's ordeal threatens the peace and security of the community. It was the place of the Old Man (Village Head) to take charge and solve the problem amicably. He did not. Ide invites the Commander instead. We only see the Village Head in one scene, using ancestral prayers to bring

Chapter sixteen	*Edet Essien, in*
	Charles Nwadigwe, Molinta Enendu & Canice Nwosu (Eds.)
	Metaphors and Climax, Reminiscences on the Drama and
	Theatre of Ogonna Agu
	London, Adonis & Abbey Publishers

back Emenike. When this eventually happens, the threat is not removed. Emenike's disposition is still the same.

Emenike seems to attribute his disposition to his involvement with the woman of the sea. Although Water Spirit devotees within Nigeria are sometimes held in awe, their goddess is believed to be tranquil and regal in outlook and not as violent and destructive as presented in popular imagination and literature. Their adherents often seek solitude where they sing and dance to themselves. Bamidele insist that "Art as a cultural system presupposes that literature as art, discusses the world view of a people in a way that is concrete and positive but not dialectical" (19). Emenike's problems can really be traced to his inability to face reality and move with time.

The Fruits of Incompatibility

The cardinal effect of Emenike's non-reconciliatory disposition is that, he becomes a terror to the community. In an encounter, he nearly shot one of his relatives. People became apprehensive over issues concerning him, including his relatives. As such, he lost the support which would have come to him from members of the community by way of advice and guidance. The African social environment is a communal format where integration and support from the components is of immense value.

Emenike himself could not live a free life rather that of fear and aggression. He was fighting battles from different fronts. The Commander and his soldiers were after him. It was a stroke of luck that in one of the encounters, he escaped. They nearly caught him:

EMENIKE: (*irritably*) Don't tell me! I asked you, who were you talking to? Decent wife? Nwaanyi di mma o kwa ya? Look, let me tell you, my goddess still lives. If not in the river, on the trees. (*Trumpet sound is heard*)

Chapter sixteen | *Edet Essien, in*
Charles Nwadigwe, Molinta Enendu & Canice Nwosu (Eds.)
Metaphors and Climax, Reminiscences on the Drama and
Theatre of Ogonna Agu
London, Adonis & Abbey Publishers

EMENIKE: Gosh! Here they come again. *(The sound of boots approaching is heard. Emenike looks up, calculating. Then he makes a swift escape. Commander now enters, followed by Ide and two soldiers. There is jubilation, from a few hangabouts).* (Agu, 27)

Emenike's hut was later pulled down by the soldiers. Nevertheless, his belief and driving force remained a barrier to his reintegration into his community after the war. Even though the origin of his involvement with the goddess remains hazy; not adequately expounded in the play, it became a blockade to his settling down with a wife. Iluka his mother attempted to remedy this but the step was slightly faulty. Every god or goddess within African communities have priests or priestesses or other intermediaries. She should have availed herself of this avenue knowing her son's professed involvement with the water goddess. She should not have stopped at marrying for him. Perhaps a better solution would have been reached because marrying for him alone did not stop his antics.

Akudiri, Emenike's wife through Iluka could not actually savour the bliss of matrimony. She was affected by the behaviour of Emenike. Sometimes, he was violent with her. Sometimes, he tried to be nice but the image of the sea woman still lingered. When she became pregnant, the attendant love and care for women in this condition from the husband, was not there. Emenike collapsed and left her when she was heavily pregnant. The trauma can only be imagined.

Emenike disregarded norms and values. He got Okobe to give him an anklet which is reserved for *Ozo* title holders. The playwright's presentation seems to aptly portray the irreconcilable nature of Emenike and his disregard for normalcy and maintenance of status quo.

Chapter sixteen | *Edet Essien, in*
Charles Nwadigwe, Molinta Enendu & Canice Nwosu (Eds.)
Metaphors and Climax, Reminiscences on the Drama and Theatre of Ogonna Agu
London, Adonis & Abbey Publishers

Reflections

Any story concerning the arts, including drama relates to us as a people; our perceptions of the world as we have come to see and respond to it. The arts go further to express our understandings of the world (Sporre 12). Furthermore, playwriting (the art of putting together drama pieces) would remain an exercise in futility if it fails to portray and draw attention to certain anomalies in the society-the world we find ourselves (Essien 107).

The play under study has shown that every blot starts with a dot. It expresses the need for individuals as sub-sets of the society to reconcile themselves to the environment and the prevailing circumstances. It seems to reiterate the fact that change is constant. We should lend ourselves to it or slip into oblivion. We should follow the current and trend or be left wallowing in the corridors of stagnation. Emenike's incompatible disposition in the play became a stumbling block and affected not only himself but the family and community at large. Discussing characters in dramas, Wallis and Shepherd opine that, we expect them to adapt to changing circumstances, to develop (19). Thus, without adapting to the prevailing circumstances, the character does not develop. This is the case with the personality of Emenike. The play is a lesson in selflessness; the need to harmonize with the wishes and aspirations of others within the society and the need to suppress individual disposition (self) in favour of a common one. If Emenike had this realization and suppressed his own desires in favour of the prevailing circumstances, he may not have met the tragic end.

Emenike was not alone in the Biafran War and he is not the only one affiliated to the goddess. He seemed to carry his beliefs to extremes without cognizance of what transpires around him. Being the only child of the family, the continuance of the family line and

Chapter sixteen | *Edet Essien, in*
Charles Nwadigwe, Molinta Enendu & Canice Nwosu (Eds.)
Metaphors and Climax, Reminiscences on the Drama and
Theatre of Ogonna Agu
London, Adonis & Abbey Publishers

Iluka's hope and consolation lie squarely in him. Instead of realizing all these and facing reality, he carried his philosophy beyond reasonable boundaries to his detriment. He could not control or master himself.

Conclusion

The society is composed of interrelated and dependent members. None of the constituents can exist and function in isolation. The emphasis is harmonious existence; regard for the opinions and existence of other constituents is the watchword. The individual in the society cannot exist without cognizance of the environment including other people and the prevailing situation. Emenike and characters of his type in the wider society need to realize and come to terms with the above mentioned components. Failure would always result in fatal consequences.

Works Cited

Anaagudo-Agu, Ogonna. *Symbol of a Goddess*. Calabar: University of Calabar Press, 2005.

Bamidele, L. O. *Literature and Sociology*. Lagos: Stirling–Horden, 2003.

Essien, Edet. "*The Squeeze*: A Virtuosal Presentation of the Nigerian Project." *The Dramaturgy of Liberation and Survival: Festschrift Essays on Chris Nwamuo's Scholarship*. Eds. Andrew Esekong and Babson Ajibade. Calabar: University of Calabar Press, 2009. 99-108.

Iji, Edde M. *Towards Greater Dividends: Developmental Imperatives*. Calabar: BAAJ, 2001.

Chapter sixteen | *Edet Essien, in*
Charles Nwadigwe, Molinta Enendu & Canice Nwosu (Eds.)
Metaphors and Climax, Reminiscences on the Drama and Theatre of Ogonna Agu
London, Adonis & Abbey Publishers

Sporre, Dennis J. *Reality Through the Arts*. 4th Edition. New Jersey: Prentice-Hall, 2001.

Tse, Andera P. "The Role of Drama and Theatre in Stabilizing the Nigerian Polity". *Makurdi Journal of Arts and Culture* 6 (2006): 68-77.

Wallis, Mick and Shepherd, Simon. *Studying Plays*. 3rd Edition. London: Bloomsbury Publishing Plc, 2010.

Chapter sixteen | *Edet Essien, in*
Charles Nwadigwe, Molinta Enendu & Canice Nwosu (Eds.)
Metaphors and Climax, Reminiscences on the Drama and Theatre of Ogonna Agu
London, Adonis & Abbey Publishers

Chapter Seventeen

Seniority in Igbo Culture: An Existentialist Reading of Ogonna Agu's *Cry of a Maiden*

Anthony Ebiriukwu

Introduction

"Why do siblings fight one another?" This is a fundamental question raised by Ogonna in his "Dramaturgist's Note" to *Cry of a Maiden*. The exploration of this thematic strand is apt due to its socio-political relevance in traditional African society. Hence, seniority based on age, ranks and ranking as precipitates of social and political instability in African societies become the focus of this chapter. Ogonna's exploration of these issues in *Cry of a Maiden* is metaphorical, therefore, it may be argued that the playwright does not make a categorical condemnation of the cultural practice of seniority by age in traditional African societies. Nevertheless, its meaning and application in the thought and thematic fixation of *Cry of a Maiden* remain palpable. Dobie affirms that "unlike the scientist, who strives for directness and similarities of meaning, the poet, who speaks of experience, uses ambiguity to reach for meaning through language that is suggestive, compressed and multi-leveled" (43). Similarly, Nwabueze declares that:

> . . . meaning is always deferral and cannot be completely grasped because there is no fixed system of knowledge and therefore no finite, absolute meaning in a text. The deconstructionist believes that there is a multitude of competing meanings in a text, each of which denies the primacy of the others. (18)

Chapter seventeen | *Anthony Ebiriukwu, in*
Charles Nwadigwe, Molinta Enendu & Canice Nwosu (Eds.)
Metaphors and Climax, Reminiscences on the Drama and Theatre of Ogonna Agu
London, Adonis & Abbey Publishers

Thus, it follows from the above postulations that meanings, especially in dramatic texts, are indeterminate, and journey through a transformational presence. The playwright treats the issues of power, authority and inheritance on the basis of seniority by age as a major cause of social and political conflicts in Igbo society. In *Cry of a Maiden*, one of the characters, Chidum, the second son, cannot take a wife because Okolo, the first, has not taken. Though tradition are on the side of Okolo, Chidum in a typical manner of an existentialist hero, revolts against this age-long cultural practice standing between his lover and himself. The situation becomes dicey enough to trigger conflict and social chaos as the elders in the bid to keep to the mores of their community appear to sympathize with Okolo. Agu is not alone in the treatment of this issue. In J.P. Clark's *Ozidi*, it was the underlying factor that strains the relationship between Temugedege and his brother Ozidi. In Duruaku's *Silhouette*, seniority by age questions the traditional stipulation of the "second line" right (the right of the second wife) to produce the successor to the throne. Even in some classical tragedies like Sophocles' *Oedipus at Colonus*, the issue of seniority by age forms the thematic force that triggered the conflict between the two sons of Oedipus, Polyneices and Eteocles that accelerated the tension in the already shattered home of the ill-fated Oedipus. The Nigerian Home Video Films also utilize the issue of seniority by age as conflict generation mechanism as reflected in Amaechi Ukeje's *His Majesty, Her Holiness* and in Ugo Ugbo's *Last Battle of Honour*.

Societal Mores and Existentialist Principles

The human person has always protested against any form of restriction to his freedom. Many philosophers of old have found discursive insight in exploring the issue of man's freedom especially in a hostile and indifferent universe. Such philosophers

Chapter seventeen | *Anthony Ebiriukwu, in*
Charles Nwadigwe, Molinta Enendu & Canice Nwosu (Eds.)
Metaphors and Climax, Reminiscences on the Drama and Theatre of Ogonna Agu
London, Adonis & Abbey Publishers

include, among others, Kierkegaard, Dostoyevsky, Nietzsche, and Sartre who according to John MacQuarrie, despite doctrinal differences "shared the belief that philosophical thinking begins with the human subject – not merely the thinking subject, but the acting, feeling, living human individual" (MacQuarrie 14-15). Soren Kierkegaard, one of the first existentialist Philosophers proposed that; "each individual not society or religion-is solely responsible for giving meaning to life and living it passionately and sincerely" (Lowrie 38). Thus, the concept of freedom is the individual's awareness of self and the giving of meaning and value to his life without any form of external influence and inhibition. Crowell explains in an online article that though arising out of historical convenience, existentialism nevertheless:

> Was explicitly adopted as, a self-description by Jean-Paul Sartre, and through the wide dissemination of the postwar literary and philosophical output of Sartre and his associates – notably Simone de Beauvoir, Moris Merieau-Ponty, Albert Camus. (np)

Crowell argues further that the importance of contemporary inquiry into the subject matter of existentialism is not only because of its roots in existence;

> But rather its claim that thinking about human existence requires new categories not found in the conceptual repertoire of ancient or modern thought; human beings can be understood neither as substances with fixed properties, nor as objects interacting with a world of objects. (np)

The existentialists' view therefore is that neither the world of psychology nor of the natural sciences stands to know or understand the composition of the human person. Thus, it is the existentialist's preoccupation to put man at the fore-front of philosophical thinking that is at every life's endeavour whose starting point is characterized by what has been described as "the existential attitude", free-will or choice. The overriding purpose of

Chapter seventeen | *Anthony Ebiriukwu, in*
Charles Nwadigwe, Molinta Enendu & Canice Nwosu (Eds.)
Metaphors and Climax, Reminiscences on the Drama and
Theatre of Ogonna Agu
London, Adonis & Abbey Publishers

Sartre's "An Essay on Phenomenological Ontology" is to assert that the individual's existence precedes his essence. That is to say primarily that the "free-will" exists. For Sartre, man is a creature in constant search for fulfillment, he is continually haunted by crave for "completion;" since there is always a project for man yeaning for completion.

Sartre observes in "Being and Nothingness," that the human person is born into the material reality of his body, and in a universe that is highly materialistic, and from which man discovers himself to be inserted into being. It is this finding that raises man's consciousness imbued with the ability to conceptualize possibilities and to enliven them; a consciousness that is in constant motion, and in pursuit for an unattainable unifying completion. By this virtue therefore, man continuously strives to move himself forward moment by moment in a bid to free himself from societal inhibitions and thereby gain fulfillment. Barnes Hazel observes that:

> If we leave the level of abstraction and attempt to see what Sartre means in terms of ordinary human experience, we find a radical affirmation of human freedom and a view of self as a value to be pursued rather than either a determining nucleus of possibilities or a hidden nugget to be discovered. (13)

For Sartre, existence precedes essence which ultimately means that it is the human individual that creates significance to his own life. He was to achieve it and not wait for it to be bestowed on him. In his awareness of his being and in his effort to create possibilities for himself, he determines how to relate with his society. Barnes goes further to posit that "we are in our inmost being, a power of choosing again at each moment the relation which we wish to establish with the world around us and with own past and future experiences in the world" (13).

Chapter seventeen | *Anthony Ebiriukwu, in*
Charles Nwadigwe, Molinta Enendu & Canice Nwosu (Eds.)
Metaphors and Climax, Reminiscences on the Drama and
Theatre of Ogonna Agu
London, Adonis & Abbey Publishers

The mores, customs and taboos of the society are impediments on individual freedom and goals. Contrarily, the existentialist philosopher does not believe that the society, religion, tradition or custom should define for the individual how to give meaning and value to his life, since the world he found himself is already meaningless, hopeless and absurd. Therefore Barnes elucidates that "man exists in a situation, but he internalizes that situation and bestows on it a particular meaning and significance. He lives it by transcending it" (14). Hence, the individual person in the world is a temporal consciousness in the universe; he lives in transcendence on an earth he is meant to subdue.

However, so long as he lives, he is continuously aware of objects in the world and how they relate to him and how he in turn relates to them. His interest in these objects (material things), is determined partly by his conviction of the satisfaction he thinks are derivable from them; the aesthetic value of the objects and their value to his life, especially their contribution towards creating a meaningful and valuable world for him. Individual understanding and interpretation of the above variables to some extent determine personal principles and constitute what becomes ethical. Thus, what is ethical is subjective and not externally imposed on the individual. On what constitutes the ethical, Barnes states that:

> It includes as essential the belief that the pattern of meaning and significance which one has imposed upon his existence is what he wants it to be. This complex of feeling and reflective judgment derives from the fact that we are each one a temporal consciousness in the world. The ethical resides in the unity of the individual's past, present and future. This is a unity which consciousness itself imposes. (15)

Thus, the decision to live ethically or unethically are all aspects of individual freedom because they involve a process of choice to live according to the tenets of the societal mores, customs and taboos or shun such communal laws. Barnes expatiates that:

Chapter seventeen | *Anthony Ebiriukwu, in*
Charles Nwadigwe, Molinta Enendu & Canice Nwosu (Eds.)
Metaphors and Climax, Reminiscences on the Drama and
Theatre of Ogonna Agu
London, Adonis & Abbey Publishers

The choice to be ethical embraces both the recognition that one is free and the acceptance of the responsibility which freedom entails. It is an authentic choice, for it recognizes that the decision to justify one's life derives from one's own spontaneous desire and is not imposed from the outside. (19)

The existentialist hero abides by these ethical standards proposed by Barnes; he lives by his own principles, obeys no (societal) laws and conventions and is sometimes seen as a social outcast. What is thus unethical is that which society imposes on the individual from the outside which inhibits the freedom-seeking-enterprise. If a man is "born slave" – which he must not be said to be – it is ethical then that he should strive to become king since kingship is an attainable goal denied him by tradition and culture. To claim it therefore; " is a freedom itself which he chooses as the value so far beyond others that he pits it against all possible values which might in the future result from submitting his freedom to any sort of calculated restriction external or internal" (Barnes 19).

There is no objective hierarchy of values which must be the same for every individual. Thus, not even tradition should debar each individual from exercising his freedom. This is obviously an existentialist principle, accepted by the existentialist hero as the locomotive engine of the liberating enterprise. It also helps to debunk the traditional and conservative view that one cannot transcend beyond the level one finds oneself or where the strata of the society and hierarchical rankings placed him. The desire to transcend beyond paternal and communal inhibitions is born out of the recognition of external object standing as an irresistible magnetic force to one's pursuit of personal values. It is this irresistible desire for this object that gives rise to self-awareness which consciousness presupposes. At the point of recognition of this object of interest and pursuit, man is free to make a choice.

Chapter seventeen | *Anthony Ebiriukwu, in*
Charles Nwadigwe, Molinta Enendu & Canice Nwosu (Eds.)
Metaphors and Climax, Reminiscences on the Drama and
Theatre of Ogonna Agu
London, Adonis & Abbey Publishers

This is the foundation of existentialist ethics as proposed by Barnes who contends that "at no point will we admit the validity of any position which either denies the reality of this freedom or deliberately ignores it. To do otherwise would be the equivalent of a present-day scientist's assumption that the earth does not move in space" (58). Freedom for the existentialist is freedom of choice which also has responsibility and does entail that "my choices here are intertwined with those of others" (Barnes 59). To promote one's own freedom one must, "simultaneously affirm the value of others' freedom".

However, Jean Paul Sartre explains that "freedom as the definition of man does not depend on others, but as soon there is engagement, I am obliged to want the freedom of others at the same time that I want my own freedom. I can take my freedom as a goal if I take that of others for a goal as well (6). Therefore, one cannot deny others' freedom if he recognizes it as an essence nor "allow simultaneously that my freedom holds no privileged place over this assertion when it is made to someone else" (Sartre 62). It then follows that the societal code or law which holds one to a particular system should not be so rigid as not to allow him freedom when the individual desires to bend towards an entirely different and personal perspective.

Hence, there is a tug-of-war-like relationship between communalism and individualism in the existentialist thought similar to the egalitarian Igbo society upon which Agu based his *Cry of the Maiden*. Agu shows that despite the highly cherished communalism in Igboland, individual freedom remains a value which the people's culture must recognize probably because of the egalitarian values of the Igbo worldview. According to Nwosu, "Igbo worldview is parallel to the worldviews of most African tribes. However, it is among the most egalitarian, responsive,dynamic and accommodating *worldviews*" (130).

Chapter seventeen | *Anthony Ebiriukwu, in*
Charles Nwadigwe, Molinta Enendu & Canice Nwosu (Eds.)
Metaphors and Climax, Reminiscences on the Drama and
Theatre of Ogonna Agu
London, Adonis & Abbey Publishers

Therefore the Igbo society is progressive, it is not built on permanence rather, it thrives on change and transformation as reflected in Chidum's desire for change. So, any individual, despite his position in the family, social rank and class can rise to prominence and heroic stature. Chinua Achebe affirms that:

> The Igbo society says no condition is permanent. There is a constant change in the world . . . There is no attempt to draw a line between what is permissible and what is not, what is possible and what is not possible, what is old and what is new . . . Everything plays a part. (56-57)

Ironically, the same Igbo society appears to be an ardent promoter of classical ideology-the class consciousness and adherence. It holds tenaciously to traditions considered to be obnoxious by all forms of modern sensibility without some degree of flexibility. But everyone should, without restriction, be allowed to rise to desired positions as to contribute to societal development. Arthur Miller reiterates this concept of existential heroism and argues that the hero's "stature as a hero is not utterly dependent upon his rank that the corner grocer cannot outdistance the tragic figure providing, of course, that the grocer's career engages the issue of, for instance, the survival of the race (qtd. in Bigsby108).

The society should therefore be an open construct, not a predetermined artifact. Bob Corbeth, while making reference to Sartre's famous lecture, "Existentialism is Humanism" concludes in an online article that:

> There is no absolute certainty . . . Thus human acts are the full responsibility of the individuals – he talks about creating oneself in action. What he means is that I, the human am free. I can make up my own mind about my acts. What I will be in some final sense is what I make myself . . . put in the shortest form: living without certainty and with personal responsibility is a nearly unbearable burden. (np)

Chapter seventeen | *Anthony Ebiriukwu, in*
Charles Nwadigwe, Molinta Enendu & Canice Nwosu (Eds.)
Metaphors and Climax, Reminiscences on the Drama and Theatre of Ogonna Agu
London, Adonis & Abbey Publishers

Between Communalism and Existentialism: *Cry of a Maiden* as a Social Commentary

Cry of a Maiden is a realistic play of protest predicated on the reaction to continued "rigidification" and eventual perpetuation of a tradition that is inhibitive to self actualization and freedom. Metaphorically, it calls for a re-configuration of tradition to recognize individual sense of freedom as proposed by the existentialist.

Chidum spent three years fighting on the side of the French Army in the jungles of Burma and Palestine war zones during the First World War. He arrives home to take as wife, his loving damsel, Ada so that he can settle down to a joyous married life. But this desire is not to come true because tradition demands that his elder brother, Okolo, must take a wife before him. Spurred by impatience and the fact that Okolo does not seem to consider taking a wife too soon, Chidum summons some notable elders of the land to help him prevail on Okolo to allow him go ahead with his marriage as he wished. Presenting the matter before the elders, Chidum pleads; "All I am asking my brother in your presence is to let me get married now that I'm ready" (10). Responding, one of the elders says: "At this point, we will seek his opinion again." turning to Okoro he says, "Now Okolo, you are directly concerned" (10). Okpala retorts. Okpala's reaction and statement reveals that this debate must have been going on ever before now, and Okolo is adamant and insensitive to the feelings of his younger brother. At last, Okolo opens up and responds to Okpala's questions and says; "A major task stares us in the face . . . [t]he task of reconstructing our cottage first" (10). From all indications, if Okolo must yield, a condition must be attached to it. Consequently, Okolo presents his conditions hidden under the

Chapter seventeen | *Anthony Ebiriukwu, in*
Charles Nwadigwe, Molinta Enendu & Canice Nwosu (Eds.)
Metaphors and Climax, Reminiscences on the Drama and
Theatre of Ogonna Agu
London, Adonis & Abbey Publishers

cloak of tradition; Chidum must acquiesce to the reconstruction of the family cottage, if he is to meet his desire of getting married.

Okoro's demand may be inconsequential to outsiders who do not understand or grasp the importance of the *Obi* in traditional Igbo society; hence such people may not appreciate the degree of Okolo's irresponsibility. Basically, the *Obi* is a man's reception hall, meant for the abode of ancestral gods and goddesses and a meeting place for visitors and the visible and invisible owners of the compound. It is a temple for the keeping of antiquities and traditional relics. Religiously, it is a place where ancestral spirits are worshipped and libations poured for the progress and continuity of the lineage. Customarily it is the responsibility of the first son as the holder of the family *Ofo* to take care of the *Obi*. Thus, the negligence of such an important ancestral place by Okolo is a mark of irresponsibility which exposes the family to imminent danger. Socially, the *Obi* serves as a meeting place where discussions for family progress and peace talks are held. It is "... a cultural centre; a museum of antiquities ..." (iv). Agu makes reference to the importance of the *Obi* in the dramatist's note as follows:

> The point therefore is that a homestead without an "Obi" is a dead place, since it is the hub of activities of the house-hold . . . The collapse of one's "obi" under whatever circumstance portends danger for the family. It literally spells death for the head of the family. (iv)

Chidum knows that his elder brother will not bulge; moreover, he appears to understand the implication and importance of reconstructing the cottage; therefore while maintaining his existentialist position he considers the freedom and comfort of others and responds: "Don't worry, uncle. We'll rebuild our cottage first" (10). The young ward accepts. Despite this acquiescence, his elder brother is not satisfied; in Okolo's usual

Chapter seventeen | *Anthony Ebiriukwu, in*
Charles Nwadigwe, Molinta Enendu & Canice Nwosu (Eds.)
Metaphors and Climax, Reminiscences on the Drama and
Theatre of Ogonna Agu
London, Adonis & Abbey Publishers

antics, he comes up with another condition; insisting that, Chidum will first of all marry Ada, Chidum's fiancée for him and then find another girl to marry. Chidum is faced with another hurdle to cross. He must forfeit his darling to his elder brother, Okolo, who suddenly awakes to the realization that he needs a wife. Chidum would rather die than accept such humiliation. The law stating that Okolo as the eldest brother should marry first, must be broken, and the existentialist must assert his will. But to assert his will in the face of a charlatan – hero like Okolo is not an easy hurdle to cross. Okolo in a soliloquy makes reference to Chidum's decision, which he considers to be a contemptuous act, but retorts. "The child that probes into the mystery of night thinks he's right. The stubborn he-goat has sought the storms, has also sunk with the flood . . . Chidum is the cog in my system. The headache in my stomach" (27) and consequently "I have you battered for this," (30) he threatens.

Unlike Okolo who is lazy, docile, gluttonous and selfish, Chidum is a refined man of no mean character; he is vigorous, promising and focused. For Chidum, "Our duty by our fathers is to honour them" (8). His practical and dutiful nature reflects in his relationship with people. Like an archetypal existential hero, Chidum fights for his welfare and also contributes to the general well-being of the society. For instance, he gives wine and tobacco to Okpala, guardian and custodian of their ancestral shrine since their father died. This is akin to the existentialist's demand for a heroic aspiration triggered by the individual's contribution to societal well-being. Okolo is boastful and full of empty promises. One who defies tradition when it makes demand on him; and yet would want others to follow traditional dictum. Udoka captures this when he admonishes him:

> Since Adigwe died, you've refused to fulfill the tradition of home-seeking. You've refused to ask how grey heads are fairing. We said no.

Chapter seventeen	*Anthony Ebiriukwu, in*
	Charles Nwadigwe, Molinta Enendu & Canice Nwosu (Eds.)
	Metaphors and Climax, Reminiscences on the Drama and
	Theatre of Ogonna Agu
	London, Adonis & Abbey Publishers

Instead we would come and know how young bloods are doing. And you send us no tobacco (38).

This sums everything about Okolo, the man to whom tradition bestows with leadership responsibility; one on whom others are supposed to lean and one whose failure will make others powerless.

Okolo is a failure. His preoccupation is to sing the praises of others and celebrate their success. He bloats himself for giving their sister, Ekemma, to Okafor, a family he adjudges as powered with strong economic base. He says of Okafor;

Like his father, I discovered he's hard-working. Has already extended his father's barns to accommodate another three - two hundred yams. Since I gave Ekemma to that family, they've not failed to call me in for wine on big market days. (7)

For Okolo, suffering is not part of life; "God forbid my sister going where she will ever suffer in life" (7). He forgets that hard-work and suffering are indispensable parts of life. This metaphor of hard-work as basic and paramount to one's success re-echoes in Okpala's admonitory dialogue with Okolo:

OKPALA: (Sips) Ach, the wine is good. Looks every inch Anene's handiwork.
OKOLO: Anene does a fine job indeed
OKPALA: He works hard. At thirty he has tethered another sheep.
OKOLO: You've often said it (*Exit Mgbochi*).
OKPALA: Not without a purpose. At your age you should have done more. (9)

Okolo lacks the vigour and guts to face the reality of traditional ethics and responsibilities. He sees it as platitudinous for Okpala to remind him that it was high time he took a wife. He is afraid he cannot face the hurdles of a breadwinner. He expresses his fears thus: "But the sheep... such a difficult creature! Do as you can you

Chapter seventeen | *Anthony Ebiriukwu, in*
Charles Nwadigwe, Molinta Enendu & Canice Nwosu (Eds.)
Metaphors and Climax, Reminiscences on the Drama and
Theatre of Ogonna Agu
London, Adonis & Abbey Publishers

can't pleasure her." (9). Okolo is intolerable, jealous, greedy and hyper-temperamental "I mean the very thought of bearing the brunt of a goat chewing on your head" (9).

The return of Chidum from Burma awakens Okolo's consciousness. He has been a wayward, carefree and docile man. Now he awakens to the consciousness of the reality facing him and the family. He now realizes that the family *"Obi"* needs to be reconstructed, and that it's time for him to get married. Such attitudes to existence are marks of failure and irresponsibility. They replicate constancy which the existentialist abhors. Moreover, in this sudden conscious awakening of Okolo and his resolve to assert and realize these goals, does he simultaneously, like the existentialist, consider the goals of others? For the existentialist insists that "I am obliged to want the freedom of others at the same time that I want my own freedom. I can take my freedom as a goal if I take that of others for a goal as well" (Sartre 6).

Okolo is aware of the imminent danger of the dilapidated cottage to his life, hence he wants it reconstructed at all cost. But on whose cost must he have his desire fulfilled? Would it not be better that by defining his own value, he should have simultaneously defined the value of his younger brother, Chidum even when there was engagement? It was the fragrant breaking of this engagement that results to chaos and consequent instability. Injustice therefore breeds instability which is the exact case here. Okolo becomes an over-lord. Ada, the maiden even observes this when she proclaims: "How you swell . . . Like a Lord", to which Okolo replies, "Of course I'm the Lord of this household. And you haven't prostrated to me like the wayfarer did?", thus referring to Chidum. Therefore, Okolo fails to recognize the goals of his younger brother, while pursuing his own goals. This is a departure

Chapter seventeen | *Anthony Ebiriukwu, in*
Charles Nwadigwe, Molinta Enendu & Canice Nwosu (Eds.)
Metaphors and Climax, Reminiscences on the Drama and
Theatre of Ogonna Agu
London, Adonis & Abbey Publishers

from the existentialist demand and the main action that actually triggered the conflict in the play.

One may be tempted to say that such images as calabash, clay-pots and fire woods that recur in the play are metaphors suggesting the fragility of the society and the fear that the imposition of norms that are antithetical to the assertion of human free-will and choice, may lead to the destruction of the fragile society. While the images of items like jack-knife, aluminum pot and hard-boots, which Chidum came back with from France, are suggestive of an overriding superiority of a new tradition and culture to those of his native home. It is Chidum's resolve to dismantle such obnoxious laws. The irony of the whole experience is that Chidum does not triumph as a revolutionary hero. He gets subdued by the repressive embodiments of the charlatan hero, Okolo. Thus, the playwright shows through characterization, the superiority of African culture which Chidum strives to change. Unfortunately he lacks the will to transcend and reconfigure the repressive cultural practices of his people. However, the existentialist hero does not suffer guilt; he must not always triumph, in recognition of this, Chidum is resolute and maintains his existentialist stand to the end of the play even though he fails to pursue his goal to a completion.

Conclusion

Metaphorically, Ogonna Agu's portrayal of the character Chidum is a reflection of a Marxist inclination that does not support unnecessary stratification of the society and bourgeois ideology. The relationship between injustice and instability may sometimes be described as causal, because every human phenomenon has a limit to which it may be stretched. Globally, injustice and instability are ravaging many nations. However, the situation is

Chapter seventeen | *Anthony Ebiriukwu, in*
Charles Nwadigwe, Molinta Enendu & Canice Nwosu (Eds.)
Metaphors and Climax, Reminiscences on the Drama and
Theatre of Ogonna Agu
London, Adonis & Abbey Publishers

worse in Africa where acrimony, bickering and revolts have become the order of the day. Notable among the root causes of these conflicts is Africa's cultural practice in value distribution system based on seniority by age. This aspect of African culture tends to limit individual freedom and self-actualization. Ogonna, in a critical but realistic manner raises this issue in his *Cry of a Maiden*, where traditional and cultural forces combine to impede the progress of the hard-working and determined second son-Chidum.

Simultaneously, the same culture empowers Okolo, the lazy and complacent first son at the detriment of Chidum. This study highlights the playwright's condemnation of inhibitive traditions that advocate progressive and liberal cultural practices to ensure socio-economic and political stability in society. Ogonna Agu's *Cry of a Maiden* promotes the illusion of life-like experiences the reader/audience encounters in an African milieu. It calls to mind the political and cultural implications of the African experience simulated from a society that is tradition-bound and whose norms are inhibitive to social advancement since Chidum, the second son, now questions the rationale behind the sustenance of a tradition that places stricture on his bid for self-actualization. Thus, there is in the play some degree of revolutionary aesthetics even though the playwright ended at critical realism because he made his hero succumb to external pressure.

From an existentialist perspective, the play, *Cry of a Maiden* is topical for its questioning of the cultural practice of seniority by age in Igbo-land. This it achieved through the problematization of the subject. The fabrics of realistic elements in the play only provided a framework for a different mode of perception. The society is in constant motion and to be stable it must flush out laws and traditions that are detrimental to human advancement. Things do change and traditions should be limited by their times and

Chapter seventeen | *Anthony Ebiriukwu, in*
Charles Nwadigwe, Molinta Enendu & Canice Nwosu (Eds.)
Metaphors and Climax, Reminiscences on the Drama and
Theatre of Ogonna Agu
London, Adonis & Abbey Publishers

dynamism of the society under which they operate. African cultures and traditions are not guided by scientific determinism and should not be seen as such. It should be capable of transcending with the dynamic world.

Works Cited

Achebe, Chinua. *There Was a Country*. London: Penguin, 2012.

Anaagudo-Agu, Ogonna. *Cry of a Maiden*. Calabar: Wusen Press, 2000.

Corbett, Bob. What is Existentialism? www2.webster.edu/../whatis. html, 1985.

Crowell, Steven. "Existentialism" *The Stanford Encyclopedia of Philosophy* (Winter 2010 edition) URL=>http://plato.stanford/arc hives/win2010/entries/existentialism/>.

Dobie, A.B. *Theory into Practice: An Introduction To Literary Criticism*. California: Wadsworth, Cengage Learning, 2012.

Hazel, Barnes. *An Existentialist Ethics: The Choice to be Ethical*. Washington DC: First Vintage Books, 1971.

Lowrie, Walter. *Kierkegard's Attack Upon Christendom*. New Jersey: Princeton University Press, 1969.

MacQuarrie, John. *Existentialism*. New York: Harper & Row Publishers, 1972.

Nwabueze, Emeka. *Visions and Revisions*. Enugu: Abic Books, 2011.

Nwosu, Canice Chukwuma. "Evolving a Performance Oriented Critical Theory for African Postmodern Theatre Practice." A Ph.D. Thesis Presented to the Department of Theatre and Film Studies, University of Nigeria, Nsukka. 2011.

Sartre, Jean Paul. *Existentialism is a Humanism*. www.Marxists.org/.. /srte.htm. 2005. Accessed 06-08-2013.

Chapter seventeen | *Anthony Ebiriukwu, in*
Charles Nwadigwe, Molinta Enendu & Canice Nwosu (Eds.)
Metaphors and Climax, Reminiscences on the Drama and
Theatre of Ogonna Agu
London, Adonis & Abbey Publishers

LIST OF CONTRIBUTORS

KALU UKA, is a pioneer and veteran of the Nigerian/African theatre. As a playwright, poet, teacher, critic, theatre director, researcher, orator and cultural advocate, Uka remains a leading light in Nigeria's theatre training, scholarship and professional practice. He has taught and produced many generations of Professors and senior academics, including Ogonna Agu. In his professional peregrinations from Ibadan to Leeds, Toronto to Baltimore, Nsukka to Calabar, Awka to Uyo, Uka's legacy remains evergreen. At present, Uka occupies the elevated chair of Emeritus Professor of Theatre Studies at the University of Uyo, Nigeria.

LUKE MOLINTA ENENDU (Ph.D.) is a Designer and Consultant on Theatre Technology who trained under the technical tutelage of Dexter Lyndersay. As one of the prominent theatre designers Nigeria has produced, Enendu has been commissioned to design the scenery and lighting of major national and international events including carnivals and cultural festivals. His articles on theatre design appear in learned journals and anthologies. Enendu is a Professor and currently teaches in the Department of Theatre and Media Studies at the University of Calabar.

CHARLES NWADIGWE (Ph.D.) is a Professor of Theatre Technology and Performance Aesthetics with a record of acclaimed technical direction for the stage and screen. His published plays have gained wide recognition and his scientific articles have been published in peer-reviewed journals and anthologies abroad and in Nigeria. His current research centres on digital interface and multimedia, proxemics and ergonomics in performance venues, and site-specific technical direction. A faculty member in the Theatre Arts Department, Nnamdi Azikiwe University, Awka, Nigeria, Nwadigwe is an editorial consultant to reputable journals.

List of
Contributors

Charles Nwadigwe, Molinta Enendu & Canice Nwosu (Eds.)
Metaphors and Climax, Reminiscences on the Drama and Theatre of Ogonna Agu
London, Adonis & Abbey Publishers

281

AMEH DENNIS AKOH (Ph.D.) is Associate Professor of Drama and Critical Theory at the Osun State University, Nigeria. His areas of research interest include critical theory, dramatic criticism, sociology of literature, gender and cultural studies. His is widely published and is listed in the Year's Work in English Studies (YWES) Index of Critics. He is currently the Editor of Nigerian Theatre Journal (NTJ).

CANICE CHUKWUMA NWOSU (Ph.D.) is a Senior Lecturer with the Theatre Arts Department, Nnamdi Azikiwe University, Awka, Nigeria. He obtained his Doctorate Degree in Theory and Criticism from the University of Nigeria, Nsukka. His research articles and critical essays on national and global issues of contemporary concern have been published in learned journals and academic publications. His research interests revolve around drama, theatre and society with particular focus on applied performance theory and critical discourse.

EMEKA NWOSU is a lecturer at the Imo State University, Owerri, Nigeria. He holds a Masters Degree and currently pursues a Doctoral research in culture and modern theatre production. His research interest revolves around Directing, Cultural Studies and Copyright Law. At present, Nwosu investigates the Nollywood video-film industry and new approaches to conflict resolution in Nigeria.

COLUMBA APEH teaches in the Department of Theatre and Media Arts, University of Calabar, Nigeria where he obtained his Masters Degree. Apeh currently pursues a Doctoral Programme in Technical Theatre in the same University. His research is mainly in the areas of theatrical sound application and acoustics.

ELIZABETH OLAYIWOLA attended the Kogi State University, Anyigba and the Benue State University, Makurdi, both in Nigeria

List of Contributors	Charles Nwadigwe, Molinta Enendu & Canice Nwosu (Eds.) *Metaphors and Climax, Reminiscences on the Drama and Theatre of Ogonna Agu* London, Adonis & Abbey Publishers

where she obtained the Bachelor and Master of Arts Degrees respectively. She is currently pursuing a Doctoral research in gender and film theory at the University of Abuja, Nigeria.

JOHN IWUH (Ph.D.) teaches Theatre Design and Aesthetics in the Department of Theatre and Film Studies, Redeemer's University, Nigeria. He was a Fulbright Scholar with professional engagements in stage lighting design and installation. Former Acting General Manager of The MUSON Centre, Lagos, Iwuh also worked with the Collective Artistes and Performance Studio Workshop, where he designed performances with local and international directors, among other commissioned projects. He is a member of IATC and other learned societies. Iwuh has also published plays, including *The Village Lamb*, winner of ANA Prize for 2008.

UCHE-CHINEMERE NWAOZUZU (Ph.D.) is a Senior Lecturer with the Department of Theatre and Film Studies, University of Nigeria, Nsukka. His research and scholarship centre on African theatre, performance analysis, globalization, theory and criticism. Nwaozuzu is also an artistic director with production credits on stage and the Nollywood industry.

OFONIME INYANG is of the Department of Drama & Film, Tshwane University of Technology, South Africa. His Doctoral research is at a conclusive stage. He writes plays, poetry and designs creative interventionist art and performances. He holds a Masters Degree in Theatre Arts (Directing and Script Aesthetics), teaches applied theatre and development communication and is published locally and internationally.

FRANCISCA NWADIGWE is a Costume, Make-Up and Visual Appearance designer with the Theatre Arts Department, Nnamdi Azikiwe University, Awka. She holds a Masters Degree in

List of	Charles Nwadigwe, Molinta Enendu & Canice Nwosu (Eds.)
Contributors	*Metaphors and Climax, Reminiscences on the Drama and Theatre of Ogonna Agu*
	London, Adonis & Abbey Publishers

283

theatrical costume application and currently pursues a Doctoral research on costume motifs and visual design concepts at the University of Abuja, Nigeria. She is a beauty consultant for Mary Kay Cosmetics Inc., USA.

EMEKA OFORA teaches drama and theatre in the Department of Theatre Arts, University of Port Harcourt, Nigeria. Ofora obtained his Masters Degree in the field of Applied Theatre and currently researches on Development Communication and Modern African Theatre.

TOCHUKWU OKEKE studied Theatre Arts at the University of Ibadan, Nigeria where he obtained both Bachelors and Masters Degrees. A versatile theatre practitioner, Okeke has directed theatre troupes and produced a movie titled *Wicked*. At present, he is a lecturer at the Theatre Arts Department, Nnamdi Azikiwe University, Awka, Nigeria where he also runs his Doctoral research in Design and African Performance.

CHIDIEBERE EKWEARIRI (Ph.D.) is a lecturer with the Department of Theatre Arts, Alvan Ikoku Federal College of Education, Owerri, Nigeria. Ekweariri obtained his Doctorate in technical theatre from the University of Calabar, Nigeria. A creative designer with publications in both local and foreign journals, his current research works are in the areas of theatre aesthetics, acoustics and scenography.

CHARLES OKWUOWULU is of the Theatre Arts Department, University of Port Harcourt. He is a Film Director, Producer, D.O.P and Editor, with some Nollywood video-films to his credit. His Doctoral research is on video-film directing in the Nollywood industry.

IKIKE INIEKE UFFORD is a dancer, choreographer and multi-talented instrumentalist who has won prizes in the performing

List of Contributors	Charles Nwadigwe, Molinta Enendu & Canice Nwosu (Eds.) *Metaphors and Climax, Reminiscences on the Drama and Theatre of Ogonna Agu* London, Adonis & Abbey Publishers

284

Arts. A Doctoral candidate in dance at the University of Ibadan and member of Calabar Carnival Planning Committee, Ufford has published widely with various dance and dramatic creations to his credit. He teaches Dance, Choreography and Theatre in the Department of Theatre and Media Studies, University of Calabar.

NICHOLAS AKAS holds a Masters Degree in Dance and Choreography from the Theatre Arts Department, Nnamdi Azikiwe University, Awka where he currently works as a lecturer. A creative Disc Jockey and Radio Presenter, Akas researches and publishes on dance, choreography, music and semiotics. His Doctoral research on dance is in progress at the Imo State University, Owerri, Nigeria.

IFEYINWA UZONDU is a Lecturer with the Department of Theatre Arts, Alvan Ikoku Federal College of Education, Owerri, Nigeria. Her research interests centre on women and gender studies as expressed through the creative arts.

EDET ESSIEN is a playwright and staff of the Theatre and Media Arts Department, University of Calabar, Nigeria, where he obtained his Ph.D. as well. Currently, he teaches playwriting, radio production and Art Administration. His plays have been produced on stage and he has starred in some video-films and television plays. His current research interests focus on audience engineering for stage productions.

ANTHONY CHUKWUEMEKA EBIRIUKWU is a lecturer with the Department of Theatre Arts, Imo State University, Owerri. At present, his research interests cover the areas of dramatic literature, theory and criticism with particular focus on cultural practices, existentialist philosophy, and the language question in African creative writing.

List of Contributors	Charles Nwadigwe, Molinta Enendu & Canice Nwosu (Eds.) *Metaphors and Climax, Reminiscences on the Drama and Theatre of Ogonna Agu* London, Adonis & Abbey Publishers

Index

List of Contributors	Charles Nwadigwe, Molinta Enendu & Canice Nwosu (Eds.) *Metaphors and Climax, Reminiscences on the Drama and Theatre of Ogonna Agu* London, Adonis & Abbey Publishers

Index | Charles Nwadigwe, Molinta Enendu & Canice Nwosu (Eds.)
Metaphors and Climax, Reminiscences on the Drama and Theatre of Ogonna Agu
London, Adonis & Abbey Publishers

287

List of   Charles Nwadigwe, Molinta Enendu & Canice Nwosu (Eds.)
Contributors *Metaphors and Climax, Reminiscences on the Drama and Theatre of Ogonna Agu*
            London, Adonis & Abbey Publishers

Index	Charles Nwadigwe, Molinta Enendu & Canice Nwosu (Eds.)
	Metaphors and Climax, Reminiscences on the Drama and Theatre of Ogonna Agu
	London, Adonis & Abbey Publishers

289